'This welcomed book is recommended for those who wish to consider some potentially life changing implications of, rather than use, philosophy for their therapeutic practices.'

Professor Del Loewenthal, Chair of Psychotherapy and Counselling, University of Roehampton

'By reaching outside the increasingly narrow world of psychotherapy, this book offers us much needed resources to re-examine current practice from the proper perspective of the whole of human experience. The writing here returns us to a maturity of thought that is currently lacking in the profession of psychotherapy. We are invited to expand our questions and assumptions beyond "evidence-based treatments", to include philosophical and creative insights. In the process, we regain a little of the personal humility that makes psychotherapy therapeutic in the first place. A real breath of fresh air.'

Dr Greg Madison, author and psychotherapist

'Offering a clear dialogue between therapy and philosophy, *Therapy and the Counter-tradition* is a much needed and most welcome book. In an age of what the editors refer to as "superficial pragmatism", this book promotes and provides philosophical integrity, which is often lacking in training and practice. Focusing on the work of twelve specific philosophers, a poet and a novelist, the book is wide-ranging, informative, and stimulating, while remaining coherent. This is a book for thinking and thoughtful therapists. I commend the editors and recommend it highly.'

Dr Keith Tudor, Professor of Psychotherapy, Auckland University of Technology, Aotearoa New Zealand, and co-author of Person-centred Therapy: A Clinical Philosophy *(Routledge, 2006)*

'A tour de force of critical insights – from Nietzsche to Wittgenstein, from Keats to Kierkegaard – Manu Bazzano and Julie Webb have provided a rich banquet of ideas that are orthogonal to the complacency of tradition and the banality of contemporary psychotherapy. Drawing on a wide range of themes: ethics, politics, art, poetry and language, *Therapy and the Counter-Tradition* revitalizes philosophy as a way of life, offering a new infusion of vitality into the healing of the soul.'

Ronald E. Purser, PhD, Professor of Management, San Francisco State University

'In an age when therapy's literature is dominated by programmatic, allegedly evidence-based pretensions to scientificity and control, with meaning routinely reduced to superficiality and utility, we desperately need far more material that will fructify imaginations, embrace paradox and the ineffable, and challenge the tradition of modernity and rationalism that, in the wrong hands, only impoverish the human condition. This exciting book uses engagements with key philosophers, like Nietzsche Wittgenstein, Butler, Camus, Deleuze, Irigaray, Kierkegaard, Merleau-Ponty, Sartre and Schopenhauer (amongst others), to do just that – a splendid text that is "full of being and becoming", with (thankfully) not an "evidence-based" claim in sight. My only (deep) regret is that this book didn't exist when I was training as a therapist 25 years ago.'

Dr Richard House, former Senior Lecturer in Psychotherapy, University of Roehampton, and author of Therapy Beyond Modernity *(Karnac) and* In, Against and Beyond Therapy *(PCCS)*

THERAPY AND THE COUNTER-TRADITION

Therapy and the Counter-tradition: The edge of philosophy brings together leading exponents of contemporary psychotherapy, philosophers and writers in order to explore how philosophical ideas may inform therapy work. The authors discuss particular philosophers who have influenced their lives and therapeutic practice, while questioning how counselling and psychotherapy can address human 'wholeness', despite the ascendancy of rationality, regulation and diagnosis. It also seeks to acknowledge the distinct lack of philosophical input and education in counselling and psychotherapy training.

The chapters are rooted in the counter-tradition, whose diverse manifestations include humanism, skepticism, fideism, as well as the opening of philosophy and psychology to poetry and the arts. This collection of thought-provoking chapters will help open the discussion within the psychological therapies, by providing therapists with critical philosophical references, which will help broaden their knowledge and the scope of their practice.

Therapy and the Counter-tradition: The edge of philosophy will be of interest to mental health professionals, practitioners, counselling and psychotherapy trainees and trainers, and academics tutoring or studying psychology. It will also appeal to those interested in psychology, meditation, personal development and philosophy.

Manu Bazzano is a psychotherapist and supervisor in private practice and visiting lecturer at various schools and colleges, most notably Roehampton University. He teaches philosophy in adult education and has a background in rock music and Zen Buddhism. Bazzano has authored numerous books and is co-editor of *Person-centred and Experiential Psychotherapies*, as well as book review editor of *Self & Society: An International Journal for Humanistic Psychology*. www.manubazzano.com

Julie Webb (MA, MBACP) has a background in training, literature and philosophy. She is a counselling lecturer at University Campus Suffolk and a humanistic counsellor and supervisor in private practice in Cambridge. She has previously had an established private practice in Shrewsbury and worked as a counselling lecturer for five years at Shrewsbury College of Arts & Technology, offering training and CPD. www.juliewebbcounselling.com

THERAPY AND THE COUNTER-TRADITION

The edge of philosophy

*Edited by Manu Bazzano
and Julie Webb*

Routledge
Taylor & Francis Group
LONDON AND NEW YORK

First published 2016
by Routledge
2 Park Square, Milton Park, Abingdon, Oxon OX14 4RN

and by Routledge
711 Third Avenue, New York, NY 10017

Routledge is an imprint of the Taylor & Francis Group, an informa business.

© 2016 selection and editorial matter, Manu Bazzano and Julie Webb; individual chapters, the contributors

The right of the editors to be identified as the authors of the editorial material, and of the authors for their individual chapters, has been asserted in accordance with sections 77 and 78 of the Copyright, Designs and Patents Act 1988.

All rights reserved. No part of this book may be reprinted or reproduced or utilised in any form or by any electronic, mechanical, or other means, now known or hereafter invented, including photocopying and recording, or in any information storage or retrieval system, without permission in writing from the publishers.

Trademark notice: Product or corporate names may be trademarks or registered trademarks, and are used only for identification and explanation without intent to infringe.

British Library Cataloguing in Publication Data
A catalogue record for this book is available from the British Library

Library of Congress Cataloging-in-Publication Data
Names: Bazzano, Manu, editor. | Webb, Julie, editor.
Title: Therapy and the counter-tradition / edited by Manu Bazzano and Julie Webb.
Description: Milton, Park, Abingdon ; New York, NY : Routledge, [2016] | Includes bibliographical references.
Identifiers: LCCN 2015039182| ISBN 9781138905870 (hbk) | ISBN 9781138905887 (pbk) | ISBN 9781315680194 (ebk)
Subjects: LCSH: Psychotherapy—Philosophy.
Classification: LCC RC437.5 .T48 2016 | DDC 616.89/14—dc23
LC record available at http://lccn.loc.gov/2015039182

ISBN: 978-1-138-90587-0 (hbk)
ISBN: 978-1-138-90588-7 (pbk)
ISBN: 978-1-315-68019-4 (ebk)

Typeset in Bembo
by Apex CoVantage, LLC

Printed and bound in Great Britain
by Ashford Colour Press Ltd, Gosport, Hampshire

Not how the world is, but that it is, is the mystery.
Ludwig Wittgenstein
I change too quickly: my today refutes my yesterday.
Friedrich Nietzsche

CONTENTS

Contributors   xii

Introduction   1
Manu Bazzano and Julie Webb

PART I
The threshold experience   7

1. Changelings: the self in Nietzsche's psychology   9
   Manu Bazzano

2. What can therapists learn from Kierkegaard?   23
   John Lippitt

3. John Keats and negative capability:
   the psychotherapist's X-factor?   34
   Diana Voller

4. That piece of supreme art, a man's life   45
   Nick Duffell

5. Tears of joy: Pascal's 'Night of Fire'   58
   Subhaga Gaetano Failla

PART II
Ethics and politics — 65

6 Who am I? You tell me: desire and Judith Butler — 67
Julie Webb

7 The liberation psychologist: a tribute to Jean-Paul Sartre — 76
Richard Pearce

8 Instances of liberation in Rousseau — 90
Federico Battistutta

9 A metaphysical rebellion: Camus and psychotherapy — 98
James Belassie

PART III
Self, other, world — 105

10 Desire-delirium: on Deleuze and therapy — 107
Manu Bazzano

11 A poetry of human relations: Merleau-Ponty and psychotherapy — 117
Paul Gordon

12 This culture of me: on singularity, secrecy and ethics — 129
Eugenia Lapteva

13 Energy ethics and the thought of difference in Luce Irigaray — 137
Federico Battistutta

PART IV
Therapy, language, metaphysics — 145

14 Under arrest: Wittgenstein and perspicuity — 147
Julie Webb

15 A penetrating beam of darkness — 156
John Mackessy

16 Lifting the curse: Wittgenstein, Buddhism and psychotherapy   169
    Jeff Harrison

17 Amor Fati: suffering to become the person one is   179
    Devang Vaidya

Index   *191*

CONTRIBUTORS

Federico Battistutta is a non-fiction writer and independent researcher in the area of contemporary religion. For several years, he edited the Italian review of religious dialogue, *La stella del mattino*, and writes regularly for various publications. Among his books are *Trittico eretico* (Lampi di Stampa, 2005), *Il cantico delle creature* (Pazzini, 2009), *Verità e cammino* (Pazzini, 2012), *No Man's Land* (Ipoc, 2012) and *Storie dell'Eden* (Ipoc, 2015). He coordinates the www.liberospirito.org website and the www.liberospirito.altervista.org blog – both virtual sites dedicated to the study of vital links between religion and freedom.

Manu Bazzano has a background in philosophy and rock music. He is an author, psychotherapist, supervisor in private practice and visiting lecturer at Roehampton University and various other schools and colleges. He facilitates workshops and seminars internationally and teaches philosophy in adult education. He studied Eastern contemplative practices for 35 years and was ordained as a Zen monk in the Soto and Rinzai traditions. He edited two bestselling anthologies, *Zen Poems* (MQP, 2002) and *Haiku for Lovers* (MQP, 2004) and is the author of *Buddha Is Dead: Nietzsche and the Dawn of European Zen* (Sussex, 2006); *Spectre of the Stranger: Towards a Phenomenology of Hospitality* (Sussex, 2012) and *The Speed of Angels* (Perfect Edge, 2013). He edited *After Mindfulness: New Perspectives on Psychology and Meditation* (Palgrave, 2014). He is co-editor of *Person-centred and Experiential Psychotherapies* international journal and book review editor of *Self & Society*, an international journal for humanistic psychology. www.manubazzano.com

James Belassie has a background in music and currently works as a musician and teacher. His training in existential therapy is ongoing, and he continues to write on related subjects.

Contributors **xiii**

Nick Duffell, after an Oxford degree in Sanskrit, taught at a boarding school in India before becoming a carpenter. Retraining as a psychotherapist, he then worked as a family therapist and organizational consultant. Nick has wide experience as a trainer and facilitator, writes and broadcasts on psychological issues and has two grown sons. His book, *The Making of Them*, has received wide critical acclaim, as his latest book *Wounded Leaders* looks set to do also. With his wife Helena, he founded the Centre for Gender Psychology in 1996 and co-authored the acclaimed book *Sex, Love and the Dangers of Intimacy* (available from www.genderpsychology.com).

Subhaga Gaetano Failla, after studying sociology in Urbino, has published several collections of short stories including *Logorare i sandali* (Aletti, 2002), *Il coltello e il pane* (Aletti, 2003), *La signora Irma e le nuvole* (Fara, 2007) and the novella *Il seminario di Vinastra* included in the 3x2 Collection (Fara, 2006). Some of his poems were published in the anthologies *Zen Poems* (MQP, 2002) and *Haiku for Lovers* (MQP, 2003), both edited by Manu Bazzano. He collaborates with various magazines and literary blogs.

Paul Gordon is a psychotherapist and supervisor. He is a member of the Philadelphia Association, set up by R. D. Laing and colleagues in the 1960s to challenge accepted ways of understanding and responding to emotional distress and also a member of the Society for Existential Analysis. He is the author of several books, including *An Uneasy Dwelling: The Story of the Philadelphia Association Community Households* (PCCS, 2010) and *The Hope of Therapy* (PCCS, 2009).

Jeff Harrison has a PhD comparing Buddhist and Western psychology and philosophy. He works as a psychotherapist and supervisor. He also conducts a number of therapy training courses. Among his publications are 'Meditation and Meaning', a chapter in *After Mindfulness* (2014), edited by Manu Bazzano.

Eugenia Lapteva is a London-based writer. Born and raised in Stockholm, she completed her BA in European literature at University of Sussex and her MA in comparative literature and modern literary theory at Goldsmiths. She has written for notable publications such as *Tank*, *Odiseo*, *The White Review*, *Sang Bleu*, *ELLE* and *Husk* magazine. Her main research interests revolve around questions of secrecy, the self and ethics in neoliberal culture and the impact of new technologies on the nature of our social and loving relationships today. She is currently pursuing her PhD at the University of Sussex.

John Lippitt is professor of ethics and philosophy of religion at the University of Hertfordshire and honorary professor of philosophy at Deakin University. He is the author of *Kierkegaard and the Problem of Self-love* (Cambridge University Press, 2013), *The Routledge Guidebook to Kierkegaard's Fear and Trembling* (2003, second edition

2015) and *Humour and Irony in Kierkegaard's Thought* (Palgrave, 2000). He is editor or co-editor of *Narrative, Identity and the Kierkegaardian Self* (Edinburgh University Press, 2015), *The Oxford Handbook of Kierkegaard* (Oxford University Press, 2013), *Nietzsche and the Divine* (Clinamen, 2000) and *Nietzsche's Futures* (Palgrave, 1999).

John Mackessy, before becoming an integrative counsellor and psychotherapist, studied social science, philosophy and comparative religion at City University and the School of Oriental & African Studies. His areas of interest include theories of knowledge, phenomenology and Buddhist philosophy. These interests inform his practice as a therapist, supervisor and counselling teacher in London. As a teenager, he tried to 'drop out of society' by shaving his head, joining *Hare Krishna* and dancing at airports. Tellingly, a moment of sceptical awakening whilst circumambulating a basil tree led to a lifelong disquietude regarding dogmatism and self-delusion. He is, though, still looking for a viable way to drop out.

Richard Pearce is as a psychotherapist in private practice, his third career and the one that represents a fulfilment of many aspirations. In this capacity, he previously worked for some years in a university student counselling service and privately for the BUPA Employee Assistance Programme. His first career was as a farmworker caring for his father's small dairy herd on the small-scale tenanted farm where he grew up.

Devang Vaidya is a person-centred existential therapist and supervisor in independent practice based in London. He has worked in a range of community-based counselling services and has taught in a number of counselling and psychotherapy training programmes. His clinical and academic interests include linking psychoanalysis, existentialism and critical theory with person-centred practice.

Diana Voller is a chartered counselling psychologist, an integrative psychotherapist in private practice and senior lecturer at the University of Roehampton, where she teaches and supervises students in counselling psychology and integrative counselling and psychotherapy.

Julie Webb, after working as an independent philosophical practitioner, trained at Chester University in humanistic counselling and has since worked for a number of years in private practice in Shrewsbury. She also worked as a counselling lecturer at Shrewsbury College of Arts and Technology, facilitating training for therapists and CPD events. She has recently relocated her counselling and supervision practice to Cambridge.

INTRODUCTION

Manu Bazzano and Julie Webb

Psychotherapy and psychotechnics

"I really don't see what trainees can learn from Nietzsche". These words were spoken, matter of factly, by a newly appointed professor who was busy revamping a psychology department. She had a point: psychotherapy trainees need to learn skills, build resilience and do research in order to be able to work effectively in a fast-changing world. Pragmatism, competence, evidence-based clinical interventions – these are all crucial requirements, far more important than knowledge of quaint nineteenth-century philosophy.

The professor appears to be right: there is virtually no place for Nietzsche or for any deep thinker in psychotherapy training dominated by neo-positivism and the demands of a neo-liberal agenda. But for those of us who are not prepared to abdicate the breadth of thinking and feeling that is fundamental to our profession, for those who are interested in thinking things through beyond a superficial pragmatism, a link with philosophy and philosophical practice is vital; hence this diverse selection of chapters will be of some value to them.

Because current training in counselling and psychotherapy is divorced from basic philosophical education, practitioners are prone to adopt philosophical or semi-philosophical notions implicitly and often uncritically, notions that are broadly linked to the particular orientation they study. Even when there *is* an explicit philosophical emphasis, external pressures rush in to flatten its distinctiveness. For example, it is now the norm for existentially trained practitioners to 'add a little CBT (cognitive behavioural therapy)' to their 'bag of tools' just in order to find work. And the same applies to long-term Buddhist practitioners and meditation facilitators, many of whom are compelled to train and teach simpler forms such as mindfulness, casting aside the intricate array of philosophical and ethical practices learned in studying the Dharma. This does not mean that CBT (or CBT-inspired approaches such as Mindfulness-Based Stress Reduction) is devoid of philosophical grounding or that it is an ineffective form of therapy. But it does matter that it has virtually become (alongside pharmacology) the only game in town, a clear sign that the overriding tendency is at present in favour of *psychotechnics* instead of *psychotherapy*.

There are political reasons for this: CBT and pharmacology speak a language that politicians, managers and bureaucrats understand, a language not so much devoid of philosophical complexity as one that is deeply at variance from what we call, after G. B. Madison (1981) the *counter-tradition*. This may in turn suggest that the philosophical practices associated with the counter-tradition are at odds with institutional power's agenda, targets drawn up in governmental offices and, above all, the demands of 'the market'.

Tradition and counter-tradition

What is the counter-tradition? The official history of Western thought is the history of the tradition, whose other name is rationalism: the belief that the world is an orderly cosmos, a totality (sometimes called 'Nature') with human reason as an integral part. It has been the dominant mode of thought, and it promises to overcome the contingencies of existence and achieve a science (and a technology) that will help us master our destiny. At times the tradition speaks the language of secular rationalism (an overriding phenomenon at present, after the boom of the 'God-delusion' industry), loosely inspired by the Enlightenment; at times it speaks the language of religious or spiritual rationalism, from Plato through the Judaeo-Christian orthodoxy.

Alongside the tradition, there has also been a steady current of thought and practice in Western philosophy since the ancient Greeks (beginning with Heraclitus), which continues to remind us of our human limitations and of the ungraspable nature of the world. This is the counter-tradition, whose diverse manifestations include humanism, scepticism, fideism, as well as the opening of philosophy to poetry, psychology and the arts.

Psychoanalysis has long established a productive link with philosophy, each discipline providing a different and compelling angle on the human condition. The same cannot be said of contemporary psychotherapy and counselling. This book wants to address this gap by fostering a clear dialogue between therapy and philosophy.

The conversation between traditional philosophy and psychoanalysis may have produced mixed results over several decades, yet it has been useful that each cultivated a different endeavour: philosophy largely aimed at curtailing the pathos of living with the aloofness of *logos* (sole reliance on logical and rational discourse), while psychoanalysis attempted to "tear the mask from *logos* and testify to the deranging suffering of the animal subjected to language" (Clemens, 2013, p. 13). Psychoanalysis's own fate has been ambivalent. Its rather lofty associations with philosophy, art and culture (and, conversely, the absorption of its key notions in everyday language to the point of mimetic invisibility) separated it from our pragmatist and utilitarian zeitgeist. A renowned cognitive-behavioural practitioner at an international conference a few years ago remarked that psychoanalysis was, of course, wonderful when applied to literature, film and the arts, but when it comes down to treating the mentally distressed, we would be better off applying CBT.

Psychotherapy has played a significant role in opening the field of philosophy outside the confines of the tradition. We don't think it too bold a claim to state that the informed confluence of the two disciplines – psychotherapy and philosophy – can be also advantageous to philosophy, a branch of learning traditionally relegated to prestigiously desiccated academia. There are things philosophy does not know and can learn from psychotherapy, as well as from literature and art. And there are things psychotherapy does not know and can learn from philosophy. It is our hope and our ambition that the process of cross-contamination encouraged in these pages will add flesh and blood to the ethereal body of philosophy. It may also ground current psychotherapeutic practice in critical philosophy, thus contributing to halt its current slide into psychotechnics.

This book is an invitation to open the world of counselling and psychotherapy to philosophy and philosophical practice, i.e. not only to basic philosophical knowledge but also to philosophy as a *way of life*. We believe this to be an essential antidote to a profession (and a vocation) that is currently under attack and risks seeing its rich legacy eroded.

Philosophy as affirmation of life

So what would this *philosophy as a way of life* look like, and how might the philosophers presented in this collection be helpful to psychotherapy practice?

One possible answer comes from a necessary clarification as well as reconfiguration of the formula itself. This is because *philosophy as a way of life* is now inevitably associated with Stoic serenity and neo-Stoic 'care of the self', by all means a valid philosophical stance echoed throughout this book. Yet the meaning of the philosophical life and the goal of serenity must be expanded to include a more decisive life-affirming stance. This is because implicit in the ways in which the serene philosophical life is apprehended lies a puritanical contempt (perhaps born out of fear) of *pathos* (a Greek word meaning passion, as well as suffering and the root of 'pathology'), the cure for which, as Rollo May understood well, is no-pathos, or *a-pathy* (May, 1969). 'Philosophy as a way of life' would then become subservient to the metaphysical project of the tradition, aimed at distancing the human subject from the worrisome facets of human existence. How we think this through is important to how we practice psychotherapy. There is a world of difference between a view of human beings as essentially 'fallen' from a state of 'Being' or imagined unity, wholesomeness, purity etc. (to which we may return via therapeutic realignment and healing and a discovery of a pre-existing truth) and one that understands the human as intrinsically eccentric, body and mind never quite wholly integrated or in synch and with time forever out of joint.

Regardless of the theoretic orientation, the former perspective will probably be driven by a desire to control, guide, implicitly or explicitly chastise the person and direct her along a normative agenda. The latter perspective will probably be animated by empathy, active and unconditional acceptance of contradictions, shortcomings and complexities and by the aspiration to help the person become more attuned to organismic experiencing. In short, the former position is *onto-theological*; the latter, *naturalistic*.

A second possible answer to the question, 'What would philosophy as a way of life look like?' is *articulation*, for instance in the way that Ludwig Wittgenstein argues for. Wittgenstein sets out his store in the heart of the city centre of the unsaid, the inexplicable and yet arrested state of affairs that we find ourselves in. Philosophy as a way of life here is about seeing, showing and describing accurately the scene before us from the very fabric of our lived lives. This accurate describing and our ability to be articulate as a means of living in truthfulness (ethics), and not cleverness, is our task in philosophical practice; a similarity that all too often is poisoned in the psychotherapeutic field by the illusions of scientific solving and medical fixing. At a CPD event in expressive art therapy, a facilitator once instructed participants to 'engage their right-brain to create a picture and give their left-brain a rest'. There is a problem with this sort of instruction, and it is a philosophical one. We cannot stand outside of our brain and instruct either bit of it to do anything. No doubt that when we pick up a crayon and apply it to the paper and draw something, there may be some neural firing or activity happening somewhere in that part of the brain that neuroscience considers to be our creative side. But it tells us nothing of our creative ability, emotional outpouring, the creation itself or our attachment to that creation. The value of such a creation is likely to be articulated through our subsequent critical reflection. This critical reflection, as an attempt to articulate our experience and any meaning it may hold for us, may, however, tell us a lot about the predicament we find ourselves in. It is a part of philosophical practice. It does not misappropriate the language of science or hijack the language of medicine but uses a homely language, whilst paying attention to living. Another part of that practice is to engage in the enquiry as to what it might be to be human, and that is to engage in dialogue not just with those wondrous descriptions from philosophers such as those presented here but also with art, poetry, literature and with one another on a day-to-day basis.

This day-to-day activity then becomes an ethical endeavour, for if I endeavour to engage with you, I will be more open and welcoming, with less of an agenda, prescription or prejudice. This is the language of ethics in philosophical practice beyond, though not necessarily at variance with ethical frameworks and guidelines. Ethics presented in this way is not about defending one's identity. On the contrary, in line with the philosophers presented in this collection, 'identity' is the very wedge that blocks ethics.

This book begins and ends with Nietzsche – a trailblazer, in modern times, of the counter-tradition initiated long ago by Heraclitus. Equally significant is the presence of Wittgenstein, with two chapters on a philosopher who was also, to use a label now in vogue, an 'anti-philosopher'. Between these significant voices you will hear from other formidable thinkers: Kierkegaard, Keats, D. H. Lawrence, Pascal, Butler, Sartre, Rousseau, Camus, Deleuze, Merleau-Ponty, Irigaray and Schopenhauer. There are many absences too, for whom maybe a second, even a third book would be necessary: Spinoza, Hume, Marx, Dewey, Blanchot, Arendt, de Beauvoir and Kristeva immediately come to mind, followed, in unruly succession, by Bataille, Benjamin, Adorno, Genet, Rorty, Cixous but also Latour, Bennett, Jameson, Agamben . . . The list could go on.

Some thinkers are present *in absentia*, their influence a vital atmosphere, a given. First of all, Heraclitus, the philosopher/poet of becoming, a thinker mistakenly branded as 'obscure' but one who taught us how much closer to human experience the *fragment*, rather than the *system* truly is. Then Hegel, the *early* Hegel of the *Phenomenology of Spirit*, influential in the development of existential phenomenology but strangely omitted in contemporary psychotherapy literature. His work appears as the essential backdrop of some of the chapters presented here.

The presence in the collection of a poet (Keats) and a novelist/poet (D. H. Lawrence) may surprise readers used to regard philosophy as a solely ontological or logical undertaking. But within what is often disparagingly called 'continental philosophy', particularly since the mid-twentieth century, the opening of philosophy to poetry, literature and art is a given. From their very inception, in fact, philosophy, poetry and art have been closely intertwined, linked to the pre-Euripidean Greek tragedians (Colli, 1975; Nietzsche, 1993), their union giving birth to the poetry of thought (Steiner, 2014) as well as the fever of thought (Genet, 2003).

Assembling chapters from writers and experienced practitioners, this collection aims to open psychotherapy to philosophy and, in turn, philosophy to art, poetry, and literature – all natural accomplices in offering inspiring, bold and colourful narrative on the enigma, grandeur and ambiguity of being human.

References

Clemens, J. (2013) *Psychoanalysis Is an Antiphilosophy* Edinburgh: Edinburgh University Press.
Colli, G. (1975) *La Nascita della Filosofia* Milano: Adelphi.
Genet, J. (2003) *Prisoner of Love* New York: New Royal Book Company.
Madison, G. B. (1981) *The Phenomenology of Merleau-Ponty* Athens: Ohio University Press.
May, R. (1969) *Love and Will* New York: Norton.
Nietzsche, F. (1993) *The Birth of Tragedy out of the Spirit of Music* London: Penguin.
Steiner, G. (2014) *The Poetry of Thought* New York: New Directions.

PART I
The threshold experience

We experience the threshold when we openly question ourselves. This may be deliberate on our part or brought about by a crisis. Its undertones may be ecstasy or deep sorrow. The experience of the threshold makes us (painfully, joyfully) aware of our limitations; it makes us aware of how much we can't be aware of.

At times the threshold experience is accompanied by the illusion of transcendence – the sense of a durable, stable reality outside the world of phenomena – and by a yearning to secure access to this 'eternity'. Believing the latter to be separate from this world may be the pitfall of most transpersonal psychotherapies. True, this reality is *transcendental*: it is beyond our grasp, in the way shifts of power and desire, genetic flows and geological movements are. But it is not *transcendent*. Rather, it is *immanent* – part of the same plane of reality.

Glimpsing the scale of my ignorance – sensing the hedge of my self-made prison – is both sobering and exhilarating. I feel intoxicated, struck by the distinctiveness and ambiguity of the virtual, of the Dionysian – by the flux of forces that have no need whatsoever for a subject or a self, that have no need for *me*. I cannot translate the experience in the confused clarity of my everyday dwelling. I do it anyway, promising not to give in to the siren call of literalism. Why? Because it was rupture before rapture, a point where my irrational reasoning faltered, giving way to a thirst for poetry and a poetic response. Some of the accounts in the chapters that follow can be read as poetic responses: Keats's negative capability, D. H. Lawrence's attunement to the mystery and beauty of the body, Pascal's tears of joy, Kierkegaard's openness to the lilies and the birds, Nietzsche's invitation to lean towards an abyss of light. The sleep of *logos* generates wonders.

1
CHANGELINGS
The self in Nietzsche's psychology

Manu Bazzano

Neither self nor 'no-self'

> That a psychologist without equal speaks from my writings is perhaps the first insight gained by a good reader – a reader such as I deserve him.
>
> (Nietzsche, 2004, p. 45)

A key tenet in modern psychology is the belief in the existence of a separate self (or 'subject') – of a doer behind the deed. For Nietzsche, this belief represented the core of nineteenth-century bourgeois morality and had its origins in the Christian notion of the individual soul. As an autonomous soul, I alone am responsible for my actions. The fact that I am answerable for what I do sounds obvious; so does the idea that I exist as a separate, self-governing individual. Autonomy, freedom and responsibility contribute to my sense of dignity; how can these notions be disputed? I will, however, neither dispute nor defend these ideas here: I will not assert the existence of an autonomous self, nor will I endorse a belief in 'no-self'. This is because I find both stances uninspiring, as well as one-sided. Moreover, they have been argued to death. Dualistic approaches try hard to substantiate the self (often through overidentification with Descartes' 'thinking thing' and its post-Cartesian variations, including the notion of an autonomous psyche). Other accounts choose to bypass the self, usually by emphasizing its interdependent or intersubjective nature, by describing it as 'being-in the-world' and so forth.

Obviously one cannot draw on Nietzsche to bolster a Cartesian view of the self, though many still insist on a caricature of the *Übermensch* as superman or wonder woman. Equally and less evidently, one cannot draw on Nietzsche to prop up a simplistic bypass of the self, as it is sometimes the case in 'transpersonal' perspectives. It is for these reasons that (drawing from Nietzsche's writings yet varying from familiar interpretations) I will attempt a different route.

Warning

I should warn readers at this point, especially those expecting a confirmation of their views of Nietzsche as instigator of unbridled individualism and uninhibited narcissism or as harbinger of a now rather fashionable brand of existential 'authenticity': you will be disappointed. Equally frustrated will be those who prefer to read him as an existentialist *avant la lettre*, the purveyor of a relational, spiritually tinged notion of 'no-self' or 'relational self'.

What name should one then give to the reading of Nietzsche presented here? For reasons that I hope will become clear, I suggest the term *negative psychology*.

Reading well, reading slowly

Before becoming a philosopher, Nietzsche was a precociously gifted classical philologist. Despite his later disparaging of this branch of learning's inherent sophistry, and despite the fact that the publication of his first book *The Birth of Tragedy* meant lifelong exclusion from the guild of philologists, he relied on philology's methods throughout his creative life: reading well, reading slowly and deeply, cultivating interpretative rigour. His grounding in philology provided him with the foundations for his genealogical approach to the notion of the self. In exploring the latter, Nietzsche revisits its historical formation – an almost *geological*, as much as a genealogical, approach, tracing the 'story' of the subject as we know it (i.e. the autonomous actor existing separately behind the action) as the ingenious creation of the prevailing Christian and bourgeois morality.

A thirst for enemies

The soul is not eternal but *contingent*. For Nietzsche, the very idea of a 'soul' (from which that of a self derives) is an indispensable *construct* in the development of our species, the result of a "forcible sundering from [our] animal past" (Conway, 1999, p. 55). Our 'inner life' is a by-product of inhibition.

> All instincts which are not discharged outwardly *turn inwards* – this is what I call the *internalization* of man: with it there now evolves in man what will later be called his 'soul'. The whole inner world, originally stretched thinly as though between two layers of skin, was expanded and extended itself and gained depth, breadth and height in proportion to the degree that the external discharge of man's instincts was *obstructed*.
>
> *(Nietzsche, 1996, p. 57)*

For Nietzsche (long before Freud), we were forced to partake "schizophrenically in the taboo pronounced by civil society" on "all those instincts of wild, free, prowling man" (Conway, 1999, p. 55). This was as much a process of *repression* as of *ingenuity* on our part. The ingenuity came from our ability as a species to cover up our motives with the noble and gracious gloss of moral righteousness. Here is an example: we habitually think we are free "to express or not to express strength" (Nietzsche, 1996, p. 29). Often the second option is not really a choice but a cunning move that masquerades as virtue my inability to exercise strength. Say, for instance, that during the course of a public discussion you voice a strong disagreement with what I am saying. I may defend my position and listen to what you have to say. I may notice, however, that I am now beginning to feel irritated, even angry; you clearly do not recognize the depth of my insight. My exasperation is now increased by the vague feeling that you may be right after all. I fear defeat, so I retreat, explaining my decision in terms of moral principles. 'I abhor confrontation – I will say – I am a Buddhist. It's no good wasting precious time arguing. I'll send you thoughts of loving kindness instead'. Thanks to my ostensible moral superiority, I have missed the chance of being congruent, even perhaps of reaching that greater level of understanding that comes from *real* dialogue – i.e. from a conversation that, according to Bakhtin, who first coined the term 'dialogical' (Bakhtin, 1982), does *not* end in mutual agreement or does *not* necessarily find common ground. I have also conveniently avoided confronting my inability to deal with anger in a constructive way.

I may, on the other hand, choose to pay tribute to the shallow 'pluralism' now in vogue: I will nod politely and pretend to appreciate your perspective while remaining leisurely unaffected by your intervention. I will respond to your objections with a knowing smile and conclude that there are as many views as there are people on this wonderful planet of ours. My admirably democratic position will leave both of us happy and unscathed in our carefully cultivated cocoon of 'individuality' – all the while paying lip service to a goody-goody notion of dialogue.

Or – I may accept the openly declared *agon* and be involved in the challenge you posed. I will honour my "thirst for enemies" (Nietzsche, 1996, p. 26), engage with you fully in honourable conflict – I will fight and disagree with you because I respect you.

Bluntly put: for Nietzsche, (a) civilized living imposes on us the *implosion* of natural elemental forces: thus the birth of our so-called 'inner life'; (b) the weak person's inability to engage in honourable conflict brings him/her to cleverly think of 'moral principles' that his/her separate self decides to abide by. As we shall see, a naturalistic reading of this dilemma will enable us to understand the situation more in terms of *quantum of force*, and we will refrain from placing the cause of action in a *separate* self. Here is Nietzsche:

> A quantum of force is just such a quantum of drive, will, action, in fact it is nothing but this driving, willing and acting, and only the seduction of language (and the fundamental errors of reason petrified within it), which construes and misconstrues all actions as conditional upon an agency, a 'subject', can make it appear otherwise. And just as the common people separates lightning from its flash and takes the latter to be a *deed*, something performed by a subject, which is called lightning, popular morality separates strength from the manifestations of strength, as though there were an indifferent substratum behind the strong person which had the *freedom* to manifest strength

or not. But there is no such substratum; there is no 'being' behind the deed, its effect and what becomes of it; 'the doer' is invented as an afterthought, – the doing is everything.

(Nietzsche, 1996, pp 25–26)

In sickness and in health

Weakness/strength, illness/health: these physiological as well as psychological binomials recur with regularity in Nietzsche's writings. If feeling weak, fragile, uncertain, I may choose, rather than acknowledging my weakness, to paint it with the colours of compassion or virtue. After all, this choice is tried and tested, having shored up the millenarian practices of institutionalized religion. If I happen to be allergic to long-established Judaeo-Christian pieties, I can always resort to 'mindfulness' or to equally effective secular forms of moralizing.

For Nietzsche, the notion of a self, separate from its actions, is a direct by-product of our weakness. He writes:

> There is nothing strange about the fact that lambs bear a grudge towards large birds of prey: but that is no reason to blame the large birds of prey for carrying off the little lambs. And if the lambs say to each other, 'These birds of prey are evil; and whoever is least like a bird of prey and most like its opposite, a lamb, – is good, isn't he?', then there is no reason to raise objections to this setting-up of an ideal beyond the fact that the birds of prey will view it somewhat derisively, and will perhaps say: "We don't bear any grudge at all towards these good lambs, in fact we love them, nothing is tastier than a tender lamb."
>
> *(Nietzsche, 1996, pp. 25–26)*

Weakness as freedom

What kind of person must believe in an "unbiased subject [endowed] with freedom of choice"? (Nietzsche, 1996, p. 26). Answer: one whose main concern is *self-preservation*. And what kind of organism is motivated by self-preservation? The question will be asked by neurologist and philosopher Kurt Goldstein some forty years later. And his reply is: a *sick* organism. Nietzsche and Goldstein, these two elective disciples of Goethe – the latter a precursor of *Gestalt* as well as non-reductive neuroscience – thoroughly agreed on this crucial point. Pathology is for Goldstein characterized by the *shrinking* of organismic experiencing (Goldstein, 1995). And what defines, conversely, *strength* in a healthy organism is the desire to give, even to squander one's resources: the will to power is at heart generosity (Bazzano, 2006).

Nietzsche's extraordinary suggestion is that our culture's fixation with the notion of an independent self is the product of the latter's endemic sickness, of our demand that others be in awe of our feebleness. The notion of an independent subject depends on our magnificent self-deception that sees weakness as freedom (Nietzsche, 1996).

And now for something truly objective

There is a broader association with our habitual notion of a doer behind a deed, and it has to do with *cause* and *effect*. In *The Gay Science*, Nietzsche writes:

> Cause and effect: such a duality probably never exists; in truth we are confronted by a continuum out of which we isolate a couple of pieces, just as we perceive motion only as isolated points and then infer it without ever actually seeing it. The suddenness with which many effects stand out misleads us; actually, it is sudden only for us. In this moment of suddenness there is an infinite number of processes that elude us. An intellect that could see cause and effect as a continuum and a flux and not, as we do, in terms of arbitrary division and dismemberment, would repudiate the concept of cause and effect and deny all conditionality.
>
> *(Nietzsche, 1991, p. 173)*

Nietzsche's position is not, however, straightforward naturalism. In a later work, *Twilight of the Idols* (Nietzsche, 2003), he critiques psychology *and* science in the same breath – the *soul atomism* of the former as much as the *atomism* of physicists (Acampora, 2004), both in turn dependent on the Kantian idealism of the 'thing-in-itself':

> And even your atom, my dear mechanists and physicists – how much error, how much rudimentary psychology is still residual in your atom! Not to mention the 'thing-in-itself'. . . of the metaphysicians! The error of the spirit as cause mistaken for reality! And made the very measure of reality! And called God!
>
> *(Nietzsche, 2003, p. 61)*

Our objective sciences, in other words, are anthropocentric to the core, relying on human psychology, which is in turn ensnared by the idea that spirit, self, consciousness are primary *causes*.

The trouble with phenomenologists

Nietzsche did not end his analysis here. If he had, his would have been a deterministic reading that understands deeds as activated by forces and humans as little more than fortuitous conduits. His notion alters during the course of his rigorous and, to some, vertiginous perspectivism. Before considering in what ways his perception changes, it may be worthwhile to reflect on how the idea of 'no doer behind the deed', compellingly conveyed in the *Genealogy*, can serve our aim here. The first, immediate advantage of this notion is its serving as a necessary antidote to a contemporary orthodoxy almost irrevocably ensnared by unreconstructed notions of subjectivity. I am not referring exclusively to the obvious examples summarily listed here as follows:

- State-sponsored M.O.T.-style interventions aimed at making the wounded and the discouraged fit for productivity;
- Inspirational conversations focused on helping people achieve self-actualization, authenticity, their higher or true self or their inner child (delete as appropriate);
- Archaeological excavations of intricate mommy-daddy scenarios;
- DIY manuals for successfully applying the tags *transference* and *counter-transference* over-human interactions, particularly those happening in the 'therapy world'.

I am explicitly referring to a 'school' of therapy that has claimed Nietzsche's legacy as its own, perhaps without really earning it: existential/phenomenological psychotherapy. Despite (or perhaps because of) its emphasis on the 'relational' domain and despite (or perhaps because of) its flight into *Dasein*, within this orientation the subject remains royally intact. The famed description of phenomena, trumpeted as radically and horizontally different from analysis, unfailingly goes back to the Ithaca of the subject who remains at the centre of phenomenological investigation. There may be acknowledgement of simultaneous 'inner' and 'outer' incidences, but these are all referred back to 'me'. Similarly, *epoché*, or 'bracketing', may be seen as an essentially self-centred operation, especially when abstractly conceived and without an accompanying psychosomatic form of *askesis* (self-discipline) such as meditation. Phenomena emerge incessantly and without a centre. Things happen: they arise, abide for a while and fade. They do not happen to *me*. In Nietzsche's thought, as in all non-self-centred investigation, the question is not 'Who am I?' but rather (as in Zen practice) 'What is this?' (Sunim, 2009), a question that addresses the entire (and decentred) field of phenomena.

I write these words with a deep sense of ambivalence, having practiced from within a humanistic and existential frame for several years (even though I came to psychotherapy long after studying Nietzsche). The paradox is that in Nietzsche we find not only the *basis* of existential phenomenology – in his persuasive ousting of metaphysics and epistemology – but also its anticipatory overcoming. While Husserl and Heidegger cling to the notions of *truth* and of a *real world*, Nietzsche's enquiry does not end there. If it did, his philosophy would be merely a reversal of Plato's 'two world' metaphysics (Poellner, 1995) with pride of place granted this time to the phenomenal world (whose hidden 'truth' would in turn be 'unveiled' to/by a subject). But the real world is for Nietzsche a myth – useful at times, but a myth nevertheless:

> The 'real world' – an idea no longer of any use, not even a duty any longer – an idea grown useless, superfluous, consequently a refuted idea: let us abolish it!...
> We have abolished the real world: what world is left? The apparent world perhaps?... But no! *With the real world we have also abolished the apparent world!*
> (Nietzsche, 2003, p. 50)

Belief in the existence of an autonomous self is closely associated to the metaphysical notion of *being* behind *becoming*. One of the tasks for a philosophy of becoming, as articulated by the counter-tradition, is to dispose of the idea of being altogether. In this, Nietzsche remains the most direct inheritor in modern times of the first thinker of the counter-tradition, Heraclitus.

We are not artists enough

As far as *truth* goes, the will to truth epitomized by science (championed by Husserl) and a philosophy of being (advocated by Heidegger) is for Nietzsche a manifestation of our *inability to create*. We placidly assume the existence of a ready-made truth somewhere, behind the bewildering precariousness of the world – a static truth waiting to be discovered. This view is not only complacent; it is a symptom of weakness. We nurture it because we are not daring and inventive enough – we are not *artists* enough – to *create* truth. The will to knowledge (*episteme*) and the will to truth (*aletheia*) both are born of our *fear* of becoming, "a movement proper to mediocre people who are unable to direct and dominate things and who conceive of happiness as immobility" (Vattimo, 2005, p. 18).

Incidentally, Nietzsche being Nietzsche, in his writings there is no straightforward 'relativist' rejection of truth in favour of *semblance*. Reason and the will to truth play an important role in the plurality of the psyche but certainly not the dominant role assigned to them by centuries of rationalism and metaphysics. Paradoxically, even the will to deceit (and self-deception) plays its part in our psychological landscape.

Does the therapist help her client unveil a pre-existing truth known to the therapist? My sense is that client and therapist together *create* truth by "taking the risk of communicating" (Madison, 1981). This is a risk worth taking because:

> [c]lient and therapist may come to bear witness to the evanescent coming-into-being, through dialogue, of a truth forged in encounter rather than the unveiling of a pre-existing, a-historical truth behind the course of events.
> (Bazzano, 2013, p. 207)

Lebensphilosophie or *Existenzphilosophie*?

Following on the footsteps of Jaspers and Heidegger, existential psychotherapy embraced Nietzsche – with mixed results. Other applications of Nietzsche's thought that could have potentially proved more fruitful were sadly neglected. I am thinking of the *philosophical anthropology* of Scheler (1961) and Plessner (1970), a school of thought often associated with phenomenology despite the fact that it had emerged from a distinct cultural movement of the 1920s originally associated with Nietzsche: *Lebensphilosophie*, the philosophy of biological and human life championed by thinkers such as Dilthey, Bergson, Klages and others. *Lebensphilosophie* presents us with refreshing alternatives to the interpretations of Nietzsche hypothesized by *Existenzphilosophie*. For example, for Dilthey (2010), our task is to understand the world on its own terms by developing the empathic relation one would apply to a work of art – a view close to Nietzsche's. Klages was one of the first who appreciated Nietzsche's psychological accomplishments, while Simmel, Bäumler and Joël each valued Nietzsche's relevance in various areas of knowledge and human enquiry (Behler, 1991). Bergson's own brand of vitalism was in turn to inspire the work of one of Nietzsche's greatest interpreters in the twentieth century, Gilles Deleuze (1983).

The *Existenzphilosophie* of Jaspers and Heidegger ended up overshadowing *Lebensphilosophie*, as well as Scheler's and Plessner's anthropological philosophy. Heidegger never mentions Scheler, whose far-reaching analyses of Nietzsche's thought are also virtually unknown to the English-speaking world. What is still refreshing about their approach is the absence of a reference "on first-person-singular human existing" (Schacht, 2006, p. 131). Richard Schacht writes:

> [Existential philosophers] often embraced Nietzsche avidly; but they also embraced him selectively, to suit their own philosophical purposes, which were generally hostile to any and all forms of naturalistic interpretation of human reality.
>
> *(Schacht, 2006, p. 131)*

A return to a (neglected) *naturalistic* reading of Nietzsche (in contrast to predominant *onto-theological* perspectives) may well be an antidote to the privileged role most psychotherapy orientations grant to the notion of a self whose origins are steeped, lest we forget it, in bourgeois morality. It could also form the basis, in an era of identity politics and intolerance of otherness, of a psychotherapy steeped in the more inclusive ethics of the *citizen* (Bazzano, 2015a).

In all fairness, within phenomenology there *have* been significant if unassuming signs of a move away from Husserlian subjectivism and Heideggerian mysticism. Merleau-Ponty's fertile notion of the *body-subject* (Merleau-Ponty, 1989) sheds light on our situation as incarnate beings: we are organically bound to the natural world; a sophisticated, precognitive language straddling the artificial divide between world and self *precedes* the allegedly 'free' and 'pure' consciousness, which is presumed to gaze at matter and become like a spectator. But Merleau-Ponty's thought remains marginal in conventional existential psychotherapy, partly because it resists systematization and is thus ousted by other thinkers' lofty if unfulfilled promises of bestowing on us their grand 'theory of being'. In this sense, Merleau-Ponty is a natural heir of Nietzsche: both thinkers' inherent naturalism reclaims the centrality of the body.

How to sanitize Nietzsche

A growing trend in scholarship (Abby, 2000; Safranski, 2003; Ure, 2008) sees Nietzsche's middle works (*Human, All Too Human, Daybreak* and *Gay Science* in particular) at variance both with his Wagnerian/Schopenhauerian debut and with the quasi-metaphysical pronouncements of his posthumous notes. In contrast with the Dionysian intoxications of *The Birth of Tragedy* and the ethical and political ambivalence of some of the *Nachlass*, the middle works would be animated instead by a pervasive disposition of tranquil examination and meek psychological enquiry. A central theme would be cultivation and care of the self – attitudes echoing the Stoics, the Epicureans and even Socrates – all compatible with the kind of explorations taken on a century later by Foucault (1997), Hadot (1995) and others. These later writers reconfigured subjectivity in term of *askesis* (self-discipline) and in an altogether more positive light than it had been portrayed during the 'death of the subject' heyday of post-structuralism.

It is true that the middle works register a significant, almost 'positivist' shift compared to the giddiness of *The Birth of Tragedy*. Certainly the dedication of the first 1878 edition of *Human, All Too Human* to Voltaire was more than an effective way to infuriate Wagner. Yet to read the middle works as painlessly compatible with ancient Greek rationalism seriously underplays Nietzsche's lifelong antagonism to Socratism and Platonism, and it glosses over the deep ambiguity displayed in his writings towards Greek thought (with the exception of the pre-Socratics and the tragedians). Although he admired the serene materialism of a thinker like Epicurus, he was at pains to distance himself from Socratic dialectics and Plato's metaphysics. Although Nietzsche's Dionysus undergoes a profound transformation during the course of his sixteen years' prodigious creative output (Bazzano, 2006), he remains the northern star in Nietzsche's firmament. Dionysus is a vexing presence in a present cultural landscape bent towards gaining mastery over the unruly nature of the affects that threatens the alleged solidity of the self. I wonder to what extent the attempt to turn Nietzsche into a modern Stoic philosopher unwittingly fits a contemporary ethos of control and sanitization of those aspects of human experience that are deemed problematic (Bazzano, 2012).

Appeals to Greek *ataraxia* (serenity or imperturbability) are now popular in current Buddhist-tinged literature as well as in philosophical and psychotherapeutic practices. Without wishing in any way to disparage *ataraxia* as a desirable goal (who would not wish serenity to those among us afflicted by mental anguish?), it is equally important to point out that this notion of serenity has to be uncoupled from notions of control and mastery over the passions if it is to play a role beyond the demands of the ego. The passions, these "magnificent monsters" (Nietzsche, 1967, p. 521), are endowed with an almost numinous quality. We can learn from their intensity and irreducible autonomy in the same way, say, in which we humbly *learn* from a dream rather than bending the oneiric domain to the goals and agendas of our waking life. Gaining full control over the passions (or rather mistakenly believing we have done so) is a form of *hubris*, whose other name is Titanism. In Greek mythology, the Titans were giants who defied the gods out of arrogance, mistakenly believing themselves to be more powerful than the gods themselves. Prometheus is one such Titan. There is no greater ego than the ego of the scientist who believes his research to be one hundred per cent objective or that of the pious person who truly believes he has eradicated 'negative' emotions from his psyche. There is no greater ego than that of the person who believes him/herself to be 'spiritual' and/or fully integrated.

From individual to dividual

Yet the validity and richness of his self-exploratory, pointedly 'psychological' turn in Nietzsche's middle works is irrefutable. It yielded real gems, one of which is the notion of the *dividual*. Nietzsche resorts to the scholastic words "*individuum*" and "*dividuum*" (1994, p. 54) to illustrate his point. *Individuum*, from which 'individual' derives, is that which cannot be divided without obliterating its essence; *dividuum*, from which the new term 'dividual' derives (useful in describing the self in Nietzschean terms) is an *aggregate* devoid of individual essence. This is firstly an ontological statement on the nature of the self, remarkably similar to the Buddhist notion of *skandhas* (heaps, or aggregates), one that rather than granting primacy to the 'mind' sees the self as a combination of physicality, feeling-tone, perception, impulse, and consciousness (Bazzano, 2015b). It also has a more ordinary dimension of flexibility, as a passage in *Human, All Too Human* neatly illustrates:

> *A philosophical frame of mind.* Generally we strive to acquire one emotional stance, one viewpoint for all life situations and events: we usually call that being of a philosophical frame of mind. But rather than making oneself uniform, we may find greater value for the enrichment of knowledge by listening to the soft voice of different life situations; each brings its own views with it. Thus we acknowledge and share the life and nature of many by not treating ourselves like rigid, invariable, single individuals.
>
> *(Nietzsche, 1994, p. 256)*

I am a changeling

Nietzsche's thought constitutes the beating heart of the *counter-tradition* and is profoundly *counter-cultural*: it invites limitless interpretation rather than advocating the mere renovations of cultural models. In his writings we find the seeds of important future deconstructions and negations. The death of God also signals "the definitive banishment of metaphysical forms concealed in the dialectics of self-awareness and of the subject" (Masini, 1978, pp. 21–22, my translation).

In the *Genealogy of Morals*, Nietzsche (1996) describes the self as a *changeling* (p. 26). The term has several meanings. Its archaic meaning describes one given to change, a fickle or inconsistent person, a turncoat, a renegade. It also describes a person or thing surreptitiously put in exchange for another: a child substituted for another in infancy; a half-witted person. We find an equivalent in Lacan, for whom the subject is a failure at subjectification (Clemens, 2013).

No happy endings

So far, the suggestion presented, in various guises, throughout this chapter can be summed up as follows: 'there is no doer behind the deed', and 'the deed is everything'. It is, Nietzsche tells us, a question of strength expressing itself. Is the doer (the self, subject), then, a fiction, a function of grammar, an expression of the commonsense, everyday necessity of using the word 'I' when speaking? To understand this position as Nietzsche's unambiguous viewpoint on the matter would effectively mean overlooking the multi-perspectival nature of his thought. Although it is true that for Nietzsche the deed is everything, at the same time the doer (the embodied human subject for whom the body itself, rather than the soul, constitutes the 'great reason') does not simply evaporate as a provisional choreographic prop on the stage of 'being'. If such a metaphysical bypass of the self has been ascribed to Nietzsche, this is partly due to Heidegger's influential 1936–1946 lectures (Heidegger, 1979–1987) in which, rather arbitrarily, Nietzsche is presented as a metaphysical thinker, when in fact he not only convincingly negated metaphysics but presented us with highly nuanced perspectives on subjectivity.

In *Thus Spoke Zarathustra*, Nietzsche suggests a more subtle relation between doer and deed:

> Oh, my friend, that your self be in your deed as the mother is in the child – let that be your word concerning virtue.
>
> *(Nietzsche, 1978, p. 94)*

There is a very intimate link between doer and deed, Nietzsche seems to suggest.

Taking my cue from Taylor (1977) and Pippin (2006), I propose a way of reframing the relation between doer and deed, one that goes back to the Hegel of the *Phenomenology of Spirit*:

> Whatever it is that the individual does, and whatever happens to him, that he has done himself, and he is that himself. He can have only the consciousness of the simple transference of himself from the night of possibility into the daylight of the present, from the abstract in-itself into the significance of actual being, and can have only the certainty that what happens to him in the latter is nothing else but what lay dormant in the former . . . The individual, therefore, knowing that in his actual world he can find nothing else but is unity with himself, or only the certainty of himself in the truth of that world, can experience only joy in himself.
>
> *(Hegel, 1977, p. 242)*

The view of action presented here at the very birth of (pre-Husserlian) phenomenology is based not on *intentionality* but on *expression* – a crucial difference, as Pippin (2006) explains:

> I may start out engaged in a project, understanding my intention as X, and, over time, come to understand that this was not really what I intended; it must have been Y or later perhaps Z. And there is no way to confirm the certainty of one's real purpose except *in* the deed actually performed. My subjective construal at any time before or during the deed has no privileged authority. The deed *alone* can show one who one is.
> *(Pippin, 2006, p. 381)*

The deed is inherently social and historical; an interpretation of Nietzsche's writing that was intended to emphasize expression over intentionality in the relation between doer and deed turns Nietzsche's psychology into a social as well as historical psychology. I see myself in the deed – socially, historically. The deed is an expression of me. My 'original' and 'authentic' intentions are simply "provisional starting points, formulated with incomplete knowledge of circumstances and consequences" (Pippin, 2006, p. 382). What I end up doing is the expression of my intention. In Hegel's words, "Ethical self-consciousness now learns from its deed the developed nature of what it actually did" (Hegel, 1977, p. 283).

I am aware that choosing Hegel as provisional accomplice in my interpretation of Nietzsche's psychology may be deemed objectionable by some. It is nevertheless consistent with recent scholarship and with my own championing of Hegel's early works (Bazzano, 2013). His depiction, in the *Phenomenology of Spirit*, of *Anerkennung* (recognition/acknowledgement) and of the lordship and bondage dialectic throughout history provides the missing link in contemporary psychotherapy's understanding of 'intersubjectivity'. By emphasizing the real presence of conflict in human encounter, Hegel avoided romanticizing the latter, and, although allowing for the possibility of commonality, he crucially identified the suffering and injustice present in human affairs. In fact, it could be said that Nietzsche exacerbates the conflict inherent in encounter and instrumental to the formation of self-consciousness by *not* resolving it teleologically as Hegel does, let alone allow for the pious fantasy of happy endings often envisaged in the 'Philosophy of the Meeting' championed by Buber and romanticized by swarms of imitators.

Closely linked to this is the virtual impossibility of *building* on Nietzsche's psychology, as many would like to do, imagining an uninterrupted lineage of philosophical and therapeutic practices beginning with him and Kierkegaard. In this sense, Nietzsche's psychology is a *negative psychology*. This is because Nietzsche's analysis of the self highlights a point of rupture, even of dissolution. Far from being a prototype of a new human being, the *Übermensch* signals a crisis – a *creative* crisis certainly, yet a crisis all the same – the agonizing demise of the self-as-we-know-it. A more detailed discussion of how this crisis – signalled by a 'limit experience' – comes about belongs, however, to a different essay.

Nietzsche's thought being irreducible, it is hard to build from it a philosophical school, let alone a neatly defined psychology. This in spite of the fact that many of Nietzsche's ideas can be found, among others, in Freud's psychoanalysis, Jung's analytical psychology, Adler's individual psychology, Otto Rank's notion of 'creative will', Rollo May's existential psychoanalysis – the list can go on. Nietzsche's influence is often unacknowledged, perhaps because his presence is too mercurial, his perspectivism too unsettling. Above all, he mocked the bulwarks of Western civilization – chief among them the notion of truth – unmasking the pretense hiding behind many of our cherished notions. For these reasons, Nietzsche makes for a strange bedfellow – an outsider, whose brilliance inculcates the twin feelings of fear and respect or, among 'virtuous people', the feeling of disdain.

References

Abby, R. (2000) *Nietzsche's Middle Period* London: Oxford University Press.
Acampora, C. D. (2004) 'Between Mechanism and Teleology: Will to Power and Nietzsche's Gay Science' in Moore, G., & Brobjer, T. H. (Eds.) *Nietzsche and Science* Aldershot: Ashgate pp. 171–188.
Bakhtin, M. (1982) *The Dialogic Imagination: Four Essays* Austin: University of Texas Press.
Bazzano, M. (2006) *Buddha Is Dead: Nietzsche and the Dawn of European Zen* Brighton, Sussex: Sussex Academic Press.
Bazzano, M. (2012) 'Embracing the World' *Therapy Today*, November (23) 9, Internet file www.therapytoday.net/article/show/3434/embracing-the-world. Retrieved 6 May 2015.
Bazzano, M. (2013) 'Togetherness: Intersubjectivity Revisited' *Person-Centered & Experiential Psychotherapies*, DOI:10.1080/14779757.2013.852613. Retrieved 12 March 2015.
Bazzano, M. (2015a) 'Therapy as Unconditional Hospitality' *Psychotherapy and Politics International*, February (13) 1, DOI:10.1002/ppi.1342. Retrieved 12 March 2015.
Bazzano, M. (2015b) 'The Winner of the Race: The Dharma in the Digital Age' *International Journal of Psychotherapy* – special issue on psychotherapy and mindfulness. In press.
Behler, E. (1991) *Confrontations: Derrida, Heidegger, Nietzsche* Stanford, CA: Stanford University Press.
Clemens, J. (2013) *Psychoanalysis Is an Antiphilosophy* Edinburgh: Edinburgh University Press.
Conway, D. (1999) 'The Birth of the Soul: Towards a Psychology of Decadence' in Golomb, J., Santaniello, W., & Lehrer, R. (Eds.) *Nietzsche and Depth Psychology* Albany: State University of New York Press pp. 51–72.
Deleuze, G. (1983) *Nietzsche and Philosophy* London: Athlone.
Dilthey, W. (2010) *Selected Works: Volume III* Princeton, NJ: Princeton University Press.
Foucault, M. (1997) *Ethics: Subjectivity and Truth* New York: New Press.
Goldstein, K. (1995/1934) *The Organism* New York: Zone Books.
Hadot, P. (1995) *Philosophy as a Way of Life: Spiritual Exercises from Socrates to Foucault* London: Wiley-Blackwell.
Hegel, G. W. F. (1977) *Phenomenology of Spirit* Oxford: Clarendon Press.
Heidegger, M. (1979–1987) *Nietzsche* (4 volumes) San Francisco, CA: Harper & Row.
Madison, G. B. (1981) *The Phenomenology of Merleau-Ponty*, Athens, OH: Ohio University Press.
Masini, F. (1978) *Lo Scriba del Caos: Interpretazione di Nietzsche* Bologna: Il Mulino.
Merleau-Ponty, M. (1989) *Phenomenology of Perception* London: Routledge.
Nietzsche, F. (1967) *The Will to Power*, trans. Walter Kaufman London: Weidenfeld and Nicolson.

Nietzsche, F. (1978) *Thus Spoke Zarathustra: A Book for None and All*, trans. Walter Kaufman New York: Penguin.

Nietzsche, F. (1991) *The Gay Science, with a Prelude in Rhymes and an Appendix of Songs*, trans. Walter Kaufman New York: Random House.

Nietzsche, F. (1994) *Human, All Too Human: A Book for Free Spirits* London: Penguin.

Nietzsche, F. (1996) *On the Genealogy of Morals*, trans. Michael A. Scarpitti New York: Cambridge University Press.

Nietzsche, F. (2003) *The Twilight of the Idols and the Antichrist: Or How to Philosophize with a Hammer*, trans. R. J. Hollingdale London: Penguin.

Nietzsche, F. (2004) *Ecce Homo: How One Becomes What One Is*, trans. R. J. Hollingdale New York: Algora.

Pippin, R. B. (2006) 'Agent and Deed in the Genealogy of Morals' in Ansell Pearson, K. (Ed.) *A Companion to Nietzsche* Oxford: Blackwell pp. 371–386.

Plessner, H. (1970) *Laughing and Crying: A Study of the Limits of Human Behaviour* Evanston, IL: Northwestern University Press.

Poellner, P. (1995) *Nietzsche and Metaphysics* Oxford: Clarendon Press.

Safranski, R. (2003) *Nietzsche: A Philosophical Biography* New York: W. W. Norton.

Schacht, R. (2006) 'Nietzsche and Philosophical Anthropology' in Ansell Pearson, K. (Ed.) *A Companion to Nietzsche* Oxford: Blackwell pp. 115–132.

Scheler, M. (1961) *Man's Place in Nature* New York: Noonday.

Sunim, K. (2009) *The Way of Korean Zen* New York: Weatherhill.

Taylor, C. (1977) *Hegel* Cambridge, MA: Cambridge University Press.

Ure, M. (2008) *Nietzsche's Therapy: Self-cultivation in the Middle Works* Lanham, MA: Lexington Books.

Vattimo, G. (2005) *Dialogue with Nietzsche* New York: Columbia University Press.

2

WHAT CAN THERAPISTS LEARN FROM KIERKEGAARD?

John Lippitt

Introduction

Why should therapists read Søren Kierkegaard? In our largely secular age, in which the latest generation of religion's "cultured despisers" often seem to speak for the cultural mainstream, what has psychotherapy to learn from an unorthodox nineteenth-century Lutheran with an uncompromising view of the importance of a proper "God-relationship"? There can be no denying the influence of Kierkegaard on important psychotherapeutic figures as diverse as Ludwig Binswanger, Rollo May, Carl Rogers and Ernest Becker (Stewart, 2011). His insightful diagnoses of anxiety and despair have been a significant influence on existential psychotherapy. As one therapist recently told me, Kierkegaard is a source of great insight, provided we "ignore the religious stuff". Yet therapists who insist on taking their Kierkegaard safely secularized are missing a trick. In this chapter, I shall argue that it is in some of his less well-known, explicitly "religious" writings that Kierkegaard offers some of his most important insights for therapeutic practice. Gordon Marino has written movingly about his experience of reading Kierkegaard's *Works of Love* in the wake of a marital break-up and grasping from it the important insight that psychological suffering is something that can be done well or badly (Marino, 2014, pp. xxii–xxiii). Marino explicitly compares Kierkegaard to a therapist, adding:

> [h]is way of recasting the landscape of human existence helped float my spirit when I was going under in ways that were positively chilling to everyone around me.
>
> *(Marino, 2014, p. xxiii)*

Also relevant here is the fascination of readers, including novelists, with the details of Kierkegaard's own biography (including the infamous broken engagement to Regine Olsen). In a number of very different but highly engaging novels, reading

Kierkegaard serves as an important part of a process of therapeutic self-discovery (e.g. Lodge, 1995; Kimmel, 2003).

I have argued elsewhere (Lippitt, 2013) that Kierkegaard offers a rich conception of proper self-love that I believe has important implications for therapy. Central to this account is the application *to ourselves* of the trust, hope and forgiveness that are central to his accounts of love of God and neighbour. But here I shall concentrate primarily on a perhaps surprising theme from this famous diagnostician of anxiety and despair: what the reflections on "the lilies and the birds" in Kierkegaard's *Upbuilding Discourses* can teach us about contentment and self-acceptance and their relation to gratitude and patience.

Outline

Here's the plot. I shall first outline something of the way that Kierkegaard is typically presented to psychotherapists: as an insightful diagnostician of anxiety. I shall then suggest how some of the *Upbuilding Discourses* serve as an important complication to this picture. The perhaps unexpected theme of *contentment* will emerge as crucial here. Then, I'll mention some of the other themes relevant to therapy in Kierkegaard's discourses, such as cultivating gratitude and learning patience, and how they might both be rooted in the contentment discussed.

Kierkegaard: the anxiety guy?

Most students of existential psychotherapy will probably at some point have encountered Heidegger's brief, pregnant remark that "the man who has gone farthest in analyzing the phenomenon of anxiety – and again in the theological context of a 'psychological' exposition of the problem of original sin – is Søren Kierkegaard" (Heidegger, 1962, p. 452). And it is as an insightful analyst of anxiety (and sometimes despair) that Kierkegaard is typically presented in this context. Emmy van Deurzen, for instance, notes that for Kierkegaard anxiety is essential to spiritual life:

> Anxiety as the basic experience of our confrontation with our essential paradox cannot be avoided without cost. If we try to avoid it, we will either go under in it or we will be simply insensitive to existence and unable to truly live.
> *(van Deurzen, 2010, p. 13)*

Van Deurzen claims that this "remarkable insight" is "of great relevance to twenty-first century psychotherapy" (van Deurzen, 2010, p. 13). Whereas most contemporary psychotherapy treats anxiety as a problem to be reduced to as minimal a level as possible, for Kierkegaard it is "a sign that the struggle with human paradox is taken seriously" (van Deurzen, 2010, p.13). (By "paradox" here I take van Deurzen to mean the various ostensibly opposed elements in the human being [eternal/temporal; finitude/infinitude; possibility/necessity] that Kierkegaard discusses.)

I have no wish to deny that Kierkegaard offers insightful analyses of anxiety and despair (the latter concept, explored in detail in *The Sickness unto Death*, being one that largely displaces the former in his writings). Certainly there is no shortage of quotes that would support such a view – and Kierkegaard must be one of the most *quotable* thinkers in the history of philosophy. For instance, he remarks (under the guise of his pseudonym Vigilius Haufniensis) that "[w]hoever has learned to be anxious in the right way has learned the ultimate" (Kierkegaard, 1980a, p. 155) and associates the lack of anxiety with spiritlessness: "If . . . the speaker maintains that the great thing about him is that he has never been in anxiety, I will gladly provide him with my explanation: that is because he is very spiritless" (Kierkegaard, 1980a, p. 157). But this does not mean that Kierkegaard just leaves us with – or in – anxiety. Nor does it mean that anxiety can straightforwardly be appropriated by existential psychotherapy without reference to Kierkegaard's theological background: to become anxious "in the right way" means, for him, to be anxious about sin (rather than about, say, sex or guilt) (Emmanuel, McDonald & Stewart, 2013). In what follows, I shall suggest that in his less well-known *Upbuilding Discourses* – particularly those on "the lilies and the birds" – Kierkegaard offers a way of addressing the problem of anxiety that is significantly at odds with the popular picture of him as the theorist of anxiety par excellence. Moreover, this proposal for how to learn to live with – and in a sense *transcend* while not attempting to *root out* anxiety – is a method at least significant parts of which are accessible to those of all faiths and none. We might even suggest that it offers a version of what Rollo May claims to be the therapist's task: "to reduce anxiety to tolerable levels and then to use the anxiety constructively" (Yalom & Josselson, 2011, p. 301, citing May, 1977, p. 374).

Another Kierkegaard: the *Upbuilding Discourses*

Kierkegaard's discourses address a variety of recognizable human problems – such as anxiety, cowardice, the difficulties of learning to be patient and various forms of self-doubt. In this way, they clearly issue an invitation to test their ideas against the reader's life, an invitation that echoes the famous motto that ends the second volume of *Either/Or*: "only the truth that builds up is truth for you" (Kierkegaard, 1987, p. 354). George Pattison has suggested that, although billed as Kierkegaard's "religious" writings, all that the early discourses really assume is that readers have become seriously concerned about the meaning of their lives and is willing to consider what they – the discourses – have to say about:

> where such concern is pointing them and how it is misconceived if it ends up in anxious self-absorption when its real function is to help them find a deeper and more solid foundation for their lives.
>
> *(Pattison, 2010, p. xv)*

Pattison further characterizes this in terms of the images of the gift, creation, and love. In other words, Kierkegaard counterposes to anxiety a fundamental trust in the goodness of the life that we have been given. Built into this is a complex kind of self-acceptance. To say this is not to underestimate the enormous difficulty that this will pose to many, in the face of seemingly overwhelming suffering. Kierkegaard recognizes that accepting the gift is "the first and most difficult of the tasks with which life confronts us" (Kierkegaard, 2010, p. xx). But he insists that accepting where we are – as well as stepping forward in faith and hope in the future – is the only way of moving on. We'll explore these themes in what follows.

Unlikely teachers: the lilies and the birds

In showing how we might do so, Kierkegaard turns to some unlikely teachers: the lilies of the field and the birds of the air mentioned in Jesus's Sermon on the Mount. What Pattison calls creation might (as he notes) also be understood merely as nature, and human psychology is part of this. We shall shortly see how Kierkegaard suggests we might use the lilies and the birds as our teachers. The overall message, I shall suggest, is the possibility of opposing debilitating anxiety with a certain kind of contentment. Kierkegaard's message in the discourses is not, as some might expect, to lay guilt upon us. Indeed, he urges self-forgiveness. Kierkegaard does not hesitate to talk of sin, but the most important message about it, for him, is the message that *one's sins have been forgiven*. This crucial, liberating fact gives us all the licence we need to forgive ourselves – a task that Kierkegaard recognizes (not least from personal experience) to be extraordinarily difficult. Any account of Kierkegaard as the thinker par excellence of anxiety that does not also stress forgiveness and self-forgiveness will remain a one-sided account (Lippitt, 2013). This brings us to what is, perhaps, the most important of all the concepts Kierkegaard discusses: love. The way that we ultimately get beyond guilt and sin is in the faith that we are loved. Kierkegaard's message is that you are loved, so love. You are forgiven, so forgive.

Kierkegaard's first three discourses on the lilies and the birds comprise the second part of the 1847 text *Upbuilding Discourses in Various Spirits*. They serve as a commentary on Matthew 6: 24–34 (part of the Sermon on the Mount), a passage that so intrigued Kierkegaard that he returned to it on several occasions. He describes the lilies and the birds alluded to there as our "divinely appointed teachers" (Kierkegaard, 1993, p. 157), and the discourses go on to consider what they teach. The theme of the first discourse is "to be contented with being a human being" (Kierkegaard, 1993, p. 159, 162), and both it and the biblical passage on which it reflects address *the worried* (Kierkegaard, 1993, p. 160). The first thing we are to learn from the lilies and the birds is their *silence*, through which we humans might learn a kind of self-forgetfulness that counteracts the destructive self-centredness and self-absorption that are, for Kierkegaard, at the heart of so many human ills. The distressed person can achieve this by contemplating the lilies and the birds and in so doing at least temporarily forget himself – and yet he, "unnoticed . . . learns something about himself" (Kierkegaard, 1993, p. 162). What does he learn?

Kierkegaard here seems to be arguing for a parallel between the beauty of a lily and that of a human being (Kierkegaard, 1993, p. 165). The sheer wonder of being alive, of being human, is typically forgotten through the "worried inventiveness of comparison" (Kierkegaard, 1993, p. 165). *Comparison* now becomes a crucial theme in the discourse, and the kind of damaging self-focus that it encourages inspires one of the most moving passages in the discourse literature, on "the worried lily".

In this parable – a lovely example of Kierkegaard's literary inventiveness, of playing with and riffing on a biblical passage – the life of a beautiful, carefree lily is complicated by the arrival of a little bird who visits, stays away, and then returns. The lily, initially puzzled by the bird's comings and goings – why doesn't it, like the lily, stay in one place? – falls "more and more in love with the bird – precisely because it was capricious" (Kierkegaard, 1993, p. 167). Instead of delighting in the lily's beauty, the bird stresses its difference (its freedom of movement) and – worse still – waxes lyrical about the beauty of other lilies it has encountered on its travels. It typically ends its chatter with the remark that "in comparison with that kind of glory the lily looked like nothing – indeed, it was so insignificant that it was a question whether the lily had a right to be called a lily" (Kierkegaard, 1993, p. 167).

Unsurprisingly, the lily becomes worried, and its self-doubts disturb its previously carefree existence. Now its static life starts to seem restrictive. Influenced by the bird's destructive chatter, the lily starts to feel humiliated and to wish it were a Crown Imperial, which the bird has told it is the most gorgeous of all lilies, envied by all others. Now comes a subtle twist in the tale. The lily convinces itself that its desire is not so unreasonable, since it is not "asking for the impossible, to become what I am not, a bird, for example. My wish is only to become a gorgeous lily, or even the most gorgeous" (Kierkegaard, 1993, p. 168). It is as if the lily has been reading self-help literature, with its advice to "be the best *you* can be".

Eventually, the lily confesses its worries to the bird, and together they hit upon a solution. The bird will peck away the soil restricting the lily to its spot, uproot it, and together they will fly to where the most gorgeous lilies grow:

> in the hope that with the change of place and with the new surroundings the lily might succeed in becoming a gorgeous lily in the company of all the others, or perhaps even a Crown Imperial, envied by all the others.
>
> *(Kierkegaard, 1993, pp. 168–169)*

Of course, we know how this turns out. Once uprooted, the lily withers and dies. The parallel that Kierkegaard draws is that the lily is the human being, while the "naughty little bird" is "the restless mentality of comparison, which roams far and wide, fitfully and capriciously, and gleans the morbid knowledge of diversity" (Kierkegaard, 1993, p. 169). Further, the little bird is "the poetic and the seductive in the human being" (Kierkegaard, 1993, p. 169), and the poetic is a mixture of truth and untruth. While the diversity it notes between human beings is not a falsehood, the poetic "consists in maintaining that diversity . . . is the supreme, and this is eternally false" (Kierkegaard, 1993, p. 169). The problem arises from stressing the diversity that results from the spirit of comparison more than our common humanity. This seems to speak to all kinds of issues about "status anxiety". Relatedly, the lily's key mistake seems to be to fail to recognize its earthbound nature and to refuse to be what it was intended to be (Kierkegaard, 1993, p. 170). Hence Kierkegaard concludes:

> if a human being, like the lily, is contented with being a human being, he does not become sick with temporal worries, and if he does not become worried about temporal things, he remains in the place assigned to him; and if he remains there, then it is true that he, by being a human being, is more glorious than Solomon's glory.
>
> *(Kierkegaard, 1993, p. 170)*

Human freedom is *rooted*. From the lilies, we can learn to be contented with being a human being, not to fret over diversity (read: status anxiety), and to be able to think "as inspiringly about being a human being as the Gospel speaks tersely about the lilies" (Kierkegaard, 1993, p. 170). The key message is that in an important sense, our common humanity transcends the diversity between us.

Kierkegaard also brings out the risks of comparison in other riffs on the theme of the lilies and the birds. Take the story of an unfortunate wood dove. Initially satisfied, like our earlier lily, with living from day to day, the wild dove one day gets to chatting with two tame doves, who present him with another perspective. The preening tame doves pride themselves on always having access to the farmer's grain, in comparison to which the wood dove starts to worry about his now comparatively precarious day-to-day existence. Eventually, the envious wood dove sneaks into the dovecote – only to be discovered by the farmer and to meet his demise (Kierkegaard, 1993, pp. 174–176).

Just as the lily fell victim to its own anxious vanity, so the wood dove falls victim to *worry about earning a living*. Ultimately Kierkegaard takes this discussion in the direction of our dependence on God and – this time stressing differences as well as similarities between human beings and the birds of the air – reflections on *work* as a human being's "perfection" (Kierkegaard, 1993, pp. 177, 198). But here I want to stress that in this story too the problem arises from *comparison*, "insofar as the worry about making a living is not the actual pressing need of the day today but is the idea of a future need" (Kierkegaard, 1993, p. 198):

> Worried about making a living, the worried person is unwilling to be contented with being a human being but wants to be different or to have diversity, wants to be rich, independently wealthy, prosperous, fairly secure, etc. In other words, he does not look at the bird of the air – away from the diversity of human life – but he looks comparingly at others, at the diversity, and his worry about making a living is a relation of comparison.
>
> *(Kierkegaard, 1993, p. 179)*

This also trails a theme that Kierkegaard will stress when he returns to the lilies and the birds in later discourses, where he insists that from these teachers we can learn to be *joyful*. Joy is explained as being "present to oneself", which in turn is unpacked as "truly to be today" and to view as irrelevant "tomorrow" (Kierkegaard, 1997a, p. 38–39). The *joy* that the lilies and birds teach puts "the whole emphasis on: *the present time*" (Kierkegaard, 1997a, p. 39). In a related discourse, Kierkegaard describes "the next day" as "the grappling hook with which the huge mass of worries seizes hold of the single individual's little ship" (Kierkegaard, 1997b, p. 72, my translation); thus "if a person is to gain mastery over his mind, he must begin by getting rid of the next day" (Kierkegaard, 1997b, p. 71). The *silence* that the lily and bird also teach human beings is explicitly linked to *forgetting oneself and one's plans* (Kierkegaard, 1997a, p. 19).

Does all this depend upon sharing Kierkegaard's Christian faith? Actually, I don't think so. Pattison & Jensen (2012) rewrite some of these polyphonic discourses as dialogues between "SK" (a believer) and "KS" (a non-believer). Certainly, much in the discourses depends upon taking a religious perspective seriously. On Kierkegaard's telling, we can learn from the lilies and the birds to cast all our sorrows upon God (Kierkegaard, 1997a, p. 41); that freedom is achieved only by acknowledging that God, not I, provides for my well-being (Kierkegaard, 1993, p. 177); and that the *silence* that we can learn from the lilies and the birds is associated with becoming nothing before God (Kierkegaard, 1997a, pp. 10–11). But as Pattison points out, these ideas are not introduced dogmatically, and Kierkegaard, consistent with his claim to be "without authority", is not so much "teaching" as "raising questions, offering new and unexpected perspectives on familiar problems, subverting expectations" (Pattison & Jensen, 2012, p. xi). Most important is Pattison's observation that insofar as Kierkegaard is a Christian writer, his concern is less with instructing his readers about the content of Christianity than with alerting them "to why the questions addressed by Christianity should matter to them" (Pattison & Jensen, 2012, p. x). Tellingly, he adds that for Kierkegaard, "the point is not to get a 'message' across, it is to engage readers in a process of change and, *like a therapist*, help them to become alert to the movements and needs of their own hearts" (Pattison & Jensen, 2012, p. xi, my emphasis).

For this reason, I think that much in the discourses can "build up" believer and non-believer alike. Jensen reports having found a reading group with no theological background being "fired up" by themes the discourses raised (Pattison & Jensen, 2012, p. xiii). In particular – and this will be my main focus for the rest of this chapter – I think there is much in what Kierkegaard says about contentment being threatened by the "naughty little bird" who embodies "the restless mentality of comparison" that will strike a chord with those of all faiths and none. This bites most of us in ways we might not like to admit. Of course, we would chuckle at those who judge their self-worth in terms of the number of their Facebook friends. And I found rather absurd the attitude of a fellow academic who seemed to value himself in significant part by the number of followers he had acquired on academia. edu (helpfully, he kept me appraised of the figure on a regular basis). And yet I will confess to having recently felt pleased on noting, in an update to my profile on that site, that it was rated in the "top 2% by 30 day views" – shortly followed by a twinge of envy at the colleague who, it turned out, was in the top 1 per cent. "Comparison" feeds both anxiety and vanity.

What the naughty little bird homes in on is our vulnerability to how what we think of ourselves can become a function of what others think of us. During a brief period in therapy, I found myself musing on the fact that in some circumstances I do, and in other circumstances I don't, care much about external opinions of me. Reflecting on what the difference was, I concluded that the former applies when I suspect that the view of me – my flaws and inadequacies – might be accurate. This is when I feel the need to justify myself to myself, and also where countervailing opinions portraying me in a more favourable light become something for which I can be – almost pathetically – grateful. All this shows, perhaps, the grip the naughty little bird has over me.

Of course, the relation between diversity and our common humanity is a matter of emphasis: Kierkegaard has no wish to deny the importance of uniqueness or singularity. He speaks of how God gives in such a way that each individual "becomes a distinctive individuality" (Kierkegaard, 1995, pp. 271–272) and claims that "at every person's birth there comes into existence an eternal purpose for that person, for that person in particular" (Kierkegaard, 1993, p. 93). In *The Sickness unto Death*, we read:

> Every human being is primitively intended to be a self, destined to become himself, and as such every self is certainly angular, but that only means that is to be ground into shape, not that it is to be ground down smooth, not that it is to utterly abandon being itself out of fear of men, or . . . not to dare to be itself in its more essential contingency.
>
> *(Kierkegaard, 1980b, p. 33)*

The discourses we have been discussing make the point in a similar way: do not mistake being "ground into shape" – *formed* – for being "ground down smooth" – crushed or annihilated. To be taken out of yourself in the way the lilies and birds inspire, to focus on being glad to be alive, is not to *lose* one's essential individuality but to see it in a fresh light, a light through which the anxieties of particularity can be challenged – and even silenced.

Gratitude and patience

Finally, how else might we take up Kierkegaard's invitation to treat the lilies and the birds as our teachers? What else can they teach?

First and foremost, as we have seen, they confront us with the possibility of being content just to be alive and to be our "given" selves. This alone might be an important message – encouraging "reframing" – to any of us who typically "want to manage our lives and write our own script in ways that are just not realistic" (Pattison & Jensen, 2012, p. 96).

At this point, some might wish to talk of "mindfulness". But Kierkegaard would, I think, want to place a greater focus than this tradition necessarily does on *gratitude*:

gratitude for all that is good in our lives and for life itself (Pattison & Jensen, 2012, p. 97). So the lilies and birds perhaps also teach an attitude to life that shows how gratitude might have the power to drown out a feeling of overwhelming anxiety. John McLuckie, a pastor who works with cancer patients, reports on how often such an attitude has helped such patients to live with the enormous life changes that such a diagnosis brings about (Pattison & Jensen, 2012, p. 128). Nor is this necessarily limited to those with a religious faith: it is notable that secular existential therapists such as Irvin Yalom also focus at this point on the value of "counting your blessings" and becoming aware of your natural surroundings (lilies and birds included, no doubt!) (Yalom & Josselson, 2011, p. 306). Kierkegaard would perhaps discuss this in terms of a move beyond resignation to grace.

The point here is that the *contentment* we have discussed is made easier if we are able to view *life as a gift*. And receiving this gift in gratitude involves accepting myself, warts and all, as I currently am. While this certainly does not rule out trying to improve, to get out of our ruts and "move on" with our lives, it does raise what is, for Kierkegaard, an important distinction between a *problem* and a *burden* (Pattison & Jensen, 2012, p. 32). What is the difference? The answer, I think, is that to describe something as a problem already implies that there must be a solution and that this is what one is seeking. Whereas to recognize the same thing as a burden suggests a different approach: the question now becomes how I am to shoulder the burdens that life necessarily brings me. For instance, how am I to live with my memories of my own past failures? Should I be aiming to *overcome* my faults – all of them? – or to find a way of learning to live with them? My suspicion is that many clients come to therapy to deal with what they perceive to be problems and look to therapy – or, worse, to the *therapist* – for a solution. In such a case, part of a successful therapeutic process might involve helping them to reframe their issues as *burdens*. Perhaps there is a kind of contentment that could grow from this very realization?

The link between contentment and finding the best in one's situation – learning to live with one's burdens – is nicely brought out in Kierkegaard's *Works of Love* parable about two artists. One travels the world and yet fails to find a face with such perfection that he considers it worth painting. The second stays at home, but in his small circle finds each face, for all its flaws, to have a beautiful and glorious side, such that his art "satisfies me without making any claim to be an artist" (Kierkegaard, 1995, p. 158). It is just this, says Kierkegaard, that shows the second to be the true artist. The parable is meant to illustrate the difference between foolishly searching for someone worthy of one's love and finding something lovable in everyone one meets, but it also seems relevant to our topic here: the contentment that the second artist has found in his humble craft.

Plenty more could be said. A related theme central to the discourses is *silence*, one manifestation of which is the way in which our need to be "noticed", recognized and appreciated might add to our anxiety. This issue warrants more nuanced treatment than I have room for here, but one aspect of the "silence" that we may learn from the lilies and the birds is the courage to perform small actions of great significance to our self-development that are not noticed by others (and in this sense are done *silently*). If we cash out our value in terms of being noticed by others (living our lives as perpetual teenagers?), we are doomed not to recognize the importance of such small steps. There is a clear link here to another important theme in the discourses, namely *learning patience*. This warrants an essay of its own, but let me here make two observations. First, note that *Taalmod*, the Danish term for patience used by Kierkegaard, literally refers to the courage to bear or endure. Thus, as Pattison and Jensen note, to be patient is "to be able to bear with ourselves and to accept who we are with endurance" (Pattison & Jensen, 2012, p. 49). Second, consider how the contentment I have tried to sketch might give rise to patience. As Steve Porter suggests, while the two are distinct, "patience emerges under the influence of contentment. We can be patient when we are content but it is difficult to be patient when we are discontent" (Porter, 2012, p. 129n5). McLuckie (Pattison & Jensen, 2012, p. 128–129) notes the importance of themes in Kierkegaard's discourses on learning patience – learning simply ways to endure – to the experiences of those living with cancer.

Please don't misunderstand me. It has been no part of my aim in this chapter to claim that a recipe of contentment, gratitude and patience is the panacea to all the issues that therapy clients present. But I suspect that many might find considerable solace, inspiration and – dare I suggest it? – even *joy* in reflecting on the message of this strand of Kierkegaard's writings. a strand we might well describe as "therapeutic". Along the lines of what I have been suggesting here, let me leave the final word to Pattison and Jensen:

> [W]hereas many readers imagine Kierkegaard as being especially preoccupied with the darker side of life, these writings [the discourses, especially those on the lilies and the birds] show clearly that his aim is precisely not to leave us brooding on whatever darkness afflicts us, but to accompany us on our way to a more open, freer, and more joyous way of living in the world.
> *(Pattison & Jensen, 2012, pp. 99–100)*

References

Emmanuel, S. M., McDonald, W., and Stewart, J. (2013) 'Anxiety', in Jon Stewart (ed.), *Kierkegaard Research: Sources, Reception and Resources, Vol. 15, Tome I: Kierkegaard's Concepts: Absolute to Church*. London: Ashgate, pp. 59–64.

Heidegger, M. (1962) *Being and Time*, trans. John Macquarrie and Edward Robinson. Oxford: Blackwell.

Kierkegaard, S. (1980a) *The Concept of Anxiety*, trans. Reidar Thomte. Princeton, NJ: Princeton University Press.

Kierkegaard, S. (1980b) *The Sickness unto Death*, trans. H.V. and E. H. Hong. Princeton, NJ: Princeton University Press.

Kierkegaard, S. (1987) *Either/Or*, Volume II, trans. H. V. and E. H. Hong. Princeton, NJ: Princeton University Press.

Kierkegaard, S. (1993) *Upbuilding Discourses in Various Spirits*, trans. H. V. and E. H. Hong. Princeton, NJ: Princeton University Press.

Kierkegaard, S. (1995) *Works of Love*, trans. H.V. and E. H. Hong. Princeton, NJ: Princeton University Press.
Kierkegaard, S. (1997a) *Without Authority*, trans. H.V. and E. H. Hong. Princeton, NJ: Princeton University Press.
Kierkegaard, S. (1997b) *Christian Discourses*, trans. H. V. and E. H. Hong. Princeton, NJ: Princeton University Press.
Kierkegaard, S. (2010) *Kierkegaard's Spiritual Writings*, trans. George Pattison. New York: Harper Perennial.
Kimmel, H. (2003) *The Solace of Leaving Early*. London: Flamingo.
Lippitt, J. (2013) *Kierkegaard and the Problem of Self-Love*. Cambridge: Cambridge University Press.
Lodge, D. (1995) *Therapy*. London: Secker and Warburg.
Marino, G. (2014) *The Quotable Kierkegaard*. Princeton, NJ: Princeton University Press.
May, R. (1977) *The Meaning of Anxiety*, revised edition. New York: Norton.
Pattison, G., and Jensen, H. M. (2012) *Kierkegaard's Pastoral Dialogues*. Eugene, OR: Wipf and Stock.
Porter, S. L. (2012) 'Contentment', in Michael W. Austin and R. Douglas Geivett (eds.), *Being Good: Christian Virtues for Everyday Life*. Grand Rapids, MI: Eerdmans, pp. 126–144.
Stewart, J. (ed.) (2011) *Kierkegaard Research: Sources, Reception and Resources, Vol. 13: Kierkegaard's Influence on the Social Sciences*. London: Ashgate.
van Deurzen, E. (2010). *Everyday Mysteries: A Handbook of Existential Psychotherapy*, second edition. London: Routledge.
Yalom, I. D., and Josselson, R. (2011) 'Existential Psychotherapy', in Raymond J. Corsini and Danny Wedding (eds.), *Current Psychotherapies*, ninth edition (international edition). London: Brooks/Cole, pp. 310–341.

3

JOHN KEATS AND NEGATIVE CAPABILITY

The psychotherapist's X-factor?

Diana Voller

Introduction

The following is an exploration of the role of the therapist's 'identity fluency' in therapeutic practice, drawing on Keats's concept of 'negative capability' and adapting it to describe an aspect of the psychotherapist's process using an inherent but often undervalued aspect of their personality structure. Two modes of inhabiting uncertainty, being *in* and being *with*, are identified and described. The negative capability process of moving between the two positions is illustrated through an analysis of Keats's 'Ode to a Nightingale' (Keats, 1977, pp. 346–348), making links to clinical practice. The chapter proposes that the therapist's capacity to be *in* uncertainty is an important but previously under-represented aspect of practice, because of both its elusive nature and its connections to the therapist's permeable sense of self.

It is elusive because essentially it is about being capable of working with a 'negative' quality. An analogy of negative might be of the hole in a donut, which can't be described, except in terms of the form around it. We have yet to develop research methods for describing this quality that are superior to literary description, and so negative capability is rarely attended to in psychological literature, with its emphasis on empirical or quantifiable research-based evidence.

Exploring the paradox of active passivity goes back at least as far as *The Cloud of Unknowing* (Spearing, 2001), a fourteenth-century classic of devotional literature, in which the unknown author recommends that an individual deliberately enters into a place of spiritual darkness in order to develop a relationship with God.

Several hundred years later and in a different context, the poet John Keats termed negative capability the quality of a "Man of Achievement especially in Literature & which Shakespeare possessed enormously . . . of being in uncertainties, Mysteries, doubts, without any irritable reach after fact & reason . . ." (Keats, 2009, p. 41). Keats is referring to a fluidity of identity that enables a creative and deeply empathic appreciation of others. It was a quality he had noticed, particularly in literary people of 'achievement', such as Shakespeare, who demonstrated an extraordinary capacity to understand his characters and situations from an inside perspective.

I suggest that this paradoxical phrase has resonance for psychotherapists too. The negative aspect of negative capability refers to an individual's capacity, or emotional range, for being actually *in* uncertainty, by which I mean having an openness to being impacted and yet actively not knowing. This is consistent with Carl Jung's proposal that, as a therapist, one can exert no influence unless one is also susceptible to influence. The capability aspect of negative capability denotes a person's ability to tolerate and to creatively embrace that uncertainty and permeability of identity in a professional context, to the benefit of the client. Importantly, capability includes the ability to come out of the negative or in-uncertainty state as well, since temporarily loosening the hold we have on our sense of self can be disturbing.

Modes of inhabiting uncertainty

Inhabiting uncertainty in some form or another, whether it is personal, theoretical or related to the client, is an inherent aspect of psychotherapy and life itself. It involves straddling the tension between embracing the aliveness and opportunities that arise through change and uncertainty, as well as addressing the challenges of uncertainty. These are not inconsiderable – fear of the unknown, fluidity of identity and awareness of death, to name but three. Relating to uncertainty in this particular way is a distinguishing feature of humanistic-existential approaches to psychotherapeutic practice in particular.

Some time ago, I undertook a qualitative research study amongst senior practitioners from a variety of orientations about how they inhabit uncertainty in clinical practice, and this revealed that rather than being an inherent quality or unitary attitude, 'negative capability' in a psychotherapeutic context may be more accurately understood as a dynamic process of movement, undertaken by the therapist, between two distinctly different modes of inhabiting uncertainty; these could be identified as being *with* uncertainty and being *in* uncertainty.

Being *with* uncertainty, as the term implies, refers to a kind of instrumental form of uncertainty. Even though there may be a felt sense of uncertainty in being *with* uncertainty mode, it is a 'you'- rather than 'I'-orientated uncertainty because the uncertainty is located elsewhere – when, for instance, the uncertainty is related to the situation being grappled with or a client's experience of being in uncertainty. Being *in* uncertainty is, however, a qualitatively different mode, a personal and more directly experienced way of inhabiting uncertainty that opens the therapist to numerous possibilities. This could well include experientially touching into the therapist's vulnerability and existential anxiety, or vicariously experiencing the client's world, or creating a space for imaginative exploration and play.

In terms of therapy, these two modes of inhabiting uncertainty, *with* and *in*, are necessary but not consistently equal. The emphasis will shift depending on the client, at different points in the therapy relationship and indeed within each session. Each mode has the potential to be extremely facilitative or inhibiting. Too much of the skilled containing and knowledge-based enquiry that accompanies being *with* uncertainty can become functional and close down the liveliness of the therapeutic space. Too much being *in* uncertainty is confusing and frightening, which also closes down the space; hence the task for the therapist in negotiating the dialectical relationship between them. Some modes of being with and being in uncertainty might be professional and personal; unknowing and un-knowing; technique and imagination; science and art. These modes could be used to compare and contrast the distinction between *with* and *in* in psychotherapy:

'Negative capability', in the sense that it has been adapted here, means the movement between being *with* and being *in* uncertainty, and in that sense it is a process, or verb, as well as an adjective describing a personality quality as Keats first intended. The term describes an aspect of the therapist's intrapersonal process that is largely intuitive, sometimes intersubjective, and almost always subjective as well. It is an ephemeral phenomenon; the shift between modes can be fleeting and microscopic or conscious and significant. It is therefore a process that is rarely made explicit, despite the fact that capacity to move in and around and between these different modes of uncertainty is a fundamental feature of psychotherapy, or at least as it is conceptualized here.

Keats was a poet who had extraordinary access to the working of his own mind, which enabled him to know how, why and what he was doing, and so the character and fluidity of his negative capability may perhaps be best described by looking at one of his poems and considering how this process could translate into clinical practice.

Negative capability: description of process

'Ode to a Nightingale' is a subjective description of the intrapersonal process of the poet that illustrates negative capability in action, and parallels to the process of the therapist can be made. The nightingale represents the paradoxical nature of the negative capability concept. The nightingale sings only at night, so its presence is heard in the silence of the dark hours; it is vocal without being verbal or visible. The nightingale is also associated with love, which could be referred back to the understanding of the concept in *The Cloud of Unknowing*.

'Ode to a Nightingale'

1
My heart aches, and a drowsy numbness pains
My sense, as though of hemlock I had drunk,
Or emptied some dull opiate to the drains
One minute past, and Lethe-wards had sunk;
'Tis not through envy of thy happy lot,
But being too happy in thine happiness, –

That thou, light-winged Dryad of the trees,
In some melodious plot
Of beechen green, and shadows numberless,
Singest of summer in full-throated ease.

2
O, for a draught of vintage! That hath been
Cool'd a long age in the deep-delved earth,
Tasting of Flora and the country green,
Dance, and Provencal song, and sunburnt mirth!
O for a beaker full of the warm South,
Full of the true, the blushful Hippocrene,
With beaded bubbles winking at the brim,
And purple-stained mouth;
That I might drink, and leave the world unseen,
And with thee fade away into the forest dim:

3
Fade far away, dissolve, and quite forget
What thou among the leaves hast never known,
The weariness, the fever, and the fret
Here, where men sit and hear each other groan;
Where palsy shakes a few, sad, last gray hairs,
Where youth grows pale, and spectre-thin, and dies;
Where but to think is to be full of sorrow
And leaden-eyed despairs,
Where Beauty cannot keep her lustrous eyes,
Or new Love pine at them beyond tomorrow.

4
Away! away! for I will fly to thee,
Not charioted by Bacchus and his pards,
But on the viewless wings of Poesy,
Though the dull brain perplexes and retards:
Already with thee! Tender is the night,
And haply the Queen-Moon is on her throne,
Cluster'd around by all her starry Fays;
But here there is no light,
Save what from heaven is with the breezes blown
Through verdurous glooms and winding mossy ways.

5
I cannot see what flowers are at my feet,
Nor what soft incense hangs upon the boughs,

But, in embalmed darkness, guess each sweet
Wherewith the seasonable month endows
The grass, the thicket, and the fruit-tree wild;
White hawthorn, and the pastoral eglantine;
Fast fading violets cover'd up in leaves;
And mid-May's eldest child,
The coming musk-rose, full of dewy wine,
The murmurous haunt of flies on summer eves.

6
Darkling I listen; and, for many a time
I have been half in love with easeful Death,
Call'd him soft names in many amused rhyme,
To take into the air my quiet breath;
Now more than ever seems it rich to die,
To cease upon the midnight with no pain,
While thou art pouring forth thy soul abroad
In such an ecstasy!
Still wouldst thou sing, and I have ears in vain-
To thy high requiem become a sod.

7
Thou wast not born for death, immortal Bird!
No hungry generations tread thee down;
The voice I hear this passing night was heard
In ancient days by emperor and clown;
Perhaps the self-same song that found a path
Through the sad heart of Ruth, when, sick for home,
She stood in tears amid the alien corn;
The same that oft-times hath
Charm'd magic casements, opening on the foam
Of perilous seas, in faery lands forlorn.

8
Forlorn! The very word is like a bell
To toll me back from thee to my sole self!
Adieu! The fancy cannot cheat so well
As she is fam'd to do, deceiving elf.
Adieu! Adieu! Thy plaintive anthem fades
Past the near meadows, over the still stream,
Up the hill-side; and now 'tis buried deep
In the next valley-glades:
Was it a vision, or a waking dream?
Fled is that music: – Do I wake or sleep?

Stanza 1

The poem begins with Keats describing a feeling of the mind being dulled; the sense of knowing that one is not thinking clearly, there is "a drowsy numbness" (1:1) we could associate with the darkening of understanding. In psychotherapy this could be related to a therapist subjugating his or her 'knowing' or intellectual understanding in order to enter the client's world. At this point, it is also the dullness of ignorance he seems to be describing; he wonders if he has been poisoned or drugged. Keats's reference to the "Lethe-wards" (1:4) at the beginning anticipates Wilfred Bion's famous comment about approaching sessions without memory or desire (Bion, 1967). (Lethe is one of the rivers that Hades claims the dead have to drink from in order to forget everything said and done when alive.)

A key issue (and difficulty) with the negative capability concept is the potential to confuse it with a justification for ignorance, which would be a serious misinterpretation as it disregards the capability aspect of negative capability. The subjugation of knowledge here is chosen in the interests of opening up to another aspect of understanding and then being capable of applying that to the creative discipline of poetry, or indeed knowledge-based therapy.

Keats goes on to contrast the dull heaviness of his feeling with the ethereal ease and vitality of the nightingale, noting their separateness. As in a psychotherapy session, one can read the poem in terms of process and structure as well as content. It can be seen here how Keats starts to give himself over to being drawn into the nightingale's world. He notes his awareness of having no particular desire to possess the nightingale's happiness for himself, but at the same time he is eager to share in the feeling and seems to merge into the world of beauty represented by the nightingale.

Stanza 2

Here Keats fully enters and becomes overwhelmed in this state, which he is thoroughly enjoying. He refers to Hippocrene, the fountain associated in Greek myth with poetic inspiration. In therapy, this might be the point at which the therapist, having found him/herself immersed in a slightly altered state, makes imaginative associations or connections, as Keats does, to personal experience or to the body of psychological theory and literature. From a developmental psychotherapy perspective, there are associations here to Bion's notion of maternal reverie (Bion, 1962, p. 183).

Stanza 3

Then, Keats starts to notice himself dissolving into this other world altogether and begins to think he would like to disappear in this way, starting to tap into his own uncertainties, which thought brings him back to his earthbound reality: "the weariness, the fever, and the fret … where youth grows pale, and spectre-thin and dies" (3:6).

40 Diana Voller

This was something he knew well, At the start of his career, Keats worked for a surgeon at St. Thomas's hospital, and shortly after this poem was written, he nursed his dying brother, which ultimately caused his own death as well. This movement – back and forth, death and life, in and out of the client's world, one's imagination and the reality of the present – is very illustrative of the therapist's process too.

Stanza 4

Having returned to the reality of mortal existence, Keats shifts back again towards the nightingale, demonstrating the fluidity of negative capability – in his process but also the content. Again, as at the beginning of the poem, the process starts with the thickening of the cognitive intellectual aspects – "the dull brain" (4:4). Now it is no longer associated with wine, sunshine and the countryside. Time has moved on. It's night. Paradoxically, although he is aware of the moon and stars, there is no light, and he vividly intuits rather than sees where he is, just as one might during a therapy session.

Stanza 5

Again, he is overwhelmed in the peaceful sweetness of his experience, "an embalmed darkness" (5:3), and then, as he reflects on the beauty of the natural world that he finds himself a part of, he becomes aware of its transience. There are "fast fading violets" (5:7) and an awareness of the existence of the future in the present, with "the coming musk-rose" (5:9) and "the murmurous haunt of flies on summer eves" (5:10).

Stanza 6

Once more Keats shows us his process, as this leads him on to thinking about death. It's also worth noticing here how he doesn't differentiate among the senses. His experience is so intense – for instance in stanza 5, the "soft incense hangs on the bough" (5:2) – the smell so powerful that it is physically tangible. In that stanza, the aural evoked the visual at the beginning of the poem, and the nightingale's song took him deep into the country, as far as the south of France, which he described visually; now, at the beginning of stanza 6, the visual evokes the aural, as he *listens* to the darkness "Darkling I listen" (6:1). The parallels between Keats's process and clinical work are clear here as the practice of listening to the almost tangible *quality* of an atmosphere is familiar territory to psychotherapists.

Stanza 7

The darkness associated with his earlier sense of time passing and the intense poignancy of his experiencing lead him to think about death: "It would be rich to die" (6:5). Here there is another shift back to the paradoxical reality of life, as he realizes that if he were dead, although he would be free of pain, it also means he wouldn't be able to enjoy the poignant ecstasy of the nightingale's song. He contrasts his mortality with the immortality of the nightingale's song, becoming aware of their separateness as he wonders about joining the bird, or his ill brother, making reference to the biblical figure Ruth (an iconic and therefore immortal representative of loyalty and loving kindness in human beings, who said, "Where you go, I go …" [Ruth 1:16–17]). In therapy, fleeting and random connections between the world of the therapist and the client can occur, or the shared existential concerns can be made apparent, accompanied by awareness of otherness.

Stanza 8

Keats's process leads him to think about powers in the universe that can be operating that are beyond our knowledge. He refers to "Charm'd magic" (7:9) in the midst of perilous seas, in "faery lands forlorn" (7:10), or perhaps that magic is the human capacity for hope and love that emerges in the midst of difficult times. In clinical practice, one could relate this to 'trusting of the process', in the sense of relying on or hoping for a power that is not directly accessible to sustain the therapist through times of stuckness and frustration.

Then Keats finds himself called back to himself again; the words "bell" and "toll" are reminders of our earthly mortal existence. We can think here of the call that brings one back to awareness, often accompanied by uncertainty or anxiety, and that also brings clients into therapy. This seems to be Keats's experience; he uses the term "sole self" (8:2), which sounds as though it could refer to both our essential aloneness, that our existence is only ours, but "sole self" could also be a reference to our soul, or psyche, to whom Keats wrote another ode. Psyche, in Greek mythology, was eventually granted immortality following her period of suffering after Cupid left; perhaps here Keats caught a glimmer of hope for something beyond too.

It's worth noting at this point that in Greek, *therapeia*, from which the term therapy is derived, is associated with attendance, therefore making psychotherapists 'attendants to the soul' (*psyche* = soul and *therapeia* = attendant), which underlines the case for the kind of sensitive attuned movement that negative capability implies.

That was a rather tangential comment, and at this point Keats also wonders if he has strayed too far. Creative doubt, a key characteristic of negative capability, sets in. Is all this an evasive deception? He wonders if the imaginative powers he described earlier as "the viewless wings of Poesy" (4:3) (poesy = the art of writing poetry), which as therapists we might understand as professional neutrality, are actually just imagination, a fancy, "a deceiving elf". This sort of doubt is not unfamiliar to most therapists at times. 'What is psychotherapy? Am I a fraud? Is this of any help at all? How real are our therapeutic relationships?' He wonders if all this that he has so intensely experienced is a vision or a waking dream.

'Ode to a Nightingale' is a subjective poem; it starts with "My heart aches" and ends with "Do I wake or dream?", illustrating how the poet (and also the psychotherapist) paradoxically draws on what is most personal, to communicate in a way that resonates with others. The poem shows the scope for movement between different positions enabled by his negative capability. Within this short poem, he moves around from joy to despair, from mortal to immortal and from reality to imagination, and here too parallels can be made to a therapist's allowing him/herself this sort of scope within a session and having the emotional agility to use it.

Whilst in many ways this poem can be understood as an ode to the benefits of being in uncertainty and a celebration of the freedom of doubt and mystery, it also warns that the desire for imaginative transcendence should not replace focusing on the truth of human suffering or the need for discipline, rigorous knowledge and structure to support the wandering into the realms of uncertainty. Keats's work here is grounded in the very disciplined poetic format that holds it all together, and his attention to technical detail in terms of his precise use of grammar, language and depth of knowledge regarding the historical references, translated into the terms of psychotherapy, would also include theoretical knowledge base and adherence to therapeutic conventions.

Negative capability: duality and identity

Negative capability, understood in this way, is clearly a complex and multifaceted process of movement between the *with* and *in* uncertainty modes and rests on the therapist's capacity for being *in* uncertainty mode.

Being *in* uncertainty is a deliberately disempowered mode. It can involve imaginative associations and fantasy, the relevance of which to the work with the client is not immediately apparent. It can also involve feeling lost in direction; one can feel ignorant and stupid; it can evoke shame; there can be a loss of sense of self and a merging of identities; and it can feel scary and disturbing as well as thoroughly enjoyable and like playing.

As such, being *in* uncertainty can appear to be in conflict with a therapist's professional identity: a sense of fraudulence that as the therapist, trained and knowledgeable in the art of being *with* uncertainty, he/she can also be in this somewhat altered state. However, to integrate the *in* uncertainty with the *with* uncertainty would mean that the authenticity of the *in* uncertainty disappears and becomes transmuted into *with* uncertainty. In order for the paradox of active passivity to be effective, it needs to remain a paradox, in which *with* and *in* uncertainty are qualitatively different states. Each different mode of inhabiting uncertainty requires the other. Consequently, it is the *in* uncertainty mode that forms the basis of competence because it is the therapist's negotiation of their duality that forms the basis of negative capability.

Therefore, rather than overlaying *in* uncertainty with knowledge and vulnerability with competency or making attempts to integrate them in some way, the 'double agent' status of being alternately and variously *in* or *with* uncertainty needs to be embraced as it is, despite the ostensible feelings of fraudulence, ignorance and lack of evidence associated with the *in* uncertainty mode. This is because, I would argue, the capacity to be precisely *in* this uncertainty is a foundational aspect of the work of being a therapist. As a double agent, the therapist can move fluidly between two often contradictory and mutually hostile territories but operate like a native in both.

The conflict regarding *in* uncertainty and professional identity is reflected institutionally, as well as being a personal concern of therapist, and this is evidenced by the current debates around regulation and protected titles. Being *with* and being *in* uncertainty are based on different underlying philosophies of what constitutes a professional. If it is accepted that a considerable part of the expertise in psychotherapy is concerned with being able to *not* know and to be *in* uncertainty, how can this be communicated to those outside the field without appearing vague and unprofessional? How transparent is it possible or desirable to be? If the *in* uncertainty is operationalized, then has it lost its essence?

It is particularly appropriate that the therapist is enabled to grapple with this uncertainty tension since, in the context of our postmodern culture that emphasizes plurality and multiple identities and in which the only certainty is uncertainty itself, it parallels the challenges that are confronting many clients. Whilst they may come to therapy initially in search of the certainty that is inherent in consulting a professional, they will ultimately be more enriched by developing ways of relating to uncertainty as a result of seeing and experiencing it in action through the therapy process.

Negative capability: the *X*-factor?

An online search reveals that the 'X-factor' (I am not referring to the TV show) is a term for the unknown factor. It is also defined as a hard-to-describe influence, an explanatory thing that adds a certain value to that object, element or person, or an important element with unknown consequences. On the basis of these definitions, it would appear that negative capability qualifies as a psychotherapeutic X-factor.

Negative capability is a "hard-to-describe influence" because it is a paradox, as it is largely about being capable in *not* doing or being something. This *not* quality means that it is difficult to write or theorize about, and when one gets close to articulating the phenomenon, of course, it loses its *not* essence and tends to disappear. However, indirect appreciation of how negative capability might operate in clinical practice has been attempted drawing on Keats's poem, which describes his own particular process.

Negative capability is an important element with unknown consequences because it is an aspect of clinical process that is always present and active, but since it is hard to describe and therefore rarely articulated, the consequences and role negative capability plays in the process are largely unknown. It could be one of those important elements that tends to get taken for granted, a bit like health or breathing – something that tends to be noticed by its absence rather than by its presence – and it is interesting to note that the topic of the role of uncertainty in clinical practice arose in response the current evidence-based certainty-orientated culture.

Conclusion

I have attempted to describe the 'negative capability' process with a view to making it a more explicitly appreciated aspect of the therapeutic process. Although it seems particularly important to retain a space for uncertainty in the current evidence-based culture, reflecting on ways to creatively engage with being both *in* and *with* uncertainty has a long history in psychotherapy – Freud's construction of the unconscious or Rogers' development of the core conditions are also illustrations of their ways of relating to uncertainty, which have since become crystallized as part of the body of theoretical knowledge without reference to their founders' particular capacity to be *in* uncertainty, without which they would never have been developed.

It is hoped by apprehending the role of the therapist's capacity to be *in* uncertainty indirectly, by drawing a poet's description of the process, rather than a therapist's, such reification has been avoided but will nonetheless be sufficiently evocative to resonate with other practitioners and contribute to safeguarding and promoting this key therapeutic X-factor.

References

Bion, W. (1967) *Notes on Memory and Desire the Psychoanalytic Forum*, Vol. 2, No. 3. London: Tavistock.

Bion, W. R. (1962) 'A Theory of Thinking'. In E. Bott Spillius (ed.) *Melanie Klein Today: Developments in Theory and Practice. Volume 1: Mainly Theory. 1988*. London: Routledge pp. 178–186.

Keats, J. (1977) *The Complete Poems*. Edited by J. Barnard. London: Penguin.

Keats, J. (2009) *Selected Letters*. Oxford: Oxford University Press.

Spearing, A. (trans.) (2001) *The Cloud of Unknowing*. London: Penguin.

4

THAT PIECE OF SUPREME ART, A MAN'S LIFE

Nick Duffell

Introduction

If philosophy is the study of life, then D. H. Lawrence is a practitioner, for he saw a person's life in itself as supreme art; it mattered to him how we lived, what we thought and how we expressed ourselves.

Ill health, restless wandering, a passion for ideas, a yearning for a better society and a tendency to mystify or upset his contemporaries marked his own short life. His constantly rewritten works were credos, efforts to make the world wake up, clarion calls for vitality. Regularly misunderstood – especially by his own countrymen, who never forgave his critique of their morbid rationality – they still offer an alternative path into history, psychology and the mystery of love. Forging an uncharted way through the Oedipal tensions that birthed his genius, Lawrence emerged with an unprecedented understanding of both genders, even if his vision of instinctual maleness is prone to misinterpretation. Intimate relationship – his own was both faithful and liberal, tender and violent – was central to his life art. His early take on the unconscious has been overlooked. His politics proclaimed a variant of socialism that, unfashionably, required leadership, but Lawrence articulated the need for inspired, not *wounded* leaders (Duffell, 2014). This writer proposes we might count him a philosopher, and this chapter aims to explain why.

Life or death philosophy

With a triumphant swoosh of his shabby black gown, the slight middle-aged professor rolled back the revolving blackboard to his starting point and, emerging with supreme confidence from a cloud of chalk dust, proudly pointed out the flow of his argument that had taken two successive weeks to set out, declaring: "*Ergo*, God exists."

The room erupted. Most of the assembled congregation, a large group of young men – and some young women – crammed into a Victorian lecture hall in England's medieval home of intellectual orthodoxy, leaped to their feet in boisterous but reverent applause for A. J. Ayer, the famous British logical positivist.

Or was it, "God doesn't exist"? I forget. It was 1968 and I was nineteen.

Certainly 'Freddie' Ayer (as we called him) is best known for his atheism, so I would now imagine the latter deduction, but it is not what my memory retains. Besides, just before his death, twenty years later, he is rumoured to have had a near-death experience in which he claimed meeting a 'Divine Being' (Cash, 2009). What I do remember with utter clarity is the rational triumphalism, the lack of emotion. My body still recalls the horror of the attempt to define God by means of formal logic, that dry mathematical schema for reason, whose foundation stone, the Law of Excluded Middles, contradicted my growing belief, born out of dabbling in Hinduism, that paradox might be the key to unlocking the world's mysteries.

It was this lecture, building on my rejection of excessive rationality and amplified by my teenage arrogance, that led me to the decision to follow my heart and abandon my course of study. Oxford philosophy seemed to consist of mind-numbing epistemology – and I had imagined it was going to be about *life*. Many years and several breakdowns later, I am still in awe of the paradox at the heart of life, and I find literature more reliable than academic philosophy. In later years, as a trainer of psychotherapists, I often wished I still had my adolescent courage to run a course that relied on novelists and poets rather than psychologists.

Chief among those I would have chosen would be two contemporaries whom I never met but whose prodigious insight and prophecy bear remarkable similarities. Both expounded a philosophy prioritizing life, the body, love (as in sexual relationships), feeling, work and awe at creation sufficient to inspire me, both as a man and as a psychotherapist. They were born during the Age of Privilege, when the rich partied like never before and the poor slaved or starved; both lived through the horrors of the Great War but on opposite sides. Both died much too young at a time of political and artistic ferment, when experiments in education and sexual relationships, the birth of feminism, the rise of Socialism, the 'discovery' of the unconscious and the influence of 'Oriental' thought began to rock the foundations of rational civilization. The backdrop to the lives of these two men was an epoch that abounded in new ideas, in artistic creativity, as if it had to escape the sterile rationalism of the Victorian period. But the outdated Imperialism of ruling classes held on for grim death, to implode in the folly of catastrophic world war whose lessons it duly ignored.

The two I have in mind are Rainer Maria Rilke and D. H. Lawrence. The latter is the more accessible – to me – and bears the difficult distinction of being badly understood in his homeland. So I propose Lawrence as a hearty guide to a psychologically informed philosophy of life – especially relevant a century later.

The D. H. Lawrence legacy

Dying at forty-four, Lawrence's legacy is hewn out of persistent labour on his constantly reworked poems, novels, essays, plays and, later, paintings. From humble beginnings in a world where class represented unforgiving barriers, Lawrence used his own experience to assert his place and vision. Today, his imperfect works still radiate truth, with life and tenderness as the central principles in opposition to materialism and rational flight. For Lawrence, the novel operated on the conscience of readers, purposefully drawing them to health and vitality in body and soul by means of the imagination, which did not just serve conception or expression but rather was a channel into life for the world to be renewed.

But if Lawrence's works are accessible, they are not simple. In 1932, shortly after his death, the critic, author and early feminist Catherine Carswell, one of the several women who knew and cared about him and one of the two who wrote biographies, hit the nail on the head when she stated, "His books are easy to read but hard to understand. Therein lies part of their potency" (Carswell, 1981, p. xxxix).

Born into a famous and aristocratic family, Lawrence's German wife Frieda had left her comfortable marriage and children to elope into poverty with this unknown man five years her junior. She expressed her dismay that Lawrence was so little understood much less calmly:

> When I think that nobody wanted Lawrence's amazing genius, how he was jeered at, suppressed, turned into nothing, patronized at best, the stupidity of our civilization comes home to me. How necessary he was! How badly needed! Now that he is dead and his great love for his fellowmen is no longer there in the flesh, people sentimentalize over him.
>
> *(Lawrence, 1934, p. 137)*

Thus Frieda began her short account, *Not I but the Wind* (Lawrence, 1934), written in the high desert cabin near Taos, New Mexico, where they had hidden from the world and to which she returned after his death in the South of France. In it she fails to hide all her contrary unconventionality, which her husband both loved and was infuriated by, and displays her enormous respect for his unwavering commitment. Carswell, only half hiding her jealousy of their intimacy, knew Frieda's limitations but respected her solidity:

> A daughter of Baron von Richthofen, who had been Governor of Alsace-Lorraine after the Franco-Prussian war . . . she expected to rule but could not resist this man who had discovered the secret of her wildness.
>
> *(Carswell, 1981, p. 10)*

Lawrence and Frieda's relationship was passionate and stormy – an enduring crucible of both their personalities:

> She loved Lawrence and depended on him totally; [her] affairs did seem to her to affect that relationship. Lawrence from the first tried to bully her; she took her revenge in several ways. If Lawrence was an irresistible force, Frieda was an immovable object.
>
> *(Sagar, 2003, p. 66)*

Frieda and Carswell, both knowing his human but flawed character, understood in their bones that this man had found some kind of key to life. This was rooted in work and love – the same two concepts that occupied Freud but that were to find in the Austrian a different, if no less important expression. "In these two ways – never being idle, yet never seeming to labour – he was unlike anybody else I ever met" (Carswell, 1981, p. 16).

Lawrence was compelled to share what he had discovered, less out of a lust for recognition or a saintly rejection of fame than out of the profound human decency in which his special talents resided and the need to survive: "He had to reckon with poverty, with illness, with the misapprehension of friends, and the malice of strangers" (Carswell, 1981, p. xxxvii).

My memories of how Lawrence was portrayed, from when I was at school in the early sixties, are as an eccentric romantic nature poet and a novelist in the realist tradition, who wrote about ordinary life in the way that Dickens, Thomas Hardy and Arnold Bennet had. Of course, what marked him out was that he was – like Hardy – a class escapee, one who had come from the rural working poor and who had reinvented himself by dint of his own genius. Again like Hardy, his mother's ambition propelled him to navigate the perilous route across the British class divide. Even to this day, it is always challenging to talk about class in Britain for the fear of admitting that it actually *does still exist* and utterly dominates our way of life. So this wasn't discussed, nor was his ecstatic notion of the value of the human body and sex. Undoubtedly fine poems like 'The Snake' (1923) were taught to us schoolchildren, and we were led to admire his ability to enter into the natural world. Lawrence's oeuvre was still framed within the genres of either romanticism or realism; yet, though he admired both Shelley and Bennet, he was not in either category.

Lawrence is hard to pin down. His untutored knowledge – his academic heights consisted of a school teacher's certificate obtained in 1908 – came out of his direct experience amplified by insight that seemed to have come, as it did to several other luminaries of the day, almost as revelation. Lawrence stood for soul, but not as one of the Georgian poets or even the war poets. For Lawrence, soul was something I suggest is best described as *indigenous*. It is the counterpart to what I call the *hyper-rational* and Lawrence called 'the Ideal'; it is what Victorian civilization had set itself to overthrow. Only William Blake occupies similar territory. Just as Blake saw the enemy in Newton, Lawrence fought the separating Cartesian dominance. He refused to assert himself *objectively*, but rather as a *subject*, as were his characters. For Lawrence, it was experience that counted: "Non cogito, ergo sum/I am, I do not think I am" (Lawrence, 1994, p. 389).

Central to Lawrentian philosophy was a horror of becoming machine-like, wherein lay his criticism both of capitalism and socialism. The theme of the man or woman who had turned into 'a machine' and lost the ability to love runs through his oeuvre: through Ursula Brangwen's schoolmistress-lover Winifred Inger in *The Rainbow* (Lawrence, 1915), her sister Gudrun's lover Gerald who eventually kills himself in *Women in Love* (Lawrence, 1920) and the paralysed Clifford Chatterley of the final novel.

The domestic life *was* life, as many of his later paintings show. Here is Winifred describing the trap:

> It is the office, or the shop, or the business that gets the man, the woman gets the bit the shop can't digest. What is he at home, a man? He is a meaningless lump, a standing machine, a machine out of work.
>
> *(Lawrence, 1915, p. 242)*

Although Lawrence had a phenomenal work rate, he turned away from social gatherings, preferring to take his part in cooking, cleaning, decorating, fixing up their temporary homes, cutting piles of firewood, having time for writing long letters to his wife's mother. But neither was he a Proustian stay-at-home, in fact the Frenchman's withdrawal from life disgusted him. But nor was he a Romantic. Life feeds on the imagination, but Lawrence is not interested in the image as a metaphor. For Lawrence, the image is a pathway, a drop of liquor distilled from the essence to be re-presented in story form, in the hope that it may appeal to a forgotten part of the reader's consciousness.

Perhaps his most enduring legacy (and most distressing to public sensibility) was that Lawrence spoke openly about sex and desire. Today's readers are more likely to be amazed at his delicacy rather than shocked by his directness. Lawrence wanted to share – it seems to me – what he had observed about the deep currents of life in order that we might be encouraged to create *new life*. The women who knew him on a daily basis understood it because it was not divorced from his everyday actions, even if being himself frequently caused trouble. In Lawrence there was no separation between the man who lives and the man who creates – this was "the supreme art."

The philosopher poet

It was not until the late eighties that, under the influence of Robert Bly, I came across a different kind of Lawrentian poetic, mostly from his later years. Many of these poems are omitted from the most common anthologies, either in print or online. Several took my breath away with their subtleties towards love relations, especially the projected field between men and women and the balance between tenderness and violence. One of these is 'Intimates'.

> Don't you care for my love? she said bitterly.
> I handed her the mirror, and said:
> Please address these questions to the proper person!
> Please make all requests to head-quarters!
> In all matters of emotional importance
> Please approach the supreme authority direct!
> So I handed her the mirror.
> And she would have broken it over my head,

> But she caught sight of her own reflection
> And that held her spellbound for two seconds
> While I fled.
> *(Lawrence, 1930, p. 498)*

Such works have to do with the vulnerability that relationships subject us to, where trust and fear can swap places with each other in bewildering Catherine wheel rapidity. Lawrence articulated for me both the honesty and dishonesty that has to be faced when engaging in the reality of emotions arising in a relationship. I found his sanguine approach helpful in my own difficult personal struggles. Professionally, I found it essential and grounding when trying to articulate a theory and methodology for working with couples, which elsewhere I called a "couplework that works" (Duffell, 2005), that privileged the idea of relationship as a mirror towards self-knowledge, that was both aspirational and realistic, that could account for failure and turning away.

The British public's inability to accept Lawrence could be perhaps ascribed to the stupidity of our civilization, as Frieda would say. But his choice of a German wife, his ambivalence towards his own country, his criticism of English reliance on rationality, his refusal to avoid discussing sex made him seem very scary at home. Lawrence was a partial outsider because he had crossed the class barrier, and so he had a view from just 'outside the box'. He was vehemently opposed to bullying, even if he was not entirely free from it is in his own life.

Not being a real gentleman, like the gamekeeper in *Lady Chatterley*, a self-made officer in the war and like Thomas Hardy, the son of a jobbing builder, Lawrence was a kind of foreigner and could still *feel*. But unlike Hardy, who was desperate to become a gentleman, Lawrence was not ashamed to talk subjectively about feelings. A theme of feeling *over time* connected to wounds of the soul is one that profoundly occupied him.

Tenderness

For Lawrence, both art and sex had to have a purpose; self-expression was not enough, as it would only serve the ends of ego. In this, as in so many other ways, he was misunderstood. Towards the end of his life, frustrated by the world's inability to learn the lessons of the Great War and to choose love and life, Lawrence went for broke with a final novel, as Sagar recounts:

> What Lawrence had seen in England had convinced him that the country was on the brink of a class war. He began a story about how two people through their sensitivity and respect for life above all else might bridge that fatal class chasm, and bring their own little ark against the coming flood; a story to be called *Lady Chatterley's Lover*.
> *(Sagar, 2003, p. 232)*

Lawrence had originally wanted to call the book *Tenderness*, but he was always unsure about his titles. *Lady Chatterley's Lover* was to be his last major work and therefore his most mature. We tend to think of *Chatterley* as being all about sex, remembering as we do the obscenity trials of the 1960s and the ushering in, as Larkin sang, the beginning of a greater awakening about sexuality (Larkin, 1974). But to me it is not really *about* sex but about *feeling*, about how we treat one another. It is an appeal for the quality of tenderness to counteract the ghastliness of war and the ugliness of industrial slavery.

While England wanted to move on, occupied as it was with motorcars, semi-detached housing estates and metropolitan railways, Lawrence, with the sensitivity of a consumptive, was not deceived. Prophetically, Lawrence, who died just as the Blackshirts began their rise to power, sensed that disaster would come again if we did not learn the lessons of the war. For him, they were *psychological* rather than political lessons. For Lawrence, only a return to love, to tenderness, to sympathy and to soulful sexuality would do. Doris Lessing, writing in an introduction to a new edition, sees *Chatterley* as an attempt to heal the problem of the First World War and all that it stood for:

> [A]nd if talk of the war was being channelled safely into war memorials and Remembrance Days, people who had been near to the nightmare would have had to remember. And against the horrors Lawrence proposes to put in the scales love, tender sex, the tender bodies of people in love; England would be saved by warm-hearted fucking.
>
> *(Lessing, 2006, p. xvii)*

In this masterpiece, Lawrence shows us money and class bound together in a feudal hangover, the alienation of women and workers, England ruined and "emasculated." This last, difficult word needs unpacking. Lawrence is not, I think, proposing a new machismo but rather that men might become less *rational*, that they might *feel* and *love* women and sex as an expression of the highest value, which for him is tenderness. He is proposing an antidote to the mindset of the age, the machismo of the classist public school ethos disguising emotional crippledness, still not rejected by us today.

This we find embodied in Sir Clifford Chatterley, landowner and coal mine proprietor, sent back from Flanders in 1918, "more or less in bits," paralysed and confined to a wheelchair, diverting himself by writing fashionably vacant stories. The novel centers round his wife Connie's feeling of isolation: she cannot get through to or feel loved by this man. Clifford has become both a physical and emotional cripple; his inability to love drives his wife into the arms of another, more instinctual – and shockingly – lower-class man. Living in a hut, Mellors stands for a kind of Green Man figure.

We are offered a picture of a divided nation, highlighted by the blind coldness and lack of tenderness in the upper classes. It depicts their retreat from the life of the body and how this, hand in hand with profit-led industrialization, has despoiled England's green and pleasant land, broken its people and "emasculated" her leaders.

"Oh God," gasps his heroine, Connie, as she is being driven out of her husband's estate through the grim village, home to the miners of Clifford's colliery, seeming "more as objects rather than men." Inwardly, Connie wails:

> What has man done to man? What have the leaders of men been doing to their fellow men? They have reduced them to less than humanness, and now there can be no fellowship anymore! It is just a nightmare.
>
> *(Lawrence, 2006, p. 153)*

Lawrence's remedy is simple enough, if too romantic for some: *love*. Not an idealized love that marked both warmongers and conscientious objectors to Lawrence but a fierce volitional love that embraces femininity, empathy and sexuality. Squarely condemning the class-divided society and the entitlement of the ruling classes, his revolutionary attitude may have been another reason the book was banned for so long. Lawrence gave the book all he had got, as if this passionate novel about a woman yearning for love might just bring life back to England before he himself dies. Its psychological precision is staggering.

Clifford's maimed state represents both the reality of the ghastly war and, more importantly, a symbol for the paralysed nature of the British upper classes, fed on a strict diet of entitlement and hyper-rationalism. For Clifford is not just physically wounded; like many ex-public school men, he is internally crippled in his inability to receive and give love. He can only *survive* by maintaining an illusion of control. He cannot and *will* not grieve.

But Clifford's coldness is not just personal – it is *systemic*. Connie ends up standing for all the disowned qualities – the age's wholesale rejection of all the feminine, evoking vulnerability and love. She becomes increasingly depressed until she receives some tenderness from Mellors. Ignored and objectified as she is by her crippled husband and his effete friends, Connie comes to acknowledge that she is being *damaged* by the absence of sensitivity from her husband.

The 'wounded leader' type described in Lawrence's book is still very much with us: the kind of problems that Clifford exhibits domestically – a tendency to overvalue work or achievement, a lack of empathy, an inability to grieve, and so on – are values in today's hyper-masculine culture of work. They are still being cultivated by a private education system unique to Britain and her ex-colonies. In my practice, when working with ex-boarders and their wives, I have seen many such desperate cases as Connie's: family members who have taken on the disowned characteristics and feelings of what cannot be felt by the dissociating survivor. Even worse: I have had to acknowledge how my own cold survival personality can create misery in those I love, unless I stay its master.

On sexuality

Today, we still associate *Lady Chatterley's Lover* with sex, though his earlier book *The Rainbow* and its sequel *Women in Love* contain even more detail and precision about the changing facets of desire on behalf of both male and female characters. Desire is embodied as a central living element between men and women, and yet, in his own life, Lawrence was rather puritanical, partly as a result of his Congregationalist upbringing:

> There can be no successful sex union unless the greater hope of purposive, constructive activity fires the soul of the man all the time: or the hope of passionate, purposive destructive activity: the two amount religiously to the same thing, within the individual. Sex as an end in itself is a disaster: a vice.
> *(Lawrence, 1922, p. 278)*

A sentiment that his wife Frieda shared:

> He was sex-mad, they said. Little even now do people realize what men like Lawrence do for the body of life, what he did to rescue the fallen angel of sex. Sex had fallen in the gutter, it had to be pulled out.
> *(Lawrence, 1934, p. 144)*

Lawrence's rescue of sexuality was purposive, well thought through and cutting-edge. He reasoned that humans are governed by a series of bodily plexuses. The *sympathetic* centres, located in the upper body, such as the heart, throat and brain, and the *volitional* centres, such as the solar plexus and genito-sacral areas, could end up in conflict. The prevailing hyper-rational paradigm had colluded in disowning the sensual centres of the lower body in favour of mental ideation, which could pollute all aspects of life, including relationships:

> What we have done, in our era, is, first, we have tried as far as possible to suppress or subordinate the two sensual centers. We have so unduly insisted on and exaggerated the upper spiritual or selfless mode – the living *in* the other person and *through* the other person – that we have caused already a dangerous over-balance in the natural psyche.
> *(Lawrence, 1922, p. 105)*

Lawrence took his stand on the sacredness of gender difference, not the status quo of gender *roles*. The novels were contemporary with the beginnings of women's rights movements. Alongside this but frequently sidelined by the Suffragette campaign, was a movement to revise notions of female sexuality, and he was the first male writer to consider female desire in an honest and frank way (Edwards, 2000). Methuen published Lawrence's novel *The Rainbow* in (Lawrence, 1915), only to be prosecuted under the Obscene Publications Act. The Crown prosecutor condemned Lawrence's text for what he saw as immoral representations of sexuality sardonically described as a mass of obscenity of thought, idea and action throughout, wrapped up in language that would be regarded in some quarters as an artistic and intellectual effort (Meyers, 1990). Methuen issued a timid apology and surrendered all remaining copies to the magistrate.

Although aware of and sympathetic to women, including their dilemmas and their multifaceted desire, Lawrence was under no illusion about their emotional and sexual power; he knew how the two sexes could easily destroy each other. His women characters are not sentimental like Hardy's. I would argue that nowhere in literature has a male writer entered so deeply into a woman's psyche. Never have so many valid criticisms of male withdrawal from the life of the soul been put into the mouths of women, but one of Lawrence's boldest achievements is to feature the inner dialogue of a woman as the core of a book, as he does in *Chatterley*.

One of its jewels is a remarkable intimate exchange between two women – quite a feat for a male writer to pull off – in which Lady Constance Chatterley and her husband's nurse, Mrs Bolton, who lost her man down the pit, talk and weep together about loss, the memory of touch, the brutality of industrial work and the durability of love relations. It is an exquisite scene enlivened with a communality of feminine wisdom, in direct opposition to the masculine dedication to the machine: "When you come to know men, that's how they are: too sensitive, in the wrong place" (Lawrence, 2006, p. 163).

Psychotherapy rooted in the body

In 1922, in reaction to psychoanalysis, Lawrence surprised everyone by writing a long essay on procreative sexuality and raising children, *Fantasia of the Unconscious*, in which he set out his stall didactically about ideas he had been working into fiction and poetry. "What Freud says is always partly true . . ." (Lawrence, 1922, p. 2):

> Freud is wrong in attributing a sexual motive to all human activity. It is obvious there is no real sexual motive in a child, for example. The great sexual centers are not even awake.
>
> *(Lawrence, 1922, p. 157)*

I imagine Lawrence would have shuddered to receive the news, as I did this week, of yet another seminar by a British analyst, this time Winnicottian, on so-called 'infant sexuality'. It seems like some strange way to avoid the reality of sex in adult lives – so safe and so compartmentalized – nothing to do with teens out clubbing with alcohol-fuelled promiscuity, or their Dads watching Internet porn, or their Mums contemplating cosmetic surgery.

> What good will psychoanalysis do you in this state of affairs? Introduce an extra sex-motive to excite you for a bit and make you feel how thrillingly immoral things really are. And then – it all goes flat again. Father complex, mother complex, incest dreams: pah, when we've had the little excitement out of them we shall forget them as we have forgotten so many other catchwords. And we shall be just where we were before: unless we are worse, with more sex in the head, and more introversion, only more brazen.
>
> *(Lawrence, 1922, p. 184)*

His predictions seem to have come true. Finding no empathy in the founding fathers' concepts, psychotherapy training organizations have abandoned teaching sexuality altogether in favour of sociological perspectives on gender, leaving the interested to pursue the mechanistic models of sexologists. Lawrence had no doubt about the centrality of sex in human life as the elemental foundation. He saw the male's desire as the starting point of life, akin to post-Reichian theory, which prefers to talk about the 'priority of charge'.

> It is the pure disinterested craving of the human male to make something wonderful, out of his own head and his own self, and his own soul's faint and delight, which starts everything going. This is the prime motivity. That is, the essentially religious or creative motive is the first motive for all human activity. The sexual motive comes second.
>
> *(Lawrence, 1922, p. 3)*

Rooted always in experience, Lawrence had an overview of one of the (to my mind) most difficult problems in both couple and individual psychotherapy. It is one where, in the family of origin, a son has become the substitute husband of his mother, replacing a father who has withdrawn from the relationship with his wife. Of course, this was Lawrence's own background, which caused him for so many years to reject his father in favour of older women. He seems to have come through it by dint of writing, entry into a committed relationship, and perhaps grace. His 'Song of a Man Who Has Come Through' (Lawrence, 1917), one of his most popular poems, is, I suspect, an oblique reference to the effort needed. In the following passage, taken from a letter to David Garnett in 1912, he unpicks the psychosexual reality behind his semi-fictional *Sons and Lovers*:

> A woman of character goes into the lower class, and has no satisfaction in her own life. She has had a passion for her husband, so the children are born of passion, and have heaps of vitality. But as her sons grow up, she selects them as lovers, first the eldest, then the second. These sons are *urged* into life by their reciprocal love of their mother – urged on and on. But when they come to manhood, they can't love, because their mother is the strongest power in their lives, and holds them . . . As soon as the young men come into contact with women, there's a split.
>
> *(Boulton, 1979, p. 476)*

This is such a common story, as fathers tend toward relational passivity and have a crazy-making effect on their wives, but it is so little known in conventional current psychotherapy, except perhaps to some diehard psychoanalysts and somatic therapists. The converse syndrome, where fathers make their daughters into their little princesses, is much better understood and easier to treat: the woman simply has to grow up. The male's Oedipal entrapment is particularly hard to recognize. As far as I know, only Willem Poppeliers' Sexual Grounding Therapy has a suitable word for this mother–son wound: "heart-rape" (Poppeliers & Broesterhuizen, 2007). The result is often a passive-aggressive male who retreats, especially with sexual symptomatology such as erectile dysfunction. The withdrawal of sexual desire from the male, being at the root of life as Lawrence (I think correctly) argues, makes this one of the hardest syndromes to treat, even if it is recognized.

But along with his understanding of Oedipal difficulties, Lawrence also cherished the potential of the eternal triangle, and today's society of impermanence has much to gain from exploring his vision. Like a committed coupleworker, Lawrence proposes that, through all difficulties, a real relationship offers the simple but vast power of the soul. If a man and a woman can be truly themselves and love each other, emotionally and sexually, being real if not perfect, a huge stability is created from the strength of this bond that benefits future generations. From *The Rainbow*:

> Anna's soul was put at peace between them. She looked from one to the other, and she saw them established to her safety, and she was free. She played between the pillar of fire and the pillar of cloud in confidence, having the assurance on her right hand and the assurance on her left. She was no longer called upon to uphold with her childish might the broken end of the arch.
>
> *(Lawrence, 1915, p. 79)*

Such a rainbow might yet be Lawrence's still to be recognized legacy.

References

Boulton, J. T. (ed.) (1979) *The Letters of D. H. Lawrence*, Vol. 1, Cambridge: Cambridge University Press.
Carswell, C. (1981) *The Savage Pilgrimage*, Cambridge: Cambridge University Press.
Cash, W. (2009) 'Did Atheist Philosopher See God When He "Died"?' In *National Post*, 28 April. Retrieved 5 November 2014 from http://en.wikipedia.org/wiki/A._J._Ayer#cite_note-25.
Duffell, N. (2005) 'Searching for Couplework That Works' *The Psychotherapist*, No. 27, pp. 5–6.
Duffell, N. (2014) *Wounded Leaders: British Elitism and the Entitlement Illusion – A Psychohistory*, London: Lone Arrow Press.
Edwards, J. D. (2000) 'At the End of the Rainbow: Reading Lesbian Identities in D.H. Lawrence's Fiction' *The International Fiction Review* (27) 1–2. Retrieved January 2016 from http://journals.hil.unb.ca/index.php/IFR/article/view/7659/8716.
Larkin, P. (1974) 'Annus Mirabilis' In *High Windows*, London: Faber & Faber, p. 34.
Lawrence, D. H. (1915) *The Rainbow*, London: Methuen & Co.
Lawrence, D. H. (1917) 'Song of a Man Who Has Come Through' In Ellis, D. (ed.) (1994) *The Complete Poems of D. H. Lawrence*, Ware, Herts: Wordsworth Editions, p. 195.
Lawrence, D. H. (1920) *Women in Love*, New York: Thomas Selzer.
Lawrence, D. H. (1922) *Fantasia of the Unconscious*, New York: Thomas Selzer.
Lawrence, D. H. (1930) 'More Pansies' In Ellis, D. (ed.) (1994) *The Complete Poems of D. H. Lawrence*, Ware, Herts: Wordsworth Editions, pp. 495–573.
Lawrence, D. H. (1932) 'Intimates in Last Poems' In Ellis, D. (ed.) (1994) *The Complete Poems of D. H. Lawrence*, Ware, Herts: Wordsworth Editions, p. 498.

Lawrence, D. H. 'Climb Down, O Lordly Mind' In Ellis, D. (ed.) (1994) *The Complete Poems of D. H. Lawrence*, Ware, Herts: Wordsworth Editions, pp. 388–389.
Lawrence, D. H. (2006) *Lady Chatterley's Lover*, London: Penguin.
Lawrence, F. (Geb. Freiin Von Richthofen) (1934) *Not I but the Wind*, New York: Viking Press.
Lessing, D. (2006) In Lawrence, D. H. *Lady Chatterley's Lover, A Propos of Lady Chatterley's Lover, with an Introduction by Doris Lessing*, London: Penguin.
Meyers, J. (1990) *D. H. Lawrence: A Biography*, New York: Vintage.
Poppeliers, W., & Broesterhuizen, M. (2007) *Sexual Grounding Therapy*, Breda, The Netherlands: Protocol Media Productions. Retrieved from www.sexualgrounding.com.
Sagar, K. (2003) *The Life of D. H. Lawrence: An Illustrated Biography*, London: Chaucer Press.

5

TEARS OF JOY

Pascal's 'Night of Fire'

Subhaga Gaetano Failla
Translated from the Italian by Manu Bazzano

> *Joy, joy, joy, tears of joy*
> *(Pascal)*

The earliest hours of Monday, November 23, Anno Domini 1654, St. Clemens day, according to the calendar. Blaise Pascal, a thirty-one-year-old man with thin lips, a skinny face and wavy chestnut hair down to his shoulders, woke in the dark, in the throes of a migraine, the faithful shadow of his familiar torment. In the meeting place of the *Solitaries*, his tiny room – cell, island in an archipelago – seemed to suffocate him.

He got up moaning, face in hands, his gaze clouded by broken sleep and physical pain. He groped for the candelabrum and lit three candles encrusted with trickling wax. He reached the window, opened it mechanically, as if seeking help. The cold autumn air rushed in, carrying scents from the nearby woods and orchard of low, rare trees. Just then the sound came through the damp darkness of the bells of Mother Marie-Angelique monastery. At the same time as he had woken against his will to attend to his customary torment, his sister Jacqueline and the other nuns of Port-Royal des Champs were getting up, as they did every night, at 2 a.m. to sing the psalms. Suddenly, within the recesses of Pascal's dazed skull, the incomprehensible voices of his recent, restless dreams were joined, a ghostly disordered crowd, to discordant chants – they sounded mean, erratic – of the women's prayers, then the daytime yells of school children, the long-ago booming voice of his father guiding his child's hand to compose an unfamiliar word with a quill.

The wind blew among the skeletal branches of the plane trees carrying a spell of unexpected relief. But that was only a brief moment. It was as if a fierce claw had clasped Pascal's head with great force. Giving out another suffocated groan, he bent outwards into the darkness, shaken by steady but vain attempts to vomit.

With some difficulty he managed to shut the window. Then, bending over, he wetted a cloth and brought it to his forehead. He staggered towards his bed where he had already placed a foot warmer in order to try and reactivate the circulation in his feet (which due to another physical problem were often ice-cold). Finally, he lay on the bed as a dying man. "*Teriaca* – he thought – my only salvation".

For some time fine physicians had recommended, as an extreme analgesic, this well-known remedy – a concoction of opium, pulverized viper, St John's wort, valerian, long pepper, cinnamon and various other ingredients. Pascal bought the best (and very expensive) teriaca from Venetian spice sellers. The concoction had to be dissolved in Malvasía wine with added honey. Still moaning and with his eyes shut, he paused a little as if to gather strength for a mighty task. All he needed to do was get up and with one step reach his small table crammed with books, papers, an inkpot and in a corner two red apples, a piece of rye bread, an elegant, tightly shut glass jug and a glass. He got up, carefully opened the jug, poured the amber-coloured liquid – the very colour of which seemed to have a calming effect on him – knocked back the salutary drink, feeling its dense tang. Then he went back to bed and waited. Purged by the previous day's fast, a condition ideal for inviting the effects of the medicine, his body was ready.

About half an hour later, the claws that gripped his head slackened, and he slipped into a faint slumber of blue reveries.

There were two or three vigorous knocks at the door. He opened his eyes with an eerie feeling of apprehension and sat up in his bed. A clang, a lacerating hiss went through his head but soon the noise turned into an innocent hum.

"Who is there?" Pascal said. His own voice seemed to him remote, lugubrious. A pale, strong hand implausibly rested on the door.

"Who is it?" he asked again, trembling.

"It's me, Blaise. Let me in".

With some alarm, he recognized that voice and its boisterous tone.

"The door is ajar. Come in".

A young man smartly dressed in a large dark cloak came into sight – he might have been in his late twenties. He wore magnificent boots up to his knees. He walked a few steps in the room and placed his hat on the table. A familiar scent filled the cell.

The visitor had no face. His voice came from a grey, formless space where his face would have been.

"What do you want?" asked Pascal in a dark whisper.

"Ah", the visitor mocked him, "you did recognize your past human coil, the young flesh hurt by dissipation. But now you fear the player in that younger man; you fear the hazard, the leap in the void".

"What do you want?" he asked again, almost imploring.

"It doesn't take much: a little noise, a simple knock on the door, and the great world authority is distraught".

"You are just a figment of my imagination!" Pascal cried out defensively, urgently. "It's the teriaca, I know. You are but the teriaca's rotten fruit, a mere hallucination".

"Your imagination is rather insidious, dear Blaise, for it marks equally the true and the false. So now you fear me. What good is all your philosophy? It's a colossal heap of empty words, a huge tangle of phrases that never turned to flesh and blood.

A little breeze, and it's gone, and you find yourself alone with your fear. You run away, but your shadow follows you. How foolish, trying to shake it off, even to erase it ... You even use your philosophy to do this!"

There was scorn in the last words he spoke.

"You can't just mock my studies like that – all those years spent wearing my eyes out at the dim light of a candle. You can't make fun of my exhausting philosophical labour!"

"What a pitiable, foolish man you are, still defending your anodyne words. The day you realize that mocking philosophy is what true philosophizing is all about, only then will you have a chance to win, and only then will you throw the die with trepidation".

The owl's melancholy song was heard in the night between the trees and the cloudy sky; it reached the room in hushed, constant bursts. Pascal turned his gaze towards the source of that sound. Then, like a drowning man who for an instant emerges from the water in the last attempt to safety only to be plunged back even deeper, he went back to look inside the room. He fervently hoped to see the visitor gone, dissolved at last into thin air, like a bad dream vanished at dawn.

But the visitor was still there. He now sat at the small table, bent over, deep in thought. He sighed.

"You see how difficult this is, Blaise . . ."

Gone the nasty tone of his preamble, he now spoke gently, almost with affection.

"Teriaca has erased your physical pain, but you are still restless, a victim of loneliness and sloth, unacknowledged sources of inner wisdom. I have found a simple truth, Blaise: people's unhappiness comes from one thing alone: the inability to remain still in a room".

"But I am not alone in this cell", mumbled Pascal. "*You* are the cause of my restlessness".

Again the visitor sighed.

"My absence would have frightened you even more", he said. "The void, do you remember? Horror of the void . . . You still need some relic to cling to".

"I would like to see a smile on your face; to see you sneer would be enough. But I cannot bear this perfect void speaking to me".

"You showed your courage a few years back, Blaise, and contradicted the sayings of the Greek who had gone about proclaiming that nature abhors a vacuum. You demonstrated it via experiments even, following the adventures of another stranger, a contemporary, that the void exists in spite of the burdening presence of that great peripatetic master whose notions, to be sure, did originate in an empty brain . . . You succeeded in perilously cracking Aristotle's statue. Our Lord the Void, alive and pulsating, is our constant cradle, our boundless tomb, forever changeable and unpredictable. You had the courage to find the void in a glass tube, but now you fear finding it in yourself".

"What I look for is truth, an unambiguous land where to find asylum and the assured hands of a mother and her welcoming embrace".

"We are faring on a vast sea, my dear Blaise, uncertain and unsteady, forever tossed about. Any reef we cling to in the hope of finding some kind of solidity gives way and gives us up, and if we run after it, it slips away from our grip and runs away in eternal flight. Nothing stands still for us. But what we truly fear is not the reef fleeing from our grasp. We have horror of this incessant vital motion. We would like to immobilize the sea, turn it into inanimate stone. This is what our thirst for truth amounts to: vilification of life and cold death".

With considerable strain and apprehension, Pascal followed the words uttered by the faceless man. Then gradually a languid tiredness and torpor descended on him. Those urgent and dangerous words became background noise; they became formless, diluted to a drone. He managed to bring the candelabra close to him and put out the candles. He let his body gently fall onto the bed and placed his head on the pillow. Muddled dreams and vivid rolling waves led him anew into strange lands. He slept for a long time.

★

Pascal woke to the queasy light of a grey, cloudy dawn. The cruel clutch over his head was now like the memory of a fresh nightmare that had left inside a vaporous space a vast and trembling bubble. He heard a distant murmured chatter coming from the barn and smelled that familiar spiced perfume that had helped him ensnare young women in his past, frivolous life, the very same perfume the visitor wore. Silent and unwearied, the faceless young man waited for him in the same place.

"You are torturing me!" Pascal said these words angrily, whimpering.

"We all are our own torturers and jailers, dear Blaise. The tormentor's tools are in our own hands; we ourselves fabricate red-hot pincers and build the walls that suffocate us. You must take your chances, Blaise, and bet on uncertainty, our sole and changeable certainty! Do you remember when, as children, we would leap from the staircase of our home? If we didn't jump right away, fear would paralyze our body and soul, and we would stay on that step forever, frightened, ashamed of our weakness".

Pascal gazed in confusion at the cloudy sky, a little clearer now, and sought a smile or a grimace on the young man's face. But in its place he again found the inexorable void. He then turned his head to the crucifix on the wall above his bed.

"How . . . how?" he groaned.

"With trust, Blaise; I speak to you as my own dear young body now aged. With trust, my dear Blaise, my own spirit, soul, vital breath now reaching beyond the thirty-one years of age of this mortal life of ours. With trust in uncertainty and a hankering for the vast sea forever changing and stable in its mutability. That is the cure, the absurd method to heal our soul. And my voice too, as a companion, to be left behind finally, to be abandoned with a bow of gratitude".

The young man sighed deeply; it was the very same sigh Pascal exhaled at the same time, and the philosopher's face seemed to relax the tension that had turned it into a mask.

The faceless man added:

"Imagine a great number of people, Blaise. They are all chained, all of them condemned to death. Some get slaughtered under the others' gaze; those who remain see their fate in the eyes of their fellows; gazing at each other, they hopelessly await their turn. This is what the human condition is like – but you, my soul … you can set yourself free".

Pascal's expression became remote, as if he were a thousand miles from that tiny, frosty cell. His mind was busy recalling an event, one that, he felt, had taken place in some other life and only indirectly to him. His mind went back to an incident of a fortnight before, when his carriage went over Neuilly Bridge and his short, peaceful journey almost turned into tragedy. For some reason, as soon as the carriage reached the bridge, the horses became frisky and jumped over the low parapet. For what seemed an eternity, the carriage hovered between bridge and precipice. Terrified, Pascal saw the abyss waiting for him: it seemed keen to welcome him in its dark belly. All of a sudden, whatever had kept him bound in nostalgia for the past or enticed by futile, wearisome desires, it all vanished. He was there now, suspended above the precipice, trembling, staring at the abyss. How could he have lived so foolish a life that he never before sensed that limit, the unambiguous measure giving at last value and sanctity to his life? In what dreamy state or slumber had he lived until now, in what distracted habits?

And yet in a short time that occurrence was already becoming a memory, slowly shaking off the very urgency that had been its strength; it was fading into some hazy dream. Fear was back once again, undisputed master, claiming its ancient dominion. Soon he would forget the abyss altogether; soon he'd go back, defeated, to his habitual, timid lethargy.

"You are saying that I can free myself. But how, when fear and suffering are still my only faithful companions? How can I?" he implored, turning a forlorn look towards the crucifix. "How can I find God?"

"He hides in the ordinary and rarely does he reveal himself to those he wants to work at his service. You will not find God through reason and the tools of science but through the secret and foreign language of the heart. But it is now time for me to leave, Blaise. I came to you because you looked for me. You may be fearful and concerned, but you did receive me; your door was ajar. We were not truly separate. You let my words into your heart. Now you don't need me anymore. The cure is over". The visitor uttered these last words tenderly.

"Will you come back?"

"Clinging to my presence would be a hindrance. An infinite journey entails infinite losses, and the intimate knowledge of farewells is the covert structure of the world".

★

The monastery bells struck nine. A gentle, mid-morning sun beamed at intervals, flickering through the grave clouds, fleeting hints of sky. The *Solitaries* of Port-Royal des Champs and the sisters of the Abbey had been awake for a while, their separate rooms and communal spaces suffused with absorbed, understated vitality. For a little while, the children of the *petites écoles* had let out their cheerful cries in the air, then they too vanished indoors. From time to time, on the few paths linking the various buildings, a lone bent figure walked by with short quick steps, a dark fluttering stain nearly dissolving in a veil of low mist until it vanished behind a door. No one had come asking for him for they knew of his voluntary seclusion. Exhausted, he drifted into a long sleep.

He woke up greatly refreshed, full of childlike vigour. Once again darkness had fallen. He leapt out of bed and lit the candles: the visitor was gone. He drank avidly a glass of water, with eyes closed. He gazed at his long, tapering fingers as if they belonged to someone else and brought them to touch his face where a sparse beard had grown. His head felt light, empty; everything he gazed at filled him with surprise. It seemed to him he had never seen the small flame of a candle, his own handwriting on the paper, the shadow fluctuating on the wall. He was enchanted by everything.

He ate the two small apples from the table, sweet as ever, and chewed on what was left of a rye bun; he even ate the fallen crumbs, which he gathered together on the scattered pieces of paper. Then he became aware of a vast, restless low sound. A straight, heavy rain heartened that side of the Chevreuse Valley, quenching the fields, the great plane trees, the orchard and the granges, filling up the buckets for the animals in the farm. The earth was breathing, and Pascal too realized he was breathing. He took in a long deep breath as if to draw air for a last breath.

"If I stay within this old drowning wreck", he thought, opening his gleaming eyes wide, "death is certain; I will go under like a mouse in a trap. The only chance I have is to gamble in this adventure, in the vast, perilous, changing sea".

A wave engulfed him as magmatic flux, incinerating fire. He thought, mistakenly, that what was happening to him now had never happened before. Then he remembered: he had been alive, once upon a time, and now life was coming back. Afraid at first, he wanted, on impulse, to escape. Then his breathing slowed down; it became calm. He half-opened his mouth, lowered his eyelids and wept. He glimpsed the Abbey shrouded in the rain, luminous, then turned his gaze inside the room in the direction of the crucifix and whispered as if mortally wounded:

"I separated myself from him".

He sighed and in a long whisper of gratitude, almost singing, he said:

"May I not be eternally separated from him. Joy, joy, joy, tears of joy".

PART II
Ethics and politics

We wish to assert ourselves, yet acknowledge that there is not really a self who can make that assertion. Accepting our entrapment in this double bind can make for a freer and more fluid existence, even if at times an unpleasant or uncomfortable one as we hold this tension. We may fall into the illusion that "I" exist as a reified entity, when it seems, as we look more closely through the eyes of Rousseau, Sartre, Butler and Irigaray, that it is always *we*.

We cannot appropriate the "I", much as we may try, and neither can we appropriate the "we": life is too mysterious for us to grasp once and for all; too untamed to be contained; and conversely too accessible to be remote. We are positioned, always situated, forever social, and sometimes the paradox of our experience as singular embodied, gendered persons, seems to reinforce the chains that bind us forever to the *other*. This paradox is explicit in therapy as the client points towards what is other whilst occupying the very terms that she/he interrogates.

The following chapters articulate a sense of not being at home within the institutions of philosophy and psychotherapy in their respective current containers, and instead reinforce our desire to persist in our own being; desire a kind of vitality that only exists because of, and is dependent upon, rupture and conflict. The chapters do not seem to gesture towards a desire to 'integrate' and compromise, but place instead importance upon inter-disciplinary engagement as a means of accommodation: in search of a home that acknowledges and embraces the other: a radical ethic which recognizes that "I" am called to respond by the sheer existence of the other, and only in that response is "I" momentarily recognized. The double helix of recognition creates sites for viable living that must first be born through conflict resulting in attunement and accommodation rather than merging.

6

WHO AM I? YOU TELL ME

Desire and Judith Butler

Julie Webb

Introduction

Judith Butler's work articulates an ethic as the *process of becoming* through a contemporary reading of the work of G. W. F. Hegel, specifically *The Phenomenology of Spirit* (Hegel, 1979). Butler argues that desire for recognition in order to live a "livable life" is our deepest desire, that like all desire, this desire is never fully satiated, and further that this livable life is always a life that comes into being in the face of the Other. In order to accept that my self-awareness is limited and reliant upon the Other *absolutely* means that ethics is a reflexive process, embedded in *relationality*, and requires me to surrender to my limited self-awareness and accept my constitutive openness. These ideas call into question the very idea that identity and autonomy are possible states or even desirable ones. Butler's work challenges the idea of knowing and has profound implications in the traditional therapy room and training environment, which have taken as self-evident the possibility of a knowable self and Other. This discussion implicitly asks, "*To what extent is therapy a quest for mutual recognition?*"

Who am I? You tell me . . .

Eighteen years ago, at the age of thirty-four, I found myself in my first philosophy seminar, having begun a belated first degree in literature and philosophy. A fire had been ignited that had been smoldering for most of my life until that point. I looked around the room at the twenty-five or so students: a handful of mature students and the rest, vibrant and energetic youths. I was excited, out of place and scared. My eyes followed a guy who, silently and lightly, walked down the isle with a tatty carrier bag in hand. He placed his bag on the table at the front of the class, took off his coat, took out some papers and began to speak. I was instantly arrested by his words. In the years to come, I discovered descriptions of the world that I had experienced but as yet had been unable to articulate. My view of the world was not so "odd" after all, and it seemed that *I* was not so "odd", or "difficult", or "deep", or "intense" either: turned out *I* was indeed human, and *I* had finally found a home to dwell in, which in a very important sense was a *no home*.

I am forever indebted to that particular tutor, for not being chained to the institution of philosophy or education, for presenting philosophical works and their creators as human beings, as critics and commentators, as artists and poets, and for leading me down a path that created disturbances and anxieties within what proved to be fertile, creative sites for own my becoming. In retrospect, it is no surprise to me now that his history was also embedded in the mental health profession, which is also where my own philosophical journey has led me so far.

It was during these studies that I was introduced to the works of Judith Butler. Butler takes up Hegel and other notable thinkers such as Foucault, Sartre, Kojeve, Lacan, Derrida and Hyppolite in her published thesis *Subjects of Desire* (Butler, 1987) and demonstrates clearly, as Philip Sabor writes in a new preface, that "contemporary reflections cannot separate themselves as much as they purport to, or would like to, from Hegelian thought of desire . . . We are (still) not finished with Hegel" (Butler, 2012, pp. x–xi). For Butler, Hegel reveals a human subject that "is never simply and immediately there" (Butler, 1987, p. 19). She states that Hegel's *Phenomenology of Spirit* "is not only a narrative about journeying consciousness, but is the journey itself" (Butler, 1987, p. 21), revealing that this is a text about movement and the fluid ungraspable subject.

Butler's discussion centres upon contemporary ideas on the nature of becoming, affirming that consciousness is necessarily *self-consciousness*: I am not only conscious of you, but I am aware that I am conscious of you, and this self-consciousness emerges "as a kind of knowing that is at once a mode of becoming: it is suffered, dramatized, enacted" (Butler, 1987, p. 28). I have often heard in the therapeutic training arena the phrase "I can only know me in relation to you" without adequate discussion about what that may mean. It is not just the case that I like potatoes and you like pomme de frites, that I am short and you are tall, that I am a woman and you are a man, or that I may be having a different experience than you. Even if all these things are true, there is more at stake than that, and these stakes are deeply rooted in the subject of *desire*. Butler articulates an ethic at play that describes desire as a deep need to be recognized in order to live out a livable life (Butler, 2004). This recognition is a reciprocal process that might be called "mutual recognition" and is an inescapable intersubjectivity based on a desire of the human that can never be fully satiated, whereby "I" can never arrive fully; "I" is a state of "perpetual striving . . . sustained in a progressive and open adventure of Spirit" (Butler, 1987, pp. 13, 14).

Desire wants "illumination of its own opacity . . . is intentional . . . reflexive in the sense that desire is a modality in which the subject is both discovered and enhanced" (Butler, 1987, p. 24). What I desire the most is to be recognized as the forming subject that I am, and more than any historical, societal or cultural situatedness, my forming is reliant upon your presence in the world: the presence of a human like me who is also my opposite and as such "keeps desire alive" (Butler, 1987, p. 15).

In *Subjects of Desire* (Butler, 1987), Butler discusses the Hegelian description of how a "self" becomes constituted in relation to what is Other and, further, how that self is also related to by that Other. Mutual recognition becomes a kind of utopian goal: that I recognize you as a non-reified forming subject, and in return you do the same for me, and between us we create a common culture around the mutual recognition of alterity, i.e. our infinite otherness. We might also call this an open-handed offer of hospitality such as the ethic that Bazzano describes as a "goddess in continuous flight, a goddess who exists in flight" (Bazzano, 2012, p. 34), a moving, ungraspable vitality: a dynamic whereby "The subject not only forms psychic relations ... but is formed by and through those psychic relations" (Butler, 2004, p. 132) momentarily and temporarily.

For Butler, the site in which recognition takes place is no static event but an *ecstatic* event, an "on-going process" of "struggle" and one that also poses the "psychic risk of destruction" (Butler, 2004, p. 132).

> Recognition is at once the norm toward which we invariably strive, the norm that ought to govern therapeutic practice, and the ideal form that communication takes when it becomes a transformative process. Recognition is, however, also the name given to the process that constantly risks destruction and which, I would submit, could not be recognition without a defining or constitutive risk of destruction.
>
> *(Butler, 2004, p. 133)*

This recognition, then, is not recognition of a secure fixed identity – that I am what I am and so are you. Rather, following Butler, recognition here is referring to what it is to be human, and the claim that this human, as a subject, is constitutively open, and therefore my claim to *being human* at all, must be to meet you in awareness of our constitutive becoming. The closing of ranks in identity categories is a closing down of the human, not just of the Other that I place outside of the category but also of myself within the confines of the category to which I subscribe. To recognize and be recognized as human, I must open myself to possibilities, even fantasies that in an important sense I will "act in concert" (Butler, 2004, pp. 1–16) with the Other, through the Other, and through my negation of the Other: in the words of Georges Bataille, "The divergent possibilities of opposed human figures confront each other and assemble in it" (Bataille, 2004, p. 193).

If I am in a continual state of assemblage, or becoming, then I am also in a constant state of undoing. To be constitutively open is also to risk. How many times as a client (and therapist) has a fragment of the "I" that I cling to in order to stave off my distress been destroyed, and how much can I bear to live in an explicit (conscious) state of not knowing that can itself create a kind of vertigo? The existential tension of accepting that I do not know, as well as the need to cling hopelessly to false knowing for comfort and safety, becomes an inescapable *performative* state. This 'false' knowing and *performativity* is not an intentional act of inauthenticity but rather a state of temporality that emerges out of norms through which we seek to make ourselves known in a way that allows us to live a "livable life": *performativity* as we engage in "a practice of improvisation within a scene of constraint" (Butler, 2004, p. 1), a scene of constraint from which none are exempt and one that for some becomes a site of punishment and/or violence. If we seek to destroy or master the Other and the difference that we encounter, then we have not recognized the Other as fully human, nor indeed would we have behaved as fully human, for instead we will have taken a dogmatic reified stance in both the self and the Other camps. Butler's work goes beyond celebrations of difference, which has been adopted by institutions including therapeutic training environments as a kind of quasi-ethic but instead seeks to take a critical look at seeking ways "to establish more inclusive conditions for sheltering and maintaining life that resists models of assimilation" (Butler, 2004, p. 4), that become conditions not just to survive in but to thrive in.

Butler discusses the idea of livable lives more explicitly through her work on gender: *Gender Trouble* (Butler, 1990), *Bodies That Matter* (Butler, 1993) and *Undoing Gender* (Butler, 2004). In asking the question, "What is it to live a livable life?" Butler discusses at length what it means to be a gendered subject and what it means to be recognized as gendered. If desire for recognition is at our heart, then the desire to be recognized within gender descriptions and as gendered beings is also the case.

Some years ago whilst working with Butler's ideas in a training session, one trainee, who had travelled through tremendously courageous changes in making his transition from heterosexual married life and fatherhood to a same-sex civil partnership, suddenly yelped and threw his hands up in the air. All eyes were upon him. He shared with us how "even now" if he is in an environment with strangers, even in a family setting with strangers present, he will "camp it up". I asked him what he meant by that, and he shared that in order to declare his "being gay", he would adopt a stereotypical feminized performance to communicate his sexuality. His reflection revealed that in his desire to mark out his difference, he adopted a ritualized stance that would place him firmly in a different identity category to others present. He came to see that he had ironically swapped one fixed identity for another and so performed a stylized recognizable and acceptable norm of homosexuality. And, of course, he did, as most of us do in order to live our lives as comfortably as possible. However, the event also illustrated how difficult and almost impossible it is to challenge gender norms outside of the binary descriptive language that we use to do so.

Consider the following familiar vignette:

The boy child is passive, funny, a joker, jack the lad. He is small in stature and because of his comic nature is singled out for bullying. A bigger boy sets about him. The comedian tries to talk his way out of the situation, at which point a crowd gathers and the comedian's father intervenes. The comedian tries to walk away. The father insists that he stand and fight – "Be a man, my son". But the son is a gentle, passive boy and wants to walk away. The bigger boy sets about him and knocks him to the ground, hitting and kicking. Eventually the father stops it, looks at his son in disgust, laughs and tuts. The boy develops a self-concept that he is not a proper boy, not on his way to being a man and subsequently develops an attitude of arrogance in order to please the father. He loses his comedic ways and grows big and strong and does "manly" things: in this case drinks and fights. His adult self-concept develops into a "man's man". However, the drinking masks what person-centred theory might call the *organismic valuing process* (Rogers, 1965), whereby the passive, comedic boy still lurks in an uncomfortable dilemma. His conditions of worth rest upon his ability to perform a particular description of manhood and on the recognition of this that he receives from others in order to experience acceptance from his chosen group. Although in an important sense it might be pertinent to question who is choosing whom here. The notion of the "group", or what we could call community, also demonstrates the need to feel a sense of belonging and highlights the precariousness or even falseness of belonging when we encounter the difficulties of leaving one group to join another. So what does this belonging really amount to if desire is always the desire to be recognized as socially viable beings? To be socially viable might mean to accept some descriptions of what it is to be human and reject others, which means that recognition may be "conferred" by some and "withheld" by others, and so it follows that recognition is also the "site of power" (Butler, 2004, p. 2).

The distinction between man and masculinity just described is artificially stylized and reified, as gender (for both father and son) is made into a "ritualized performance", yet if we are to avoid the risk of being refused a place in that list of socially prescribed roles of permissible living, we may find ourselves adhering to such roles. Femininity and masculinity get represented as "natural" but are actually a "false naturalization" and a reified or rigid gendering. In short, the fixed gender identity that Butler describes consists in a set of quasi-compulsory norms, socially produced and coercively imposed and that are taken as "natural" – how we ought to behave and how we are socially recognized and she asks:

> If I am a certain gender, will I still be regarded as part of the human? Will the "human" expand to include me in its reach? If I desire in certain ways, will I be able to live? Will there be a place for my life and will it be recognizable to others whom I depend for social existence?
>
> *(Butler, 2004, p. 2)*

What lurks in everyday statements such as "I like a man to be a man" or "This is how I like my women" or "She looks like neither man nor woman" is not just about statements of preference but statements that conceal dogmatism that renders the subject to object and therefore less than human.

The root of desire, the "I want" that belongs to me is infinite and lacks limitation, wants to be recognized and saved from the threat of reification, and implies an explicit necessity for becoming undone in the very process of our own becoming: "the desire to persist in one's own being" (Butler, 2005, p. 43). Desire then, as we know, can never be fully satiated, and if we are constitutively open, then using the example of gender, what it is to *be* a man or a woman is not fixed just by being one, and furthermore, because we never arrive fully, we are continually redefining not just what it is to be a man or a woman but what it is to be "I" at all.

However, the fixing of identity permeates all identity categories, and society is the dominant mode for assuming and relating to identity. Therefore, whoever we are, it is vital to grasp clearly what identity consists in, for as Butler points out, when I adopt one, I reject the other, and it becomes problematic if I assume that the one I adopt is an act of normalization that creates a site of superiority.

Butler argues that when normalization prohibits certain identities and defers them to the tomb of taboo, it doesn't just punish or discriminate, it also pushes them into cultural unintelligibility. If it can't prevent or suppress, it will stigmatize and punish, whilst at the same time be haunted by the Other that it punishes. This is the Hegelian reflexive process that produces the "I" that I am, and also the "I" that I am not: "it is not possible to read the profound and perhaps inescapable ways that heterosexuality and homosexuality are defined through one another" states Butler (2004, p. 139). I am inextricably bound to and for the Other. Furthermore, if that difference translates into a hatred for that which I am not, then the Other becomes a being not worthy of recognition (not human at all). The often despised and stigmatized Other seems prevalent in our everyday lives, and I have often found it to be a constant in the therapeutic environment. What seems ironic is that our Western liberal individualistic culture, which prizes identity as an individual right, is the very stuff that in therapy gets left on the floor of what in effect becomes a therapeutic cutting room. *Becoming* and *undoing* are a constant state of affairs synonymous with the existential tensions of life and death, and perhaps they are better understood by stating the tensions as becoming/undoing, life/death – the struggle that is human.

Alain Badiou states that "[t]he experience of otherness is central, because it is the foundation stone of ethics" (Badiou, 2012, p. 24) and goes on to describe how identity is the very notion that gets in the way of love and declares that it is our "existential project to construct a world upon a decentred point of view other than that of my mere impulse to survive or re-affirm my own identity" (Butler, 2004, p. 25). Of course, we can never describe a view from nowhere; we are always situated, and to deliberately knock ourselves off-centre can feel like an act of masochism and torture, and maybe it is. How we respond to the task, to this project of "human", however, may be the measure of how much we suffer and how much suffering we inflict upon others. Both Badiou and Butler claim that identity in fact gets in the way of our ethical becoming: the clinging that becomes our dogmatism. This clinging, then, also becomes the challenge of *personal development* in counsellor/psychotherapy training, where we are asked implicitly (and often explicitly) to give an account of ourselves. On the face of it, it seems a reasonable state to reflect upon; however, as Butler argues, it is "ethical violence" (Butler, 2004) to demand such an account because in a really important sense I am to an extent unknown to myself: I am a stranger to myself. This is all at once disconcerting and yet filled with excitement and surprise if I can surrender to the freedom of the project that is me and of course you: the project that is human, whereby "human" seems to be the neo-art of our times as we fight against conformity, dogmatism and reification.

As a therapist in private practice, most of what I encounter is distress around issues of identity that are necessarily born from relationship dynamics, and every other client seems to arrive in a state of deep distress because a significant relationship has broken down somehow. Given this discussion around having any sense of self in, against and for the Other, it seems perfectly reasonable that we might experience a severe sense of rupture when our significant Other departs or indeed when we feel the need to depart ourselves.

In just such a rupture, a new client whispered through his tears that he was ill. When I asked what he meant by "ill", he proceeded to share that he had lost a great deal of weight because he could not eat, was exhausted because he could not sleep and found himself frequently to be breaking down in floods of tears. Woven among these statements of distress were descriptions of a marriage in crisis. As his tears momentarily ceased, he looked up at me and repeated, "I am ill". I replied softly, "It sounds like you're ill with life". He gasped for air, nodded his head and sobbed relentlessly. We worked together for eighteen months in a space that he stated he felt seen and heard in, a space where he seemed to build strength within himself to face his crisis and his broken marriage. He became strong enough to make decisions and choices that were difficult and life-changing. My work with this client was in a way very ordinary: there were no addictions, child protection issues, historical abuse. It was simply a person experiencing a sense of rupture after twenty years of assuming that he knew who and where he was and where he was going. My client's self-structure was utterly dependent on his relationship with his wife. Of course it was, and why wouldn't he come crashing down in an acute state of vertigo, disorientated and grief-stricken, as he experienced his symbolic death. If "I" come into being in the face of the Other, then those significant, intimate, long-lasting relationships become the most fulfilling and challenging ones where my false sense of security, my false sense of identity, which are also important for my functioning with ease in the world, leave me vulnerable to a scene of disintegration when they collapse.

If my significant Other withdraws from me in some way, then the fantasy and unknowable possibilities that I have surrendered to in that significant relationship become shut down. When we attempt to hold onto the Other as we would a thing, in a way we are also trying to hold onto an idea of self that is in an important sense my "I" as a thing too. Our living paradox/tension is about our desire to be sure of a self that is never a surety. "I" am an endless possibility, a fantasy in the making that is an embodied presence, and that has visceral experiences. Sometimes the paradox sucks because in prizing your possibilities of becoming (which I must) and wishing you all that, I find my possibilities of becoming *with* you, in front of you, alongside you, abruptly dissolved, and so Kristeva (1989) is right when she describes that any loss of you is a loss of me, even if "me" is just a fantasy.

Holding onto that notion in the midst of grief is, of course, a difficult task and for some just unbearable, and yet, in all my own difficult experiences and being privy to the grief of my clients, I am constantly in awe of the human capacity to endure, to cut through, to make anew. Our trials and tribulations, anxieties and fears, grief and losses prove time and time again to be not just the occasion to survive but perhaps the location in which we may thrive.

We might want to declare that we all have a right to leave, a choice if you like, and that this is what autonomy is all about. Well, it is my feeling that "autonomy" is another word that gets used a lot without fully exploring what it might mean. In the spirit of this discussion, the notion of autonomy is challenged because if the "I" actualizes in a constant response to and for the Other, from the force of desire that can never be fully satiated and yet is life itself, then "I" am always behind "You", and in a really important sense I rely upon you to *tell* me who I am at any given moment. And so, even given the challenges and distresses described in this discussion, as well as the continued challenges that I encounter in my own life, I find myself grinning in the pantomime of it all. Even though Kuerishi's description that follows is referring to sexual desire, it is a fitting description in the wider context of this discussion and illustrates our inability to ever be beyond desire and how slippery the pole is between 'foolish' and 'fascist' polarities:

> How unsettling is desire! That devil never sleeps or keeps still. Desire is naughty and doesn't conform to our ideals, which is why we have such a need of them. Desire mocks all human endeavour and makes it worthwhile. Desire is the original anarchist and undercover agent – no wonder people want it arrested and kept in a safe place. And just when we think we've got desire under control it lets us down or fills us with hope. Desire makes me laugh because it makes fools of us all. Still, rather a fool than a fascist.
> *(Kureishi, 1998, p. 34)*

Mutual recognition and the ethic of becoming rests upon the idea that all my possibilities of becoming are reliant upon reflexivity: my encounter with the Other. All this whilst at the same time not knowing up front what my possibilities are until they are momentarily and temporarily born between us. So there is a trust and belief involved here that is about not knowing and never knowing, and as therapists, maybe our task is to surrender to this possibility that may well create the interruption necessary in our work with clients stuck in the belief that they are what they are: fixed identities pitched against other fixed identities. Therapy becomes the site for the interruption of reified states: a site that is the creative act of undoing that makes possible our becoming – becoming human.

How open can we be to the chance created during encounter to see who we may become in any given moment? What might be beneficial is a deeper exploration and understanding of what is meant in ethical terms by the clichéd statement, "I can only know me in relation to you", as well as what the challenges and consequences might be of adopting Butler's ethical stance of becoming:

> Perhaps most importantly, we must recognize that ethics requires us to risk ourselves precisely at moments of unknowingness, when what forms us

diverges from what lies before us, when our willingness to become undone in relation to others constitutes our chance of becoming human. To be undone by another is a primary necessity, an anguish, to be sure, but also a chance – to be addressed, claimed, bound to what is not me, but also to be moved, to be prompted to act, to address myself elsewhere, and so to vacate the self-sufficient "I" as a kind of possession.

(Butler, 2005, p. 136)

References

Badiou, A. (2012). *In praise of love*. London: Serpent's Tail.
Bataille, G. (2004). 'Hegel, Death and Sacrifice' in Keenan, D. K. (ed.) *Hegel and contemporary continental philosophy*. Albany: State University of New York Press, pp. 187–204.
Bazzano, M. (2012). *Spectre of the stranger: Towards a phenomenology of hospitality*. Brighton, Sussex: Sussex Academic Press.
Butler, J. (1987). *Subjects of desire: Hegelian reflections in twentieth-century France*. New York: Columbia University Press.
Butler, J. (1990). *Gender trouble*. London: Routledge.
Butler, J. (1993). *Bodies that matter*. London: Routledge.
Butler, J. (2004). *Undoing gender*. Oxford: Routledge.
Butler, J. (2005). *Giving an account of oneself*. New York: Fordham University Press.
Butler, J. (2012). *Subjects of desire: Hegelian reflections in twentieth-century F*. New York: Columbia University Press.
Hegel, G. W. F. (1979). *Phenomenology of spirit*, trans. A. V. Miller and cont. J. N. Findlay. New York: Oxford University Press.
Kristeva, J. (1989). *Black sun*. New York: Columbia University Press.
Kureishi, H. (1998). *Intimacy*. London: Faber & Faber.
Rogers, C. R. (1965). *Client-centered therapy*. Boston: Houghton Mifflin.

7
THE LIBERATION PSYCHOLOGIST
A tribute to Jean-Paul Sartre

Richard Pearce

Introduction

In this chapter, I describe how Jean-Paul Sartre's unswerving commitment to nonconformism and to the cause of the disadvantaged is linked to an existential philosophy that can provide the foundations for a coherent and practical psychotherapeutic approach. Occasionally using personal anecdotes, the chapter reflects on his investigation of what it means to be human. Key components of this investigation are reviewed, including Sartre's understanding of consciousness, the meaning of 'the other' in individual and social contexts and the dialectic of interior and exterior interactions. The sociopolitical foundation of Sartre's thought implies that psychotherapy must recognize the political underpinnings of such social interventions. The concluding part of the chapter, therefore, makes a plea for acceptance of this political dimension.

Some initial thoughts

Here I describe the circumstances that first drew me to the work of Jean-Paul Sartre and later inspired me when I became a psychotherapist. This was a relatively late career decision for me, and I was drawn to an existential training largely as a result of the iconic figure that Sartre had represented in an early, formative period of my life. Even so, that training, while recognizing his importance, laid relatively little emphasis on his oeuvre, and I felt that I pursued a lone furrow in viewing him as the major figure in existential psychology. As is common in European circles, it is his early work, particularly *Being and Nothingness* (Sartre, 1956), that receives attention, while the equally important later work, including the *Critique of Dialectical Reason* (Sartre, 2004) and the Flaubert study, *The Family Idiot* (Sartre, 1981), scarcely get a mention. Yet I believe that this more mature work, where he attempted a synthesis of Marxism and existentialism, equally informs my work as a psychotherapist.

I first became aware of Sartre's work many years ago, long before I trained as a psychotherapist – not the Sartre of *Being and Nothingness* (*B&N*) but of May 1968 and the struggles for 'third world' emancipation that he championed in his later years. Perhaps foremost among his work during this period would be the first book of the *Critique*, in particular the forward-thinking *Search for a Method* (Sartre, 1968). Even now, the latter small book remains for me the most inspiring and important tract that he wrote. This represents the essence of the 'political Sartre', the methodology of his synthesis of Marxism and existentialism, and it was this human, non-functionalist, non-determinist Marxism rather than existentialism that first drew me into his work. But why did this happen? Why should I have been drawn into and inspired by Sartre's Marxism and later by his existentialism? In order to develop this theme, I introduce an autobiographical note. I will begin with a brief vignette of my origins, drawing on the world I was born (thrown) into and the way I responded to it, in order to demonstrate both why I was inspired and drawn to Sartre's work, as well as the value of his thought for me now as a psychotherapist. I will return to this theme briefly in my conclusion. In addition, I hope to show that when I engage with others in my role as a psychotherapist, I am carrying out a political act.

A brief review of my early years

I was born into a harsh, patriarchal and petit bourgeois society of small-scale tenant farmers and, as an only son, was expected to take my place in providing continuity for its traditions. Sartre's notion of 'fundamental project' suggests that the extent to which we seek authenticity and the way we seek it are initially (and sometimes wholly) determined in the place that we first learn to 'be' in the world, where our relatedness and separateness are first experienced, both with regard to ourselves and to others. More often than not, it is within the family and its mode of existence that the parameters that shape our early existence are defined and where the foundations from which our search for 'authenticity' unfolds.

But the family, however it is constituted, does not exist in a vacuum. It is, in many ways, a microcosm of the broader social groups within which it is situated. It is the role of the family to spawn and develop future members of the dominant society, so that the values and 'ways of being' associated with the prevailing culture will be perpetuated. It is thus an instrument of social reproduction and an exercise in social control. It has two roles: to nurture and to foster. It must ensure that its offspring are sufficiently cared for, physically, socially and emotionally, so that they might grow to be productive members of that society. At the same time it must inculcate its offspring with the values and attitudes that are acceptable to that society. These roles are paradoxical. On the one hand they promote free will and autonomy; on the other they exercise control and discipline.

My parents spawned me in a post-war world, one that was different from the one they were raised in and in which their certainties no longer held. They brought to me much of their own worlds, but in a changing sociocultural context. My father was an only child. I have little recollection of his mother, but I am told that she was a gentle woman, very much overshadowed by her husband. He was an archetypal Victorian patriarch: strong and unyielding; certain of his own correctness and extraordinarily domineering. He dominated (and outlived) my father. He died at the age of ninety-eight when he was still subtly commanding those around him. My father accepted the values and certainties of his father, but struggled, often in vain, to assert his own identity within them. My mother was the third of four children whose father died when she was aged four. Consequent poverty meant that she, in common with her elder siblings, was 'farmed' out to relatives and brought up with a cousin. An unusually beautiful child and young woman, she grew up with a constant sense of insecurity and social inferiority.

Although both my parents, in their different ways, brought with them into their nuclear family an acceptance of the cultural and social values from which they came, there was an uneasiness at this acceptance, an unspoken questioning – a vestige, I believe, of the lack of autonomy that their respective family experiences had left them. The world post the watershed of the 1939–1945 war was changing, and with it ways of relating, and while they would have wanted to respond to this, they did not know how and would generally retreat into a conservative defence of the world of their childhood.

As the only son, I was raised in the expectation that I would continue the family traditions. I remember the warmth and security of my mother's love, as well as the feelings of insecurity around this love. My mother had difficulty in having children and was ill for long periods during those years. Born by caesarean and bottle-fed from birth, I experienced a succession of childminders about whom I remember very little, except a predominant feeling of guilt that I had not been 'good enough'. My mother's health returned as I got older, probably from the age of six onwards, and I recall clinging to the warmth and security she provided, possibly from a fear that she would disappear. While my very gentle and loving mother did not withhold unconditional love, it felt, because of the context, somehow conditional and insecure.

My parents were relatively poor, and there was always a pervading atmosphere of struggle. I was given the impression that my father worked very hard and that I should be grateful for what he provided. He was quite distant and preoccupied but always gentle. Nevertheless, I grew up with a sense of trepidation towards him, a fear of the world he represented and of retribution if I failed it. And I always felt I would fail it because I did not identify with that world. I was not afraid of my father, only of the world he represented within the family. This world seemed hostile and threatening, something difficult and incomprehensible. As far back as I can remember, back to early childhood, I felt this vulnerability in the face of the other. And I think my father felt it.

My teenage rebellion was keen but easily crushed, yet the sense of rebellion never left me. It was not until many years later (during therapy) that I realized that I still carried a desire to be different but that it was neither the conservativism of my village nor the authority of my parents that I was rebelling against, but the lack of autonomy, the closing off of possibilities. I left school at fifteen and went to work for my father. Although he suggested I could choose another path if I wished, it never seemed like a real option. My future had long been decided; not to live that future was unthinkable. For ten years I tried hard to fit into that world and be a part of it, but in the end I failed. I was always an outsider, or felt myself to be. I stayed because I perceived I had no other world, no other way of becoming in the world, no other potential 'identity' (I had a strong rapport with animals, which made it easier). This was a time of enormous conflict for me. There were many rites of passage traversed, initiations into the worlds of 'sex, drugs and rock 'n' roll', but all this happened surreptitiously, privately; like my inner conflict, this private world could not be revealed to the family I still strove so hard to please. But the search for authenticity over time became more focused. Eventually I went to night school and gained access to university. No one tried to stand in my way once I had decided on my pathway, but the rupture felt quite traumatic, and I suffered what would now be described as a clinical depression. Looking back on this episode, I see it as a manifestation of the guilt I felt at deserting my parents and their world. Without me, the raison d'être of their world disappeared: the continuity that is so much a part of that tradition was broken; there was no one left to carry the myth.

It was this person who became attracted to the icon that was Jean-Paul Sartre. At that time, he represented the intellectual champion of the oppressed, those whose struggle was to assert their freedom and self-expression – whether those who struggled were groups defined by race, class, sexuality or gender or indeed everyone who was marked by difference with respect to the world of the ruling elite of white, bourgeois males. I felt a sense of common cause and identity with these oppressed. But while I was interested in existential notions of freedom and authenticity, it was to Sartre's anti-authoritarian Marxism that I was principally attracted to. Nevertheless, when many years later I was to train as a psychotherapist, it was that early experience of Sartre that drew me to existential psychotherapy and, within that tradition, to his earlier work. Now, working as a psychotherapist, I find his later work not only provides a continuity of thought but also a constant source of inspiration.

A review of some concepts

In his two major philosophical tracts, Sartre moved from the individual to the social. In *B&N*, he analysed concrete personal relations before moving to the social and historical context in the *Critique*. Here I will briefly review key concepts from both of these. I emphasize, however, that not only is there continuity in thought throughout but that the later, now neglected work has at least as much to offer psychotherapy.

The distinction between pre-reflective and reflective consciousness underpins most of what follows: Sartre was, unarguably, a philosopher of consciousness. We are aware, have an understanding or sense of ourselves pre-reflectively: a way of holding, a tacit understanding of what is lived, or what is experienced. Reflection elicits knowledge; we place order on experience so that it is 'knowable' in an indirect way; as such, knowledge is not 'of ourselves' in the way that pre-reflective understanding is, but external to us. To put it simply: pre-reflective understanding is *felt*; reflective understanding is *known*. Pre-reflective awareness 'engenders' a sense of existence; reflection allows us to 'make' sense of existence. We hold a sense of ourselves in the world prior to reflection, and it is through that pre-reflective sense that we engage with the world, that we aspire towards a sense of 'identity'. Furthermore, that engagement is not random or accidental according to Sartre. We are aware of ourselves pre-reflectively, not in a self-conscious way, but through a non-directed awareness that is always intentional; it is towards something, towards that which comes into awareness, whether physical, imagined or psychological.

Sartre's description of pre-reflective consciousness provides a framework for understanding subjectivity and the contradiction between subject and object. Nowhere is this more apparent than in his discussion of the 'look' (Sartre, 1956), a concept that in turn provides a framework for understanding the experience of the other and 'being with others', or human relations. The experience or realization that we can become an object for the other, that our subjectivity is denied, can be manifest at both the pre-reflective and reflective levels. But here, I am most interested in that experience at the level of pre-reflective awareness because it is that sense of otherness, the feeling of potential subjugation and humiliation or, at the very least, non-acceptance as a result of being 'seen', whether concretely or in imagination, that has such a profound influence on our relations with others. This led Sartre to apparently very pessimistic conclusions regarding human relationships, a view that he modified in later, unpublished work where he allowed for the possibility of reciprocal appreciation of subjectivity (e.g. Sartre, 1992).

The framework of Sartre's psychological philosophy that is relevant to psychotherapy begins with the notion of the 'fundamental' (or original) project: a value-based framework that makes sense of a life. It provides both a guide to living and an aspiration. It is a notion that accrues early in life, when we pre-reflectively feel accordance with a sense of ourselves in the world. This sense describes how we choose to relate to the world, both in terms of human relations and with respect to our physical and social environments. It is the closest we get to the idea of 'self' or 'identity'. We may try to grasp this notion objectively through reflection – 'this is who I am' – but this is always a fruitless struggle. Nevertheless, that pre-reflective awareness of ourselves allows us to sense when we are acting in accordance with that project. We *choose* this project, Sartre argues, at some point early in our lives. The pathways we follow may change, but these are superficial changes and do not necessarily alter our project. Change in the original project is possible but often only after 'life-changing' events (conversion). A sense of authenticity is gained through living life in a way that feels consistent with this project.

So how do we make a choice regarding our 'fundamental project'? In his several profound psychological and biographical studies, Sartre elaborates on this in considerable depth (Sartre, 1963, 1967, 1981). Sometime in our early life, a sense of self 'adheres'. I use this word to describe the gradual assimilation of a pre-reflective set of values that describe our way of feeling 'accordant' with ourselves in the world. That is not to say that this sense describes the 'thing itself'; the way we are, the 'who we are'; rather, it describes our aspiration and sense of coherence. When we act according to that immanence, we feel that we are 'moving in the right direction'. It is important to reiterate, however, that what adheres does not do so in a reflective sense; for the most part it remains at the pre-reflective level. We know it in one sense but as awareness rather than knowledge. It is one of the invariable tasks of therapy to increase self-perception, to make the sense of self more visible, often to facilitate the discarding of misleading notions of identity, and sometimes to work towards a shift in this fundamental project.

Later work and the Sartrean Dialectic

The project is emergent through a dialectical process that engenders an aspirational way of being in the world, a sense (no more) of self or identity that carries with it also a sense of how to *be* in the world in relationship with others. But the *Critique* extends this person-to-person relationship into the social field and the possibility of both an external as well as an internal dialectic.

The idea, sometimes gleaned from *B&N*, that this pre-reflective self is immutable is modified by Sartre's later work. There is the possibility of change, but this would be part of a dialectical process. But when we make this initial (and pre-reflective) choice, it is our engagement with the other in the broad sense that is determinant: an engagement not only with *other* people, particularly significant people, but also with our social and physical environment and with our history. We are part of a historical and cultural process, and when we engage with the world, we are a part of that dialectic. Sartre's depiction of the 'look' describes a powerful process; it describes how we meet others, the anxieties associated with being and observing the other as an object. His descriptions in *B&N* evoke a sense of this tension, the vulnerabilities and anxieties around acceptance reflected in the non-acceptance of objectification.

An important part of the experience of project emergence is the encounter with others, of being-for-others and the relations between subject and object. But these are found not solely in concrete personal relations but also in relations with our social and physical context. While Sartre developed a more flexible view regarding the possibility of change of the fundamental project in his later work, perhaps this possibility is best understood in relation to the Sartrean Dialectic, a concept he derived from those of Hegel and Marx. Although the dialectic was apparent in *B&N*, Sartre developed its central importance in the *Critique*. At its simplest, it describes a process, a movement of change. Viewed subjectively: an impression is formed by an event that can give rise to a predisposition to receive similar events in the same way. An experience that contradicts such an impression, however, sets up a process that leads to an adjustment in the way future similar experiences are received that allows for both the original and the contradiction. The movement is ceaseless, and the title of the *Critique* echoes his belief that to reflect dialectically is to reflect rationally. Most importantly, some sense of the original experience is always present in the new: nothing is lost. It is a developmental process based on the resolution of contradiction.

The dialectic of consciousness is apparent in B&N but not explicitly stated. We first experience something pre-consciously; a myriad of sense impressions form an awareness of something. This may then be objectified through reflective consciousness, but in this process the something becomes objectified. This process in turn may modify the pre-reflective awareness, and the movement continues. There is a dialectic of the internal and external, of subject and object within consciousness itself.

In the *Critique*, Sartre sought to integrate the role and perspective of the individual and subjective, with the social and historical perspective of twentieth-century Marxist political economy. Key to this approach is the regressive–progressive method outlined in his *Search for a Method* (Sartre, 1968). It describes a process of interiorization, when experiences of the individual's 'world' are absorbed and held. Her 'world' describes the totality of her social, physical and relational environments at any moment. The individual may then respond to that which is interiorized, in a process of interaction or exteriorization. Consequently, the individual is both changed by interiorization and changes her world through exteriorization. These processes are dialectical processes, reflecting a movement through which interacting forces are changed by encounter, blending anew as each contains the influence of the other. But the precursor of these processes is the tension of contradiction. If what is held of the experience of her world causes no grounds for reflection, then the individual is unchallenged. Similarly, if what is interiorized is not acted upon through reflection and action, then the status quo, or what Sartre termed the 'practico-inert', remains unchallenged.

Need and scarcity

'Need' and 'scarcity' are terms that Sartre uses to ground the development of his theory. In his early work, Sartre talks of 'desire'. Consciousness (being-for-itself), in differentiating from nature or what-is (being-in-itself), senses an unfulfilment, or 'lack', a bounty of possibility that is the negation of what-is: hence the root of desire. The later Sartre talks of 'need' rather than 'desire'. As social beings, we have socialized desires or felt requirements that we act towards. Need arises through our interaction with the world, and at its most basic is the desire to survive, to reproduce one's existence. Scarcity may be a condition of the material world, so that the ability of some to meet these basic requirements may become constrained, in particular, constrained by others. This creates hierarchy, class, domination and oppression – the stuff of history. But need is a social concept, as is scarcity, and beyond survival they become defined by social norms: they become subject to choice. Such reasoning Sartre took from Marx, but he added a different dimension. Need becomes socialized desire. Desire becomes social in the act of interaction with the external world: thus need and desire often become undifferentiated. And when need is socialized, it is embedded in reproduction not only in terms of survival but also in terms of the 'self', or at least a sense of self.

What is critical is that Sartre grounded the social and historical dimension of Marxism in individual consciousness. The individual's subjectivity through the dialectical processes just described becomes a pivotal actor in the historical sweep of social and physical environments. An interesting exposition of Sartre's attempts to bring subjectivity to the core of Marxism can be found in his lecture *Marxism and Subjectivity* (Sartre, 2014). Subject and object are enmeshed in a constant dialectic. In describing the way in which the individual subject becomes pivotal in this regard, Sartre introduces further key concepts that describe her interaction on the social plain. The movement of the dialectic is permeated by *praxis*, a term used to describe an active engagement with the world. Through praxis, the subject engages with the world in order to change it, an engagement guided by her pre-reflective fundamental project. The expression can be linked in a vehicular sense to that of being-for-itself, or consciousness, in *B&N*: subjectivity in the act of engagement. The material world itself is a worked process, which, without praxis, remains static, in inertia, as the 'practico-inert', which can be perceived as a social manifestation of being-in-itself, or facticity. But we may not engage with the practico-inert merely to initiate change; we may also seek to deny our needs, our desires, making them subservient to those of others. This is a denial of the aspirational future orientation of the fundamental project; he termed such a movement as 'hexis', by implying conscious action that leaves the practico-inert unchanged in the context of contradiction.

This dialectical reasoning sets out a series of constantly interacting processes involving the subject and her external world. Part of this journey for Sartre involved a critique of the more deterministic and mechanistic view of the human subject promulgated by the orthodox Marxism of that time. He perceived the subject as part of an ever interactive dialogue with the social in the making of history. But he retained the emphasis on human freedom and choice that is so passionately expressed in *B&N*, even if the social determinants and limitations are made more explicitly part of the picture. So the subject existed not in the splendid isolation as portrayed in *B&N* but as a 'totalization', an interactive unfolding or movement described by the dialectic of the internal, the external and their mutually interactive processes. Rather than an 'individual', therefore, Sartre speaks of the 'singular universal' in describing the subject whose 'lived experience' underpins the social movements and expressions of history.

From the basis of his interaction with a nondeterministic Marxism, Sartre rooted the concepts of freedom and subject–object dialogue espoused in *B&N* in the social context of history. His 'singular universal', through a dialectical relationship with the world as it is in any given moment (the practico-inert), a relationship founded on praxis (or hexis), a movement based on a 'totalization', becomes the unwitting architect of history. At the centre of praxis is the 'fundamental project', or pre-reflective, but always dematerializing, sense of self. But the *Critique* was concerned primarily with the social group and placed that sense firmly within the dynamics of collective action. It is from the vantage point of that dynamic that we best observe the political implications of his work.

The political dimension

Sartre's politics was above all a politics of liberation. He played a minor role in the resistance during the German occupation, which was a precursor to an active political life in the post-war period, an activity that continued until his death, although this involvement became more muted after he lost his sight in 1970. He campaigned always for the underprivileged, the persecuted and the oppressed. He was active in the anticolonial movement and harshly critical of the many 'unjust wars' that became so prevalent after the war of 1939–1945 (Cohen-Solal, 1987). He became an icon for struggles of liberation from oppression of all kinds, and it is this icon that first aroused my interest in his work.

He pursued his political agenda partly through his editorship of the weekly journal, *Les Temps Modernes*, and other journalistic enterprises. Among his publications, one that stands out as a political tract is the small but profound work, *Anti-Semite and Jew* (Sartre, 1948). His analysis of the roots of prejudice and his understanding of how the process of persecution arises make a valuable and insightful contribution to understanding a contemporary Western world that is currently living in the wake of the near collapse of finance capitalism. A world characterized by constant subjection to the fear of the stranger, epitomized by rising anti-immigrant fervour; by an increasing persecution internationally of minorities such as gays and bisexuals; and by the rolling back of female emancipation. We live in a world increasingly characterized by an apprehension of difference.

In *Anti-Semite and Jew*, Sartre describes a trajectory of unthinking and irrational prejudice. It must be noted, however, that anti-Semitism and notions of racial and cultural supremacy, which characterized the colonial period and still permeates European culture, are group responses and are the collective reinforcements of individual prejudice. But in looking at the roots of prejudice, we find also the source of vulnerability and anxiety.

The issues that bring people to therapy are rooted in concerns derived from relations with the other, whether (as is usually the case) other people or the other in terms of social, cultural or physical environments. When the other is not known sufficiently, it leads to existential uncertainty. Such uncertainty generates anxiety, which if unresolved or too strong to be held, turns the subject towards what Sartre describes as irrational responses, often projections of blame, anger or guilt onto the 'stranger' (or the 'strange phenomenon') because not to do so would generate a sense of self that is not acceptable, that would undermine the fundamental project. These are not responses grasped from nowhere but often poorly rationalized and emotional responses to experiences of perceived or real suffering.

The individual may equally project that (initially) pre-reflective sense of non-acceptance inwards; they interiorize the experience (a more common occurrence, I suggest, for those who come to therapy), a process that undermines (or in some particularly difficult cases overdetermines) the ephemeral sense of self that is described by the fundamental project. I would add, however, notwithstanding the interiorization of such alienation, the dialectic ensures that there is a response in terms of either praxis or, more possibly, hexis as the way in which the individual's interactions with society are reinforced. She may also respond to the possibility of group activity (a process of exteriorization) and adhere to collective manifestations of prejudice or hostility towards the 'stranger', such that the dialectic engenders a self-reinforcing process of non-acceptance towards the other.

Whether the individual responds to an experience by directing the response outwardly or inwardly makes no difference to the potential for an inauthentic response. At the same time, what is authentic is also the acceptance of freedom and with this an acceptance of responsibility for one's actions. As Sartre states in *Anti-Semite and Jew*:

> If it is agreed that man may be defined as a being having freedom within the limits of a situation, then it is easy to see that the exercise of this freedom may be considered as authentic or inauthentic according to the choices made in the situation.
>
> (Sartre, 1948, p. 90)

Arguably, we are free because we choose, and in making choices we create the opportunity to express our subjectivity in our interactions with our world. So, too, does the other. To deny our own freedom is to deny our subjectivity and is the ultimate deception. From this notion of 'freedom and authenticity', it is possible to conceive of an ethical framework and a political agenda.

Any discussion of the political nature of psychotherapy, presupposes an ethical perspective. After writing *B&N*, Sartre was intent on addressing the topic of an existential ethics, a task he was never to complete. The posthumously published *Notebooks for an Ethics* is little more than an organized collection of notes, although containing much insightful material (Sartre, 1992). Although he did not complete his ethical framework, he wrote enough for others to fruitfully develop this theme.

What these notes did suggest was a movement away from the pessimistic view of human relationships that emerged from *B&N* towards the possibility of reciprocity. This notion essentially forms the bedrock of 'good' as opposed to 'bad faith'. Sartre had argued in *B&N* that being-for-others involved ultimately either surrendering subjectivity in order to capture the other through submission or objectifying and subordinating the other to one's own subjectivity. He described this as denying one's own freedom or that of the other, through either voluntary or wilful submission of subjectivity. Freedom is an expression of the subjective. To deny one's freedom is to be in 'bad faith'. It is possible, within this rubric, to assert the possibility of a mutuality of interest or reciprocity of knowing in human relationships. If we are able to meet the other not as an object, with the implicit threat described in the 'look', but as a subject to be affirmed and accepted, then the possibility of reciprocity (and intimacy) is present. We are free to choose, while accepting the freedom of the other to do likewise.

Existentialist thought in part arose through the rejection of the conception of the human being as merely mechanistically determined. As a conscious being, she is set apart from both inanimate objects and other animals and plants. This debate is even more intense today, although the voices against this fundamentalist view of science are unfortunately a minority. The question remains: are we totally determined beings, both physiologically and concomitantly psychologically, or is there some point where we are able to break out of past conditioning and act as free and conscious agents? The message of *B&N* emphasized the latter: being-for-itself, effectively consciousness, was always free to choose. Even in passivity, we inexorably choose who we are. The notion of praxis highlighted in the *Critique* reinforces the possibilities created by conscious choice, even though in this later work Sartre was to clarify the limitations of choice and recognize the weight of conditioning, especially of the early, formative years. The latter is in fact implicit in *B&N* in Sartre's adherence to the view that the fundamental project is unchanging once chosen. There remained, however, a window for freedom and choice; without that window, how can we be held responsible for our actions? How can history not become formulaic? In the *Critique*, Sartre not only remained true to the existential tradition in this respect but also attacked mechanistic and deterministic thought within Marxism. The starting point for an existential ethics remains the concept of existential freedom.

A note on psychotherapy

I came to psychotherapy as a profession relatively late in life, as a third 'career'. From the beginning, my interest was fuelled by a fascination of what it meant to be human and the hope that I might learn something of myself, as I work with others.

I was trained as an existential psychotherapist, but my view of what this means has grown with my practice, with my encounters with these 'others' that have braved the therapy room with me, as well as with my increasingly deep encounter with the work of Jean-Paul Sartre. I believe that the breadth of Sartre's psychological thinking allows for a broader and more inclusive approach to psychotherapeutic practice than is described by the narrow thinking of much that passes for existential psychotherapy.

I believe the profession often makes a profound mistake in arguing for particular techniques that should be followed for 'true' or 'authentic' practice within a particular 'modality' of therapy. Often this smacks of arrogant elitism, the need to differentiate from the other in order to aggrandize one's chosen path (or training). In my view, techniques may vary (and undoubtedly should, given the uniqueness of each individual), but what is important is our understanding of these core aspects of how the human exists in the world. In this respect, I feel an increasing debt to the thought of Sartre and the framework of existential analysis that he provides. Although I do believe there is a divide between approaches to therapeutic work, the fault line, in my view, corresponds not to current divisions within the profession but to the divide between those who perceive human action to be grounded in human agency and reflective of conscious choice and those who view behaviour to be mechanically determined and therefore subject to 'correction'.

In addition, I suggest that the underlying philosophical framework that Sartre elucidated shows the practice of psychotherapy to be a *political* act, one that is orientated towards both freedom and authenticity in the manner in which the individual (or singular universal) expresses her dialectical interaction with the world.

Psychotherapy as a political act

In order to justify this statement, I will draw some threads together from previous deliberations. I will define a political act as a purposive intervention that impacts, in some way, on the totality of relationships that constitute a social context and one that is premised on an ethical perspective. I understand that within the therapeutic context the individual has a perspective – of a varying degree of concreteness – of themselves that is based on a dialectical relationship between the world as she perceives it and the felt sense of self described by her fundamental project. From within that process emerge the manifestations of anxiety that are her way of responding to her world. I suggest that in the context of psychological trauma, of whatever degree, there is a response that is a denial of freedom in some form, a loss of authenticity in her relations with the world, either through negation of her own freedom or that of the other. The role of psychotherapy is to enable the individual to draw down the blinds of 'fear and loathing', to achieve a heightened awareness of her transient self, and to know and accept her own subjectivity as well as the subjectivity of others.

Acceptance of the freedom of the other is a quintessential part of this. Acceptance of one's own freedom also implies acceptance of responsibility: we choose our freedom and concomitantly accept responsibility for that choice. But in doing so we recognize and accept the freedom of the other, since such acceptance is the premise upon which one's own freedom is based. As Sartre emphasizes:

> I am obliged to will the freedom of others at the same time as I will my own. I cannot set my own freedom as a goal without also setting the freedom of others as a goal.
>
> (Sartre, 2007, pp. 48–49)

As outlined, developments of Sartre's work suggest that relationships (of whatever form) are not stable unless based on reciprocal acceptance and that the achievement of the latter is the experience of freedom. It is a psychological liberation. Such an act of liberation, because we are social animals, because our praxis can and does change the world, even in an infinitesimal way, is a political act. The dialectical processes, which are an unalienable consequence of our touching of the world, engender a response and counter-response to our praxis (or hexis). They also contribute to a progressive politics, since where there is mutual acceptance there is no space for a hierarchy of needs, with the concomitant aggrandizement and exploitation, or for the exaggeration of difference and rejection of the stranger that characterizes the politics of fear and hate. Rather, it is a politics that recognizes the mutual interdependence of social relationships, one premised on egalitarian values. It is the politics of freedom and liberation, a cause that Sartre promoted for much of his life.

An addendum: making sense of myself

That I was drawn towards what I believed Sartre represented at an early and pivotal juncture in my life is perhaps unsurprising, although it is only much later, when I was to study his work in more depth, that I began to understand why this was the case. Feeling stifled by my social context, therefore rejecting of the social attitudes and cultural framework of that context, I was open to the oppositional mores of the time. But there was more than this, and this relates to the idea of project choice.

I grew up with loving parents, but in my early years their love was not expressed as much as I needed, due to my mother's ill health and the apparent reticence in my father's show of feeling. I recall feelings of vulnerability and insecurity associated with a fear of loss. But this fear was accentuated if not fostered by a contingency broader than that of my immediate family: that of village society. Even in those early formative years, I recall a sense of trepidation concerning the possibility of wider disapproval, of being found wanting by the 'others' of the community – a sense reinforced by my parents shared feelings. Yet there was a foundation of care, as well as a strong connection to nature and animal life as something to be fostered and cherished rather than exploited, even to the point of our pecuniary detriment.

I suggest that many characteristics of the way that I engage with the world were formed in that preadolescent period. Contradictions were present: between being shamed into potential conformity by the fear of non-acceptance (a combined force of social authority and familial insecurity) and a sense of compassion and belonging stemming from parental love and a connection to nature. These contradictions were sharp enough to inform a sense of restlessness from an early age, a profound insecurity engendered by the exterior world, accompanied by an adequately secure base within the family that facilitated the desire to challenge that exterior world.

It is worth repeating that a characteristic of Sartre's later thinking is that it allows a 'putting into context' of the early concepts, thus emphasizing the social context of individual experience. Additionally, the notion of a liberation psychology is built on the interface between free will and material conditioning. In this respect, I see the choices and pathways that followed my early development as influenced by that early project choice. Through the dialectic process that ensued, I 'chose' a sense of myself that was to inform the patterns of decision making that followed in a changing landscape of possibility. At times, I have chosen future pathways on the basis of that sense of myself that felt, in my pre-reflective consciousness, both liberating and authentic – but not always, and I have felt too the contradictions of both entrapment and inauthenticity. But I have carried with me at all times, some ethical sense, part of the sense of self that pre-reflectively adhered in my early years, that still makes me as a psychotherapist the libertarian socialist that I have always been.

References

Cohen-Solal, A. (1987). *Jean-Paul Sartre: A Life*. Canada: Random House Publishers.
Sartre, J-P. (1948). *Anti-Semite and Jew*. New York: Schocken Books.
Sartre, J-P. (1956) [1943]. *Being and Nothingness: An Essay on Phenomenological Ontology*. New York: Philosophy Library.
Sartre, J-P. (1963). *Saint Genet: Actor and Martyr*. New York: George Braziller.
Sartre, J-P. (1967) [1950]. *Baudelaire*. New York: New Directions.
Sartre, J-P. (1968). *The Search for a Method*. New York: Vintage Books.
Sartre, J-P. (1981). *The Family Idiot, Gustave Flaubert, 1821–1857: Volume 1*. Chicago: University of Chicago Press.
Sartre, J-P. (1992) [1983]. *Notebooks for an Ethics*. Chicago: University of Chicago Press.
Sartre, J-P. (2004) [1960]. *Critique of Dialectical Reason: Volume 1*. London: Verso.
Sartre, J-P. (2007) [1946]. *Existentialism Is a Humanism*. New Haven, CT: Yale University Press.
Sartre, J-P. (2014) [1961]. 'Marxism and Subjectivity'. *New Left Review* 88, July–August, pp. 89–111.

8

INSTANCES OF LIBERATION IN ROUSSEAU

Federico Battistutta
Translated from the Italian by Manu Bazzano

Invincible soul

In his poem 'The Rhine', Hölderlin speaks of the Genevan philosopher Jean Jacques Rousseau as an "invincible soul" and compares him to Dionysus (1990, pp. 224–225). The German poet had shared with Hegel and Schelling an enthusiasm for the French Revolution when still a young student at Tübingen; his admiration of Rousseau tells us how the latter has been perceived across the centuries with an almost mythical degree of intensity. Nowadays his thought is seen as more complex and controversial, revealing a mixture of different, even contrasting elements. From the singularity of Rousseau's thought emerges a biography that inevitably includes idiosyncrasies and contradictions. It is not surprising that late in life he felt compelled to write a systematic self-analysis, *The Confessions* (Rousseau, 1996).

In this chapter, I will not sketch Rousseau's entire philosophical itinerary but limit the enquiry to the Genevan philosopher's discussion of the relationship between nature and culture and identify possible contemporary developments in the human sciences. I will therefore focus on a few works only: the two *Discourses on the Arts and Sciences* (Rousseau, 2014) and *Discourses on Inequality* (Rousseau, 2014), belonging to the more critical phase of his thinking, and *Emile, or On Education* (Rousseau, 2004), published in 1762 after almost ten years of anguished reflections, which is at the heart of his more constructive propositions on how to retrace our lost naturalness.

Pathologies of civilization

The *Discourse on Inequality* (Rousseau, 2014a) proposes an actual genealogy of social evil, questioning society as a whole at its foundations. The second part of this text begins with a very well-known passage:

> The first man who, having enclosed a piece of ground, bethought himself of saying "This is mine", and found people simple enough to believe him, was the real founder of civil society. From how many crimes, wars and murders, from how many horrors and misfortunes might not any one have saved mankind, by pulling up the stakes, or filling up the ditch, and crying to his fellows, "Beware of listening to this impostor; you are undone if you once forget that the fruits of the earth belong to us all, and the earth itself to nobody."
>
> (Rousseau, 2014a, p. 23)

The pathogenic cell of social living begins with the loss of the natural common goods and the subsequent privatization of the means of production. With the introduction of private property and via a series of mutually affecting changes, the necessity of work comes into being – something that in turn alters the natural environment, turning the soil into a place that "man had to water with the sweat of his brow" (Rousseau, 2014a, p. 27). With work, reflective thought is born, along with a growing sense of conceit. Reason subsequently perfects itself, and egoism supplants innocent self-love. The rupture between being and appearance marks the predilection for what is false:

> It now became the interest of men to appear what they really were not. To be and to seem became two totally different things; and from this distinction sprang insolent pomp and cheating trickery, with all the numerous vices that go in their train.
>
> (Rousseau, 2014a, p. 29)

Possessing *things* became all-important, but things are obstacles between one conscience and another. Believing that possessing things is indispensable to their happiness, people began to look for their self-realization in things. With the domestication of the natural world (plants and animals), men and women domesticated themselves as well: Rousseau's analysis of the process of civilization in many ways anticipates parallel notions (including that of alienation) found in the writings Hegel, Feuerbach and Marx.

In the *Discourse on the Sciences and the Arts* (Rousseau, 2014b), we find a critique of science and of culture in general. In this work, composed at the very peak of the Enlightenment, Rousseau writes that the arts and sciences corrupt morals; as he sees it, they are means by which tyrants exert their coercive power; they garland and decorate the chains of the people, and in so doing they succeed in suppressing their inborn aspiration to an originary freedom. Going against the accepted views of his time, Rousseau celebrates the learned ignorance in which divine wisdom has placed humanity. For him, nature had wanted to preserve humans from the ills of science like a mother who snatches away a dangerous weapon from the hands of a child; similarly, all the secrets nature hides from humans are evils from which it wishes to shelter her children. As it can be easily imagined, these discourses exacerbated his connections with the philosophers of the *Encyclopaedia* given that they held a very different stance with regard to notions of science and progress.

State of nature and nature of the state

In his *Discourse on Inequality*, Rousseau (2014a) takes up his reflections on the *state of nature*, humanity's originary condition, a notion beset by numerous misunderstandings that normally interpret it as an *actual* state of being. Here is what he says:

> It is by no means a light undertaking to distinguish properly between what is original and what is artificial in the actual nature of man, or to form a true idea of a state which no longer exists, perhaps never did exist, and probably never will exist; and of which, it is, nevertheless, necessary to have true ideas, in order to form a proper judgment of our present state.
>
> (Rousseau, 2014a, p. 7)

We are dealing here with a heuristic hypothesis, a paradigm of evaluation – fairly useful in bringing to light, by contrast, a parallel state of affairs, an actual human situation. The state of nature is for Rousseau a construct on the basis of which one can observe certain characteristics in the concrete life of human beings.

Hobbes before him, particularly in his *De Cive* (Hobbes, 2010) and *Leviathan* (Hobbes, 2011), had established that the raison d'être of State power rested with human beings' need for security. Left to a state of nature, we would find ourselves in constant danger, in a situation of boundless war without any hope of resolution: it would be the *bellum omnium contra omnes* (the war of all against all), with no one ever being so much stronger than others as not to fear defeat. In order to guarantee mutual safety, humanity must therefore exit this state of affairs and give up the unlimited freedom it enjoys in the state of nature and submit instead to the absolute power of a ruler: this is the birth of the State. According to Hobbes, freedom and equality, both specific traits of the state of nature, constitute a danger for humanity.

Rousseau is at the opposite pole: for him the *bellum omnium contra omnes* does not belong to the state of nature but originates with the birth of civilization. "Peoples once accustomed to masters are not in a condition to do without them" (Rousseau, 2004, p. 2). What we call progress is in fact regression, for it produces loneliness and non-communication: "All ran headlong to their chains, in hopes of securing their liberty" (Rousseau, 2004, p 30). Progress can be achieved, for Rousseau, only by returning to nature; nature made us good and happy, and society has corrupted and made us miserable. In speaking of human goodness, Rousseau underlines the notion of the human being as having essentially positive tendencies and instincts, as being naturally cooperative and inclined to constant self-improvement.

Working on oneself

I am not going to discuss here Rousseau's political thought as expounded in his seminal work *The Social Contract* (Rousseau, 1998) or the implications and contradictions implicit in this work – as for instance his notion of a general will (opposed to Hobbes' abstract view of absolute power), which is prone to authoritarian slips especially with regard to the rapport between the personal and the political spheres. Instead, I will turn my attention to Rousseau's reflections concerning a person's development. The need for a social radical revolution is for him inseparable from psychological and anthropological regeneration. This was echoed by André Breton a century and a half later: "Marx said: 'Transform the world'; Rimbaud said 'Change your life'. These two mottoes are for us one and the same thing" (Breton, 1935, p. 68).

A person's development must be understood for Rousseau in this context. This is an ambitious project: after the denunciation of the lies on which the entire edifice of modern society is built, 'work on oneself' – as René Daumal's original expression *le travail sur soi* has it (Daumal, 1996) – is needed, in order to return to that originary transparency that, in spite of everything, never abandoned us entirely. We discover in unfamiliar corners and in our own depths that very naturalness sought by Rousseau in past epochs of history. The theme of transparency is the discontinuous element found in Rousseau's existential and intellectual trajectory. His work can be read as conflict between *transparency* and *obstruction*. We can think of the Genevan philosopher's work as revolutionary only in view of an eternal human nature rather than in relation to a notion of progress as such (Starobinski, 1971). Rather than a historical product, revolutionary praxis is seen here as a vital instinct inherent in human beings that comes to the fore in the presence of destructive sociopolitical (*thanato-political*) forms. No power in the world can silence human nature. Human nature is alive and pulsating; it will always find ways, running subterranean paths and channels, to resurface and reassert itself again and again.

Pedagogy of liberation

Émile, or On Education (Rousseau, 2004) is widely held to represent the peak of Rousseau's thought, but it would be reductive to limit this work to a specifically educational domain. Although it is fair to assess its importance from the viewpoint of the pedagogical sciences, at the heart of this voluminous book one finds an anthropological, psychological and political meditation that is impossible to ignore. "The real object of our study is man and his environment" (Rousseau, 2004, p. 10), he will say in the first volume of this work. But human existence, as presented to us by civilization, is, according to Rousseau, a collection of servile habits and prejudices that result in the restriction and subjugation along the entire arc of human existence:

> Civilised man is born and dies a slave. The infant is bound up in swaddling clothes; the corpse is nailed down in his coffin. All his life long man is imprisoned by our institutions.
>
> *(Rousseau, 2004, p. 11)*

Rousseau's educational project is therefore a social and political path of liberation from the millenary confusion our species is subjected to, towards a life that is worth living.

> Life is not breath, but action, the use of our senses, our mind, our faculties, every part of ourselves which makes us conscious of our being. Life consists less in length of days than in the keen sense of living.
>
> (Rousseau, 2004, p. 11)

Rousseau sees the human being in what we would nowadays call a holistic perspective, i.e. as a dynamic-energetic, unitary organism. This notion is at variance with Cartesian dualism and intellectualism and is affirmed by stressing the legitimacy of our instinctual life, of feelings and spontaneity. It is also substantially different from theories popular among his contemporaries, such as Condillac's notion of the 'man-statue' and La Mettrie's 'man-machine'.

Rousseau outlines a project aimed at the comprehensive education of the person, making it possible for a human being to truly feel life's vibrant stream within and without. This is education of the *human* rather than the *citizen*, for it is not possible for Rousseau to train both at the same time: the former constitutes an absolute unity, whilst the latter is only a fragmented entity. The best place for education is, for Rousseau, the natural habitat so as to protect the child from the falsities of urban living and in order to facilitate education. "Fix your eyes on nature, follow the path traced by her" (Rousseau, 2004, p. 16), he writes. And also: "The new-born child is already a disciple, not of his tutor, but of nature" (Rousseau, 2004, p. 32). Rousseau's vision is animated by the principle of self-sufficiency in human nature, by its inherent ability to promote autonomously its own potential for development. Above all, the task of education is to not interfere with it and secondarily to promote it. In this sense, a tutor does not *give* precepts but allows them to be *found*; the only habit a child needs to learn is not to have habits.

This reversal of perspective (cultivating the habit of not having habits) paradoxically sums up the Genevan philosopher's message. It is a message worth inheriting and developing further. Its bare truth can itself become an object of study and a source of endless discovery.

En route

Rousseau was at times slandered during his life and called all sorts of names: a new Cato, Brutus, Diogenes the Cynic and so forth. Through successive epochs, the defenders of order and the status quo laid it on thicker, adding new criticisms to the old ones and trivializing his thought (for instance with the myth of the noble savage). In this sense, he does belong to the philosophical counter-tradition. The questions raised by his philosophy are nevertheless well received within the vast domain of the human sciences, even though the debt and acknowledgement to Rousseauean legacy are at times not voiced explicitly. Besides, intellectual affiliations are not always manifest or fully conscious; they are often realized on the basis of common perception or barely noticeable affinities.

One writer who openly declared his debt to Rousseau is the great anthropologist Lévi-Strauss. He saw Rousseau as the founder of the human sciences and the precursor of ethnology, a discipline that can be fully conceived and realized by doing away with the tyranny of the Cartesian *cogito* and re-examining the place of the human being. For Rousseau, nature comes before culture, animality before humanity and feeling before knowledge; life in its full unfolding comes before humanity (Lévi-Strauss, 1983).

But it is no doubt in the area of pedagogy and education that Rousseauean meditations found positive reception and expression, particularly since the turmoil in France of May 1968.

The Summerhill libertarian school of Alexander Neill was founded on the principle that there is in the child an inner positive energy that supports and regulates his/her development towards a spontaneous, creative and balanced personality. The Summerhill community is inspired by principles of egalitarianism, self-regulation and self-determination. Apart from Rousseau, this experiment is also indebted to Freud and Reich, particularly to the latter's critique of the patriarchal family as bedrock of the authoritarian personality (Neill, 1960). Similarly worthy of notice is the notion of self-managed education proposed by the group clustered around Georges Lapassade and created with the intent of intervening against the institutional conditionings in schools both in terms of concrete educational praxis (actualizing the principle of 'negative education' promoted in *Émile*) as well as in more general sociopolitical terms (Lapassade, 1971). And it is virtually impossible not to associate Rousseau's pedagogical ideas and his critique of the institutional apparatus with Ivan Illich's notion of the *de-schooling* of society (Illich, 1971). Illich saw school as anti-educational for it claims to be the official and institutional place for education; it prevents the emergence of other educational contexts, and, above all, it underrates the fact that the whole of social life possesses formative value. In this way, school becomes an instrument of domination and manipulation, an essential tool of the bureaucratization of life. Illich's utopia envisions the creation of coordinated nets of learning managed by the local community outside institutional influence.

Carl Rogers' non-directive psychology and pedagogy also present traits that are easily associated with Rousseau, in spite of the fact that Rogers, like Neill, said that he could not really see himself as Rousseau's successor for he lacked a deep knowledge of his philosophy (Rogers, 1989). Nonetheless, aspects of client-centred therapy and person-centred therapy allow one to draw similarities with Rousseau: the organism's tendency to actualization and self-regulation; openness to experience felt as a process and vital continuum. Rogers' educational horizon is singularly inscribed within humanistic psychology, a field of practice that has responded effectively to the reductionism of behavioural and Freudian matrixes. As Maslow maintains, the nature of each human being does not appear to be intrinsically evil, and our needs, emotions and fundamental abilities are either neutral, pre-moral or positively good (Maslow, 1968): a perspective that is inscribed in the very same path outlined by Rousseau. With Maslow, humanistic psychology takes a particularly critical stance towards society: psychotherapy must not become a way to facilitate social integration and adaptation but on the contrary contribute to the person's self-awareness, questioning at its very root the relationship between sickness and health.

Becoming childhood

Some critics have noted contradictions within Rousseau's pedagogic discourse. In spite of its principled declarations, some have found *Émile*'s story unreal and artificial and conditioned from the outside by the presence of the tutor. On the other hand, *Émile* is also a novel with a stratified and complex narrative and a work of its time. When it first appeared, the Parisian court deliberated that *Émile* should be destroyed and burned. Rousseau himself had to flee. The same verdict was later reached by the Geneva court, something that pained him greatly. Subsequently, the bishop of Paris put the book on the Index, and finally Pope Clemens XIII condemned it (among the passages proposed for the anathema is the one stating the fact that "Émile will learn nothing by heart").

Having said that, *Émile* is not an untouchable icon; appreciating this work today also means going beyond Rousseau's limitations and those of his era. This is what, for instance, post-structuralist thinker and advocate of the "pedagogy of difference" René Schérer did, by writing a sort of *Anti-Émile* and charting the contours of a *perverted Émile* (Schérer, 1974). The author plays with the three meanings of the word 'perverted' (*perverti* in French). The normal usage alludes to an expression of sexuality that is different from dominant morality. Another connotation of the term refers to the distortion of the needs of childhood and of the child's possibilities for self-realization. Finally, the adjective points to the fact that Rousseau's theses have been revisited, moulded and altered to produce something totally new. I will not examine here Schérer's theses on the pedagogy of *eros* and childhood sexuality; some of these have attracted controversy and a great deal of polemics, while others have been accepted alongside views that affirm a mutual rapport of growth between child and adult in which both learn and become enriched (not unlike Deleuze and Guattari's discussion on *devenir-enfant*). I mention them here solely in order to hint at how Rousseau's exploration has continued along different lines, retaining their vitality, the desire to provoke and the aspiration towards new hopes. Remembering all the while how the true disciple is the one who can go beyond his/her teacher.

References

Breton, A. (1935) *Position Politique du Surrealisme* Paris: Sagittaire.
Daumal, R. (1996) *Correspondance (1933–1944)* Paris: Gallimard.
Hobbes, T. (2010) *De Cive* Kessinger: Montana.
Hobbes, T. (2011) *Leviathan* London: Createspace Publishing.

Hölderlin, F. (1990) *Hyperion and Selected Poems* Edited by Eric Santner, New York: Continuum.
Illich, I. (1971) *De-schooling Society* New York: Harper & Row.
Lapassade, G. (1971) *L'autogestion pédagogique* Paris: Gauthier Villars.
Lévi-Strauss, C. (1983) 'Jean-Jacques Rousseau, Founder of the Sciences of Man', in *Structural Anthropology*, vol. II, Translated by Monique Layton, Chicago: University of Chicago Press, pp. 33–43.
Maslow, A. H. (1968) *Toward a Psychology of Being* New York: Van Nostrand Reinhold.
Neill, A. (1960) *Summerhill: A Radical Approach to Child Rearing* New York: Hart Publishing.
Rogers, R. Carl (1989) 'A Note on the Nature of Man' in Kirschenbaum, H., & V. L. Henderson (eds.) *The Carl Rogers Reader* Boston: Houghton Mifflin, pp. 401–408.
Rousseau, J. J. (1996) *The Confessions* Ware, Herts: Wordsworth Editions.
Rousseau, J. J. (1998) *The Social Contract* London: Penguin.
Rousseau, J. J. (2004) *Emile, or On Education*. Internet file (e-book), Retrieved 20 November 2014 from http://intersci.ss.uci.edu/wiki/eBooks/BOOKS/Rousseau/Emile%20Rousseau.pdf.
Rousseau, J. J. (2014a) *Discourse on Inequality* Translated by G. D. H. Cole, Internet file Retrieved 14 November 2014 from http://ocw.mit.edu/courses/literature/21l-449-end-of-nature-spring-2002/readings/lecture10.pdf.
Rousseau, J. J. (2014b) *Discourse on the Arts and Sciences* Translated by I. Johnston. Internet file (e-book). Retrieved 14 December 2014 from https://ebooks.adelaide.edu.au/r/rousseau/jean_jacques/arts/.
Schérer, R. (1974) *Émile perverti ou des Rapports entre l'éducation et la sexualité* Paris: Laffont.
Starobinski, J. (1971) *Jean-Jacques Rousseau: Transparency and Obstruction* Translated by A. Goldhammer, Chicago: University of Chicago Press.

9
A METAPHYSICAL REBELLION
Camus and psychotherapy

James Belassie

Introduction

Albert Camus advocates a metaphysical rebellion, 'the means by which a man protests against his condition and against the whole of creation' (Camus, 2000a, p. 29). Strongly at variance with the Judeo-Christian tradition, he is comfortable in locating problems in the outside world, rejecting the injunction to 'internalize' them via notions of sin, pathology and ill-adjustment.

He offers no apology for the confusion and despair he encounters when he seeks meaning (rational order) in the world and fails to find it. He refuses to accept the need for any response to such despair that 'demands of me a resignation' or a 'negation' (Camus, 2000b, p. 42) of the despairing part of himself:

> Metaphysical rebellion is the justified claim of a desire for unity against the suffering of life and death – in that it protests against the incompleteness of human life, expressed by death, and its dispersion, expressed by evil.
> *(Camus, 2000a, p. 30)*

Consider the fear of death. Or, conversely, the desire to die. Both states, beyond a certain threshold of severity, will be considered by many professionals to be 'pathological' in nature; symptoms of inner, psychological problems. The *DSM-5* speaks of Suicidal Behaviour Disorder as a condition for further study, which seems to confirm this as an increasing trend in psychiatric thinking (American Psychiatric Association, 2013). It seems to signify a growing and more general reluctance to think of psychological suffering as arising from the hard facts of a person's existence, with professionals focusing ever more intently on responses aimed at an inner, psychological remedy, that will be inevitably felt by some as compromise, surrender or resignation. But to many philosophers, including Camus, such 'pathological' states may be considered potentially justifiable, perhaps even rational responses to phenomena encountered in the world beyond the individual that are found to be intolerable – in the one case, death; in the other, life. The options for potential responses open up suddenly and dramatically. The problem remains, but the (perhaps dangerous) possibility emerges not just that there might be no realistic remedy but that the nature of the problem is not truly – certainly not entirely – psychological. As Camus said: 'There is but one truly serious philosophical problem and that is suicide' (Camus, 2000b, p. 11).

Again, to suggest that the question of death is a philosophical question is insultingly obvious. Yet in their day-to-day work how many mental health workers throughout the UK seriously consider the problem of suicide in its philosophical, as well as its psychological context? I think not many, and I think this illustrates the enormous potential of a philosophically informed therapy to offer something uniquely useful to some clients. First of all, the mere act of examining life philosophically in therapy, rather than exclusively psychologically, is itself radical and expresses respect for and belief in a client's own perception of her life and her capacity to respond autonomously to her world (however 'ill' she may appear to be).

Beyond this, there are specific philosophical perspectives associated with specific writers that can often be felt to be of special relevance. I will discuss one perspective – that of Absurdism – associated with Camus, but first I want to put down some thoughts about the difficulties of attempting to harness philosophical ideas in a way that might usefully inform therapeutic work.

Use of imagery and metaphor in harnessing philosophical thought

I have already hinted that a philosophically informed therapeutic response is particularly appropriate to what have been (somewhat crudely) categorized as 'existential' problems in living (related closely to what Camus refers to as potential targets for metaphysical rebellion): feelings of meaninglessness, anxiety about death and so forth. Although accepting them as underlying many of the symptoms of psychological distress, I would argue that many practitioners of psychology and psychotherapy give a noticeable lack of weight to such experiences *in and of themselves*. This is understandable if we remember that this dimension of human suffering was never intended to be part of the remit of science.

Easing the task of living with these kinds of universal problems has historically been attempted through religious – faith-based – thinking. If psychotherapy hopes to address issues of existence, then it is worth reflecting upon how the consolation delivered by faith-based thinking actually operates. Few philosophers have given more thought to this question than Camus, and it is even possible to see the fruit of this reflection as having informed his whole literary style. For me, the subject is most evocatively addressed in connection with the complicated theology and character of Father Paneloux in Camus's novel *The Plague* (Camus, 2002), whose tone in preaching about the crisis, initially rather detached and cerebral, becomes more urgently personal and emotional as the epidemic escalates. Significantly, Camus is careful to focus not only on the priest's developing response to the pestilence as reflected in his sermons but also the nuances of the townspeople's changing reaction to his words.

The first striking thing about Camus as a writer is his distaste for a strenuously dialectical style. I find it easy to believe Oliver Todd's statement, in his introduction to *The Rebel*, that 'systematic thinking made [Camus] cringe' (in Camus, 2000a, p. ix). Most famous to this day as a novelist, even his explicitly philosophical writings are tied together not so much by the force of reason as by their rich, interwoven and all-pervading use of imagery and metaphor. Of his most famous philosophical metaphor – that of Sisyphus with his rock – James Wood writes:

> What moves us is not that Camus's emblem of the absurd is so entirely metaphorical, but that Camus believes in him so fiercely, and so sympathetically describes his fate and his revolt, that Sisyphus appears to be real to Camus, and becomes almost actual for us. This is the quality of Camus's thought, and it is why he is such a powerful novelist: he takes religious terms, turns them into secular metaphor, and then, by dint of his sympathetic concentration on them, appears to reconvert them back into a usable reality . . . We are reminded that his essay is not philosophy but a kind of storytelling.
>
> *(in Camus, 2000b, p. xviii)*

Two things strike me as particularly relevant here. First, the connection between religious and metaphorical thinking; Second, the connection of Camus's gift of turning ideas into 'usable reality' with the description of the philosopher as storyteller. In the rationalist tradition of philosophy, metaphor and storytelling are at best inferior literary components. The prevailing concept of traditional philosophy is that it deals purely with ideas, in abstraction. Insofar as this creates a tendency to dryness, it might be thought of as inherently problematic to emotionally based therapeutic work. In the same way, to a Christian prisoner awaiting execution, abstract theological ruminations on maintaining trust in Christ might seem to offer a colder, more cerebral consolation than immediate contact with a tangible religious artefact or meditation on a specific religious image (the cross, a saint, the gates of heaven), such as that scene depicted by Father Paneloux in *The Plague* as he comfortably surrenders to his death firmly grasping his crucifix (Camus, 2002).

The process of procuring consolation through tangible objects or images might seem childish, fulfilling a role not much different from that of a baby's teddy bear: the comfort the object provides is so irrational, so symbolic – yet so palpable, so immediate, so visceral. Nonetheless, the physical object, the image, the icon that can be encountered and related to viscerally, with 'sympathetic concentration', are connected totemically to a larger cognitive system; they represent a structure of abstract ideas that comprise, in this case, an entire religious faith.

Any philosopher who bases a work on a central metaphor or saturates it with recurring imagery-based *leitmotifs* recognizes the ability of these linguistic techniques to function in a way comparable to a religious artefact – a lightning rod that does more than summarize and point to a complex and abstract set of philosophical ideas and concepts but that also conducts in a flash some of their poetry, their beauty and their immediate emotional (and practical) significance. I am, in part, speaking of what Ricoeur, following Jakobson, refers to as the 'emotive function' of metaphor (Ricoeur, 2009, pp. 262–263). But perhaps the more important quality of metaphor in this context is that it is easily *transportable*; we can carry specific metaphors away with us as artefacts and use them to give voice to legitimate and immediate existential concerns in a way that wading through a ponderous philosophical text does not allow.

Nobody wants to do away with rationalism and dive back into a superstitious or totemic way of relating to the world. But nor would we wish to discard the immediacy of metaphorical thinking along with religious thinking. As therapeutic practitioners attempting to make use of such an unwieldy, ungraspable tool as philosophy, perhaps we should remember the power that imagery and metaphor have, not just over our mental, but over our emotional and psychological experiences of life. It might be that just as religious imagery can serve to bypass cognition and mediate direct emotional comfort, there are philosophical metaphors that can help return us, at times of deep anxiety or psychological crisis, to a more balanced emotional perspective. Can we also learn from the great literary philosophers, such as Camus – with his intuitive sensitivity to the psychological force of metaphor, allegory and storytelling – new ways of attending to and using language itself, which after all, for better or worse, represents the prime medium through which most therapeutic work is conducted?

The imagery of water in Camus's *The Fall*

"For if I try to seize this self of which I feel sure, if I try to define and to summarize it, it is nothing but water slipping through my fingers" (Camus, 2000b, p. 24).

It is in relation to all this that I now offer some thoughts on Camus's final novel, continuing a previously published discussion (Belassie, 2011). Indisputably, *The Fall* (Camus, 2006) confirms Camus as a master of the psychological and philosophical metaphor. Many have commented on the obvious Christian imagery and the importance of moral themes like guilt, innocence, judgement, penitence (Cruickshank, 1960, among others). Rather than drawing out directly the explicit philosophical themes or basing my discussion on the central allegory of the novel (the fall itself), I will examine a secondary, related, but far more pervasive system of imagery that runs through the work.

Not only the narrative but the entire philosophical content of the book, virtually every important development or intellectual diversion, is articulated in terms of imagery that centres around the element of water – human interaction with water – in its many forms.

It is clear how water is linked, on a literal level, to the most obvious aspect of 'the fall' – the leap Clamance failed to make over a bridge to save a drowning girl – and it is clear how this failure to leap led Clamance to conclude his guilt, guilt he claims is universally attached to the human race, which is his obsession, themed as judgement and regret throughout the book. Given the close psychological link in Clamance's personal world between water and guilt, it is not surprising that his monologue is infused – perhaps subconsciously – with a subtle and corresponding obsession with water symbolism.

Like Camus, Clamance describes his love of Mediterranean summers with sunlit-coated seas viewed from on high, as well as the freedom and clarity the views bring him. Perhaps, then, his preoccupation with water existed even before he encountered the drowning girl. Nonetheless, it is this encounter that turns his preoccupation into a paranoid obsession that emerges one night, two or three years later whilst river gazing, when he hears a mysterious laugh that he believes springs from the river itself. From then on, he doesn't return to the river – he avoids water and becomes nervous in high places but is not finally overwhelmed until, on the top deck of a cruise ship, he realizes that the laugh he heard lies in wait across waves and ripples and will continue to haunt him. This realization that he is not free from his haunting encourages a resignation, if not surrender, to his plight.

Clamance is uneasy in his resignation (as opposed to the ease he formerly felt on the high ridges) as he accepts in his final ironic display of penitence – only a step away from martyrdom, in fact – abandoning Paris and the twinkling Seine and settling in Amsterdam, submitting voluntarily to the bitter rain and fog, the grey ocean and dreary canals that give the greatest possible contrast to the clear blue purity of the Aegean, where he experienced a kind of innocent vitality. And, in keeping with this true commitment to his new state, he manages to take satisfaction in his new surroundings by forcing himself to appreciate the motionless, deathly fragrant canals.

It is interesting to compare Clamance's personal relation to water within the novel as significant to Camus's wider thinking and use of imagery, as well as its relation to even broader cultural archetypes to which we are all subject. Camus's visceral attention to the natural world, ancient mythology, the human body and in this case that most central, life-giving and pervasive of all the elements, water, is crucial in underpinning the broad and enduring appeal of his philosophical concerns.

It is possible that Camus has given primacy to water imagery precisely because of the intimate physical relation with it that human beings inevitably experience. If it is central to Clamance's life, it is no less central to ours. It is an aspect of his condition, just like his sense of guilt, that we have no choice but to share. For Clamance, water appears to both purify and contaminate – but there is so much more to it than this, just as there is so much more to *The Fall* than a book about judgement and human shame. The metaphor functions not just at this level of cultural (religious) symbolism but at many more tangible – embodied, instinctive – levels as well.

'Indulge in a swim'

There is a moment in the essay *Summer in Algiers* (Camus, 2000c) when Camus describes lyrically a certain type of embodied encounter with the sea: 'In Algiers no one says "go for a swim" but rather "indulge in a swim". The implications are clear'

(Camus, 2000c, p. 128). A little further on, he comments on the significant change that comes over one's perception of the world when you are at water level. Visual perspective is lost, tactile grounding is compromised and we have more difficulty perceiving our surroundings as a whole. We recognize colour vividly – 'against the sharp white background of the Arab town the bodies describe a copper-coloured frieze' (Camus, 2000c, p. 130) – but shape and form are blurred, and the concerns of land and air – our natural elements – seem far off, inaccessible and foreign, from our new vantage point. Water is not our element: to immerse ourselves in it is to surrender ourselves to it and lose all sense of our significance; yet for Camus, the need for and attraction to water – to plunge into it, sit by it, sail across it – seems a deeply ingrained and inescapably natural part of human existence.

Could it be that this paradox mirrors the kind of 'absurd' paradoxes that concerned Camus in his pre-war period – the kind of paradoxes he highlights in *The Myth of Sisyphus*?

> I can negate everything of that part of me that lives on vague nostalgias, except this desire for unity, this longing to solve, this need for clarity and cohesion. I can refute everything in this world surrounding me that offends or enraptures me, except this chaos, this sovereign chance and this divine equivalence which springs from anarchy.
>
> *(Camus, 2000b, p. 51)*

Humans are creatures drawn to meaning systems – religious, philosophical or political movements – that appear to offer clarity and a stable ground for existence but that on close inspection seem to be comforting illusions, which crack beneath us like ice and plunge us into the depths of absurdity. Viewed in this way, the 'fall' away from the stability of land, bridges and cliffs into the blinding, shifting waves would come to symbolize the necessary birth (or baptism) of the 'absurd man'. In addition, it is difficult to think of a more apt allegory for the state of constant defiance and 'metaphysical' revolt Camus demands of the absurd individual than one who finally forsakes the false surety of land and abandons himself to the true uncertainty of the water. Imagine the drowning man kicking and struggling to the bitter end, as all drowning men surely do, not in the least discouraged by the pressing awareness of the futility of his struggle but rather, ludicrously and irrationally, spurred on by it. This is the example of the absurd spirit.

Returning to Clamance, his spirit is not abandoned to the absurd. He does not leap from the bridge but crosses it and continues on his way. Would it be unjustified to suggest that, in having him cross the bridge, Camus is painting Clamance as an existentialist figure? Here is how Camus critiqued 'the existentialists' in *The Myth of Sisyphus*:

> Now, to limit myself to existential philosophies, I see that all of them without exception suggest escape. Through an odd reasoning, starting out from the absurd over the ruins of reason, in a closed universe limited to the human, they deify what crushes them and find reason to hope in what impoverishes them.
>
> *(Camus, 2000b, p. 35)*

He describes a journey – an intellectual journey *over* something that, once completed, leaves us with the feeling that a choice has been made. Something has been leapt *over* – evaded – not leapt *into*: this is Camus's primary criticism of the existentialists in *The Myth of Sisyphus*; that they came to the brink and leapt *across*, or backed away to safety, and it seems also to be Clamance's primary accusation, as he laments a re-enactment for the opportunity to leap in and save the drowning girl and, in doing so, would also save himself. Paradoxically, the lamenting is also punctuated with cries of relief for missing his chance the first time around, and so despite his clinging to firm ground, Clamance knows about the potential freedom and joy to be found in leaping into, rather than across the waves, and he also knows the regret of one who has not leapt: his condition often bubbling up in descriptions of exhilarating despair.

This imagery of exhilarating despair continues to the end of the novel, as one night Clamance exclaims his desire to venture into the new falling snow that he views through his window. It is a scene of pure-like innocence: a wholesomeness and spotlessness that is free from contaminants until Amsterdam awakens in the morning and turns the virginal into the all too familiar brown sludge.

I suggest that this can be read as part of the allegory of the fall: in the leap off the bridge into the water, into life, into absurdity, the moment of 'purity' would be the moment of true freedom between life and death – the ecstatic, ephemeral feat of floating, sinking between today and tomorrow, the surface and the murky bed. And it is the knowledge that we will end up there in the mud tomorrow that enables us to appreciate the beauty and purity of our present suspension.

References

American Psychiatric Association (2013) *Diagnostic and Statistical Manual of Mental Disorders* (5th ed.). Arlington, VA: American Psychiatric Publishing.

Belassie, J. (2011) 'The Imagery of Water in Camus's *La Chute*', *Journal of the Society for Existential Analysis* (22) 2, pp. 318–324.

Camus, A. (2000a) *The Rebel*. Translated by A. Bower. London: Penguin.

Camus, A. (2000b) *The Myth of Sisyphus*. Translated by J. O'Brien. London: Penguin.

Camus, A. (2000c) *Summer in Algiers*. Translated by J. O'Brien. London: Penguin.

Camus, A. (2002) *The Plague*. Translated by R. Buss. London: Penguin.

Camus, A. (2006) *The Fall*. Translated by R. Buss. London: Penguin.

Cruickshank, J. (1960) *Albert Camus and the Literature of Revolt*. New York: Oxford University Press.

Ricoeur, P. (2009) *The Rule of Metaphor*. Translated by R. Czerny. Abingdon, Oxfordshire: Routledge.

PART III
Self, other, world

Contemporary therapeutic discourse is unanimous in emphasizing the relational and dialogical dimensions of human experience and in underlining their significance in the therapy room. Anyone vaguely familiar with philosophy or sufficiently schooled in healthy scepticism will nevertheless know that when something is commonly and universally accepted as true, this can be taken as a reliable sign that underlying ideological agendas are at work. This is not to say that the fact that we all now agree that the relationship is the be-all and end-all of therapy is a conspiracy deliberately designed to make us avert our gaze and to distract us into complacency. However, before deciding to join the choir, we might want to reflect on what other assumptions are at work here.

Are we, for instance, relying a little too much on our early relationships with our parents or primary caregivers? What is the place of the wide world, of culture and society if it is true that we are, as Merleau-Ponty teaches us, subjects *destined* to the world? What is being neglected or glossed over? And why is it that conflict, *agon* and struggle, crucial to the very dawn of self-consciousness, have been seemingly forgotten? Is our contemporary understanding of 'intersubjectivity' too dependent on the Christian matrix of neighbourly love, as well as perhaps an extension of our 'culture of me'?

Of course 'love matters'; it matters for the encounter between you and me; it also matters for justice in the wider, unjust world we live in. But perhaps love, like that other sound principle, *non-harming*, needs a deeper recognition of difference, as Luce Irigaray reminds us – a leaning forward that suspends the very foundation of the philosophical tradition: identity.

10

DESIRE-DELIRIUM

On Deleuze and therapy

Manu Bazzano

> Every delirium invests History before investing some ridiculous mommy-daddy.
> (Deleuze, 2004, p. 235)

Broken paths

My route to Gilles Deleuze (1925–1995) has been labyrinthine: I found him, lost him and found him again several times. My first, incandescent contact with his writings happened in the 1970s, the heady days post May 1968 when he published with Felix Guattari an explosive book. *Anti-Oedipus* (Deleuze & Guattari, 1983). Too busy being alive and with little time for systematic reading, I nonetheless remember surfing excitedly through its puns, *double-entendres* and dizzying new concepts. The gleeful onslaught on academic decorum was thrilling – with Freud depicted as "a masked Al Capone" (Deleuze & Guattari, 1983, p. 118) – and I was overjoyed by the unorthodox inspirations behind the book. One of these is the work of the great playwright and certified 'paranoid schizophrenic' Antonin Artaud. He was the man who practically invented what came to be known as physical theatre and who transported Nietzsche's insights on Greek tragedy onto the stage. Artaud saw writing as "a process that ploughs the crap of being and its language" (Deleuze & Guattari, 1983, p. 134). At the time I understood *Anti-Oedipus* to be providing a sophisticated philosophical backdrop to R. D. Laing's 'anti-psychiatry' when in fact it went much further.

Anyhow, the 1970s went by in a jiffy; other anti-intellectual escapades ensued and yours truly forgot all about Deleuze – until recently.

Learning from disappointment

The basis of my current mode of life and practice is Zen, existential psychotherapy and the person-centred approach (PCA). I learned and continue to learn from all three. I am also disappointed by the ways in which all three are being assimilated into contemporary culture, their critique of the tradition conveniently adjusted to fit the *neo-positivist* view. In relation to Zen, the fashionable thing is to create links with psychotherapy in ways that bypass the Dharma's otherness. But Zen cannot be reduced to a set of 'mindfulness' techniques for well-being. This is a popular misapprehension that merely replaces techniques of hard science for 'techniques of the soul' without disputing the dominance of *techne* in human life – arguably, the very root of the problem. The ineffability of Zen teachings, their ambivalent and non-utilitarian nature simply cannot be reduced to a quantifiable and sellable product. It cannot be categorized as 'trans-personal' either, for Zen as I understand it is a somatic practice straddling spirituality and materiality, transcendence and immanence, its inspired ambiguity declining to commit to an existing metaphysics.

In the case of the PCA, Rogers' legacy of far-reaching egalitarianism and quiet, compassionate radicalism is seemingly undergoing a conservative turn, one that is obsequious to the dictates of the market. And I am under the impression that a similar development is well underway within existential psychotherapy, which is increasingly dominated by an *onto-theological* approach that pushes to the margins embodied experience and situatedness.

I am not dismissing altogether the directions taken by mindfulness, person-centred or existential therapy at present but rather registering my disenchantment with this state of affairs. The embracing of neo-positivism by many is perhaps motivated by the wish to be seen as serious professionals with respectable posts in reputable institutions or out of a legitimate aspiration to be no longer pushed to the principled and colourful margins. Some may have made this choice strategically, genuinely believing that the master's tools can be used in dismantling the master's house and out of an aspiration to offer empathic presence to a pathologized/medicalized public. Some among us attempt to quantify the unquantifiable, use right-brain via left-brain lingo and produce evidence that all boxes are ticked and moments of genuine meeting duly measured.

A traitor's quest

At this very juncture, sickened to hear what, to my sensibility, were beginning to sound like grovelling noises, it became tempting to look elsewhere.

I respectfully discarded CBT and the neuro-scientist, neo-essentialist groupings. One option was psychoanalysis. Feeling like a traitor and going against the endemic tribalism of my person-centred training, I began to look into the 'enemy's camp'. Already during my philosophy years, I had admired Freud's agility when dealing with notoriously slippery thinkers such as Goethe, Nietzsche and Schopenhauer. I had been in awe of psychoanalysis's ability to comment on bourgeois culture (of which it is an integral part), widening the view from the analyst's room to cinema, literature and the everyday. I had also noted how hopelessly naive its humanistic counterparts had been, clutching at notions borrowed from Heidegger, Buber, Levinas and presenting them as if they belonged to a matrix altogether different from psychoanalysis. At times, copious humanistic borrowing extended to writers within the psychoanalytic tradition, especially John Bowlby, Melanie Klein and the object relations theorists – with mixed results.

I began to wonder whether seeds could be found within psychoanalysis of a convincing anti-positivist stance that could temper the present makeover of psychotherapy into psychotechnics. Two notions stood out: *free association* and the *unconscious*. But what had happened to these key psychoanalytic ideas? Have they not been disowned by contemporary psychoanalysis and psychodynamic therapy? Free association robs the analyst of her claim to authority, reshuffling the cards in favour of *process*: is that why free association has almost vanished? As for the unconscious, if it is mentioned at all, it is to emphasize that its contents need to be made conscious, which in itself is a worryingly one-sided interpretation of Freud's poetic 'dictum, '*Wo Es war, soll Ich werden*' ("Where it is, I shall be"). In this interpretation, it (id) is playground for the all-conquering 'I' rather than a bewildering locus of learning and transformation. This position – making the unconscious conscious – is a concise description of the neo-positivist stance and of its fantasy of bending the ineffable to the almighty human will.

The ghost of *Anti-Oedipus*

> Say it's Oedipus, or you'll get a slap on your face.
> (Deleuze & Guattari, 1983, p. 45)

Does psychodynamic practice also dance to the neo-positivist tune? When it dawned on me that all orientations had virtually accepted neo-positivism, I felt really and truly stuck. Now I had nowhere to turn. It did cheer me up somewhat to think that all I could do now was meditate, focus on clinical work and get on with living and learning.

Then one summer night I found online an interview with Deleuze, 'D is for Desire' (Boutang, 1996); it brought it all back in a flash: the 1970s, anti-Oedipus, the phantasmagorical derision of psychoanalytic expertise, the denunciation of our societies of control, the wild, generous vagaries of a turbulent decade and above all the joyful pledge to overthrow capitalism and its ideology of greed.

In the interview, Deleuze comments on *Anti-Oedipus* and defends its main tenets. He expresses the wish that the book may be rediscovered in years to come. At the end of the twenty-minute interview, I sat mesmerized, gazing at the blank screen, feeling as if I had been reminded of something I had lost. How on earth had I managed to forget it in the first place?

In the interview, Deleuze summarizes the three (still eminently valid) tenets present in the book:

1   *The unconscious is not a theatre*, the place of representation where Hamlet and Oedipus and Ophelia go on and on playing their scenes but, crucially, *a factory*, a place of incessant production. Deleuze's tangential inspiration here is Artaud who referred to the body (and especially the sick body) as an overheated factory. From Artaud, Deleuze also borrowed the notion of the 'body without organs', which is a way of saying the body is an assemblage *with no underlying organizational principles*. This notion of the unconscious is aligned with what Deleuze (2004) calls "desiring-machine" (p. 232), a notion at variance with the biological theory of mechanism that underpins psychoanalysis and is associated with a view of desire seen as a continuous chain of flow, withdrawal, interruption and flow again – crucially, one that is entirely devoid of meaning.
2   *Delirium* (madness, profound mental distress, including schizophrenia) is not solely about the small familial scenario of our childhood. It is closely linked to desire: desiring means to a degree becoming delirious. What we rave about when we rave is the world – as well as history, geography, tribes, deserts, peoples, races, climates (Stivale, 2011).
3   *Desire* (in itself a kind of delirium) *is creative*; it is highly imaginative, it constructs *assemblages*, i.e. things in the plural, the collective and the multiple. It cannot be reduced to one thing such as mother, father, phallus and so forth. When we desire something, we set out creating a new assemblage or aggregate:

> We said something really simple: You never desire someone or something; you always desire an aggregate.
>
> *(Deleuze in Boutang, 1996)*

These three tenets are at variance with psychoanalysis, a practice that Deleuze and Guattari set out to demolish with the same vigour and panache with which Laing & Co. attacked psychiatry. Similarly, in other texts Deleuze outlines the contours of an "anti-psychoanalytical analysis" (2004, p. 276). He sees analysts act like priests and policemen in relation to desire. Not only do they find rigid explanations for it, tracing narrow origins and an equally constricted set of interpretations. They also police desire's natural tendency to create new assemblages, and this for very good reasons: assemblages have a highly *subversive* and transformative potential. The uprisings of May 1968 in Paris and elsewhere in Europe was one such example – the creation of a collective assemblage, an affirmative delirium aimed at uprooting a world that had become repressive and rotten to the core.

The notion of *desire* presented here is not that of the perennially unsatisfied craving manufactured by our consumerist society. It is also different from the hungry ghost covetousness the Buddha warns us about. Both of these are closely linked and grounded in the self's fundamental sense of *lack*. But in Deleuze's conception, there is no self behind the production of desire: desire is another name for the persistent movement of living-and-dying. Like Spinoza's *natura naturans* and Nietzsche's *will to power*, desiring-production is autonomous and impersonal. We have a choice, one that is relevant, I believe, in the therapy room: we can say *yes* to the incessant movement of becoming, and this may in turn open our experience to joy *and* sorrow. We can also say *no* to the innocence of becoming and choose instead the static consolations provided by systems of life denigration. We can affirm desire or subject it to a reductive interpretation, which eventually turns itself into pantomime:

> Desire does not depend on lack, it's not a lack of something, and it doesn't refer to any Law. Desire produces. So it's the opposite of a theatre. An idea like Oedipus, the theatrical representation of Oedipus, mutilates the unconscious and gives no expression to desire. Oedipus is the effect of social repression on desiring production. Even with a child, desire is not Oedipal, it functions like a mechanism, produces little machines, establishing connections among things. What this means in different terms, perhaps, is that desire is revolutionary. This doesn't mean it wants revolution. It's even better. Desire is revolutionary by nature because it builds desiring-machines which, when they are inserted into the social field, are capable of derailing something, displacing the social fabric. Traditional psychoanalysis, however, has turned everything upside down in its little theatre. It's exactly as if something that really belongs to humanity, to a factory, to production, were translated by means of representation at the *Comédie Française*.
>
> *(Deleuze, 2004, p. 233)*

Beyond familialism

Desire or delirium (or rather desire-delirium) is "a libidinal investment of an entire historical milieu, of an entire social environment" (Deleuze, 2004, p. 275). It cannot be understood solely in terms of the family. Mum and Dad are important to some degree. After all, we come into the world via a dwelling. At the same time, the home, "the dwelling of stone and clay and abode of primary relations" is embedded into a larger context; it is "open to a wide world into which we are thrown" (Bazzano, 2014b, p. 205). In Deleuze's words:

> We say that the problem of delirium is not related to the family, that it concerns mommy and daddy only secondarily if it concerns them at all.
>
> *(Deleuze, 2004, p. 235)*

Passing notes on longing

What Joanna liked about Akio was, among other things, how radically different he was from her: he belonged to another ethnic and social group, one that is as far removed from her own upbringing as it is imaginable. His temperament too is very different from what she had been used to before with her previous partners. They met when she was travelling in the Far East; their love affair had been short-lived and intense, and she still thinks and dreams of him. Her desire for him is visceral, overwhelming and all-consuming, but their current circumstances are in the way: the long distance, their individual work commitments as well as familial and affective attachments all create great obstacles to establishing a more 'real' relationship.

My initial understanding of this client's dilemma veered towards configurations of *lack*. Before I knew it, I was thinking of how we could trace the genealogy of her longing back to attachment issues, early familial scenarios, not least the important occurrence of her father's early death. I also mulled over more textbook-style responses: issues of self-worth and the likes, perhaps her inability to build 'realistic' relationships with people where she lives and works, plus her tendency to look for what is unreachable and even impossible. Yet there was no way of explaining away the longing she often talked about. It was vividly present in the room: the way she sighed from time to time, the way her gaze took on a remote quality whenever she talked about Akio.

She did not accept the impositions that circumstances enjoined on their love. She envisioned a life of constant travel; it was travel that brought her love, and it was travel, an existence lived outside the constraints of job and family, that made her more alert and open to her experience. I felt secretly annoyed by what I saw as a pointless rebellion and an adolescent need for a fuzzy notion of freedom and idealistic 'nomadism'.

All the same, with issues of self-worth lingering in the back of my mind, I found myself praising her sincerely, being more accurate in my interventions, offering from time to time descriptive challenges, trying to highlight the sheer impracticality of her predicament. But I also felt that I needed to bring the longing itself to the centre of our exploration. One evening after she left, I sat by myself musing over this. I felt that there was something 'poetic' about her longing. I was dissatisfied with the word 'poetic' and discarded it right away. Then I remembered a poem quoted somewhere – or was it a quote with two poems in them? – that I had read months ago. From what I remembered, it *praised* longing itself; it didn't see it as need. I could not find the quote but managed to bring back to mind their contents and their authors, their meaning and resonance indelible. The first was by Ibn al-'Arabi, a thirteenth-century Sufi poet quoted at times by Ted Hughes. It said something like '*O Lord, /nourish me not with love/but with the longing of love*'. The second quote was by the poet René Char; in speaking of poetry, Char defines it as (I paraphrase it) *the realized love of desire that has remained desire.*

Could I *be* with that longing and not be enticed to somehow pathologize it? Could I refrain from trying to bridge it with intimations of 'realistic solutions'? Could I meet Joanna's deep desire as longing for otherness, as desire for the impossible, as an aching symptom of the tragic poetry of human life? Could I be with her nomadic spirit and put aside the notion that 'psychological integration' has to mean a sedentary life with a steady job and a family? Could it be that our loves and deeds, our thoughts and dreams are conditioned by the hold of a static view of existence?

On nomadism in general, on nomadism as an exciting philosophical stimulant, Deleuze had very interesting things to say. For him, nomadism is a way of life outside of the organizational State; it is movement across space and in contrast to the rigid confines of the State. In *A Thousand Plateaus*, Deleuze and Guattari write:

> The nomad has a territory; he follows customary paths; he goes from one point to another; he is not ignorant of points (water points, dwelling points, assembly points, etc.). But the question is what in nomad life is a principle and what is only a consequence. To begin with, although the points determine paths, they are strictly subordinated to the paths they determine, the reverse happens with the sedentary. The water point is reached only in order to be left behind; every point is a relay and exists only as a relay. A path is always between two points, but the in-between has taken on all the consistency and enjoys both an autonomy and a direction of its own. The life of the nomad is the intermezzo.
>
> *(Deleuze and Guattari, 2004, p. 380)*

There are too many implications deriving from the notion of nomadism, particularly if we consider that mainstream eastern and western cultures (including biblical narratives) have opted for more reassuring notions of territory and identity instead. I have discussed some of these implications in a book that also tackles the other difficult notion closely linked to nomadism, i.e. *exile* (Bazzano, 2012). What I want to propose here is that desire, delirium and longing naturally go beyond the familial boundaries within which western psychology has chosen to inscribe its study of psyche. If so, the picture of psyche we have been painting over the last one hundred plus years will have to be modified.

From the family to the world

Foucault has shown us how nineteenth-century psychiatry connected madness to the family. Psychoanalysis has maintained this link, and, in spite of its groundbreaking potential, 'anti-psychiatry' did the same. The greatest majority of therapeutic orientations, including those stating fundamental disagreements with psychoanalysis, emphasize the central role of the family. And even when father and mother "are interpreted in a symbolic way – the father symbolic function, the mother symbolic function – [this] doesn't change a thing" (Deleuze, 2004, p. 235).

Prevailing contemporary interpretations have imploded further, towards genetic explanations of schizophrenia and other forms of acute mental suffering, making familial and systemic readings look positively left-field by comparison. I believe our task, however, lies in expanding the vision further: rather than from the family to the brain and our genes, the movement needs to expand *from the family to the world*.

There is a parallel here with the historical neglect of Hegel in phenomenological and humanistic psychotherapy (Bazzano, 2014b) and the consequent upholding of "the mother–infant dyad into which psychoanalytic understandings of intersubjectivity are normally cocooned" (Bazzano, 2014b, p. 206). This has perhaps prevented a contextualization of that very dyad within the "wider matrixes of history, society and culture" (Bazzano, 2014b).

This can be rendered in a very different way. Here is Deleuze again:

> All you have to do is listen to someone in a state of delirium: the Russians worry him, and the Chinese; I've got no saliva left. I was sodomized in the subway, there are microbes and spermatozoa everywhere; it's Franco's fault, the Jews' fault, the Maoists' fault. Their delirium covers the whole social field. Why couldn't this be about the sexuality of a subject, the relation it has to the ideas of Chinese, Whites, Blacks? Or to whole civilizations, the crusades, the subway? Psychiatrists and psychoanalysts have never heard a word of it, and they are on the defensive because their position is indefensible. They crush the contents of the unconscious with pre-fabricated statements like: "You keep saying Chinese, but what about your father? – he's not Chinese. – so your lover is Chinese?" It's like the repressive work by the judge in the Angela Davis case, who assured us: "Her behaviour is explicable only by the fact that she was in love". But what if, on the contrary, Angela Davis's libido was a revolutionary, social libido? What if she was in love because she was a revolutionary?
>
> *(Deleuze, 2004, p. 273)*

The task of a counter-traditional mode of thinking and practice is to actively resist dominant cultural narratives and to go back to the original purpose and aspiration: serving people in distress, meeting them compassionately, practising *epoché*, i.e. the suspension of prejudices and assumptions but also the suspension of pre-established ontologies. A practice inspired by the fluid parameters of the counter-tradition will suspend the axioms and signposts of the tradition in the service of the client.

Expanding on the notion of desire-delirium as something that belongs to the world rather than to a decontextualized family unit, Deleuze differentiates between two poles of delirium:

> The real problem of delirium is the extraordinary transitions between two poles: the one is a reactionary pole, so to speak, a fascist pole of the type: 'I am a superior race' which shows up in every paranoid delirium; and the other is a revolutionary pole: like Rimbaud, when he says: 'I am an inferior race, always and forever'. Every delirium invests History before investing some ridiculous mommy-daddy. And so, even where therapy or a cure is concerned – provided this is indeed a mental illness – if the historical references of the delirium are ignored, if you just go round and round between a symbolic father and an imaginary father, you never escape familialism and you remain locked within the framework of the most traditional psychiatry.
>
> *(Deleuze, 2004, p. 235)*

Creative delirium

> Priests, professors and doctors, you are mistaken in delivering me into the hands of the law. I have never been one of you; I have never been a Christian; I belong to the race that sang on the scaffold.
>
> (Rimbaud, 1986, 'Bad Blood')

Anti-Oedipus, a post–May 1968 text, reflected the assemblages of that period, a way to summarize the creative delirium of '68 and the ethos behind it, to clear the air from the oppression of a political, academic and psychoanalytic establishment who, as Deleuze saw it, had blocked off and repressed desire. Many misunderstood desire as a chance to have a party or as mere 'spontaneity', but this misunderstanding mattered little, Deleuze says, since creative assemblages were nevertheless formed (with inevitably mixed results). Critics thought *Anti-Oedipus* an infamous legitimization of permissive behaviour. Deleuze's response was that he didn't see his task as that of a policeman or a parent; he was saddened in seeing some fellow travellers taking the road of excess and failing to reach the palace of wisdom, laying themselves open instead, through the indiscriminate use of drugs and drink, to the lethal intervention of state psychiatry, which turned innocent people into a pulp state, the clinically schizo state (Stivale, 2011). Deleuze did not actively prevent anyone from doing what they wanted but felt nevertheless responsible for young people who got into trouble; he did what he could to help them.

Rather than 'party all the time', the message at the heart of the book is don't get psychoanalyzed; don't become a victim of psychiatry. Instead, "stop interpreting, go construct and experience/experiment with assemblages, search out the assemblages that suit you" (cited in Stivale, 2011).

The creation of assemblages is concurrent with a reframing of the notion of the unconscious and essential antidote in a psychotherapeutic landscape that has either reified it or dismissed it. Desire-delirium is an agent of impersonal change and collective transformation, and it can be aided rather than hindered by a psychotherapeutic practice able to recognize its emancipatory power, its ability to create the genuinely new outside the greenhouses of academia and institutions.

References

Bazzano, M. (2012) *Spectre of the Stranger: Towards a Phenomenology of Hospitality* Brighton, Sussex, and Portland, OR: Sussex Academic Press.

Bazzano, M. (2014a) *After Mindfulness: New Perspectives on Psychology and Meditation* Basingstoke, Hampshire: Palgrave MacMillan.

Bazzano, M. (2014b) 'Togetherness: Intersubjectivity Revisited', *Person-Centered & Experiential Psychotherapies* (13) 3, September, WAPCEP, Routledge, pp. 203–216. DOI:10.1080/14779757.2013.852613

Boutang, P. A. (1996) '*Gilles Deleuze's ABC Primer, with Claire Parnet*' Internet file. Retrieved 24 July 2014 from www.youtube.com/watch?v=IrZdOZzr4as.

Deleuze, G. (2004) *Desert Islands and Other Texts 1953–1974*. Translated by Michael Taormina. New York: Semiotext(e).
Deleuze, G., & Guattari, F. (1983) *Anti-Oedipus: Capitalism and Schizophrenia*. Translated by R. Hurley, M. Seem and H. R. Lane. Minneapolis: University of Minnesota Press.
Deleuze, G., & Guattari, F. (2004) *A Thousands Plateaus* London: Continuum.
Rimbaud, A. (1986) *Collected Poems* London: Penguin.
Stivale, C. J. (2011) '*Commentary and Transcripts of Gilles Deleuze's ABC Primer, with Claire Parnet, directed by Pierre-André Boutang (1996)*' Internet file. Retrieved from www.langlab.wayne.edu/cstivale/d-g/abc1.html#anchor575650.

11

A POETRY OF HUMAN RELATIONS

Merleau-Ponty and psychotherapy

Paul Gordon

In memory of Mike Fielder

Introduction

It's a Friday, early, not yet seven, mid-May and I'm on the M4. It's a beautiful morning. London, traffic-free, in this light always takes me aback. The sky, cloudless, seems to be a blue I've never seen before, and there is a clarity to all the greens of the fields and the woods that is almost overwhelming. I understand why artists become so obsessed with trying to capture these.

I'm listening to a CD, *Endless Vision*, by the Iranian lutenist, Hossein Alizadeh, and the Armenian duduk player, Jivan Gasparyan. One of the most exquisite albums I have, it never fails to take my breath away, and this morning is no exception. (I've always been grateful to the *Observer* reviewer, Carol McDaid, for her enthusiastic review several years ago, which made me get it for myself.)

Later, I switch to John Coltrane, his classic quartet at the celebrated Village Vanguard club in New York in 1961. Even with the car noise and the not very good stereo, I'm blown away, as I always am, by the energy and inventiveness of these musicians, not just Coltrane himself, but Jimmy Garrison, McCoy Tyner and Elvin Jones, that 'aching on the frontier of the possible', in Geoff Dyer's unforgettable phrase. I can think of no other group of musicians who were so attuned to each other, so musically empathic, to such profound effect. These four men would never play as powerfully as they did when they played together.

And I'm thinking about this chapter and what I want to say about this man, this thinker, who has been a quiet influence on my way of being a therapist for many years now, quiet but significant. Until relatively recently, he has been a somewhat neglected figure, at least outside the world of academic philosophy. There are a number of reasons for this; he died very young, at fifty-three, in 1961, only a few months before the Coltrane recording; unlike several of his friends – de Beauvoir, Camus and Sartre – he didn't write fiction; his writing can be difficult, although it can also be poetic, as I hope to convey; he left no memoirs, and there has not yet been a biography of him in English.

And thinking about Merleau-Ponty links me inevitably to my therapist, later colleague, Robin Cooper, hugely significant to me as a therapist-in-the-making but more importantly as a human being. It was he who encouraged me to read Merleau-Ponty, saying there was not a page of *Phenomenology of Perception* without some insight in it. Although the first book on psychotherapy I wrote, *Face to Face*, was inspired by the singular ethical thinking of Emmanuel Levinas, Merleau-Ponty's presence was a strong one, *particularly his thinking on language and his scepticism about the idea of an 'inner world'*.

Life and context

Maurice Merleau-Ponty was part of that incredibly gifted generation of intellectuals in post-war France that included de Beauvoir, Camus, Sartre and Levi-Strauss. Another contemporary, Simone Weil, died in exile in Britain during the war. With Sartre, De Beauvoir and Raymond Aron, he founded the journal, *Les Temps Modernes*, which would become one of the most influential journals of the time. It was named after the 1936 Charlie Chaplin film, *Modern Times*, which Sartre loved, in which Chaplin's character struggles against the depredations of the machine age. They edited the journal together until 1953, when Merleau-Ponty resigned over differences over the Soviet Union, about which he had become highly critical.

He was born in Rochefort in the Charente-Maritime area in western France in 1908. His father was killed in the First World War when Merleau-Ponty was eleven. (Camus and Sartre, later to be his friends, also grew up without a father.) He and a brother and sister were brought up by their mother in Paris. He would recall later the happiness of a 'prolonged childhood' lasting twenty-five years (Merleau-Ponty, 2012, p. 361). His early academic interest was in psychology, especially the Gestalt psychology of Aron Gurwitch, whose lectures he attended. But he also attended the 1929 lectures given by Edmund Husserl in Paris. Ten years later, the year after Husserl's death, he would visit Louvain to study Husserl's papers, apparently the first person to do so. The documents had been gotten out of Nazi Germany by a courageous priest, Father Herman Van Breda, with the involvement of Husserl's widow, Malvine, and the cooperation of the Belgian government. Thousands of papers were saved from certain destruction, smuggled out under diplomatic protection.

His first major philosophical work was *The Structure of Behaviour*, completed in 1938, while his magnum opus, *Phenomenology of Perception*, was completed in 1945. The book was first translated into English only in 1962, with a new translation in 2012.

He had met Sartre during the war and had joined his Socialism ou Liberte resistance group to produce anti-German propaganda. The group had its first meeting in de Beauvoir's hotel room.

He was appointed professor of psychology at the Sorbonne in 1950 and two years later took up the most prestigious post of professor of philosophy at the College de France. (Later holders of these posts would include Roland Barthes, Michel Foucault and Pierre Bourdieu.) His inaugural lecture in January 1953, 'In Praise of Philosophy', was dedicated to his mother who had died the previous year. This propelled him into a deep despair from which, it seems, he never recovered. Sartre reported him meeting de Beauvoir and saying, 'But I am already half dead'. In fact, he lived on for several years, a semi-recluse. He died on 3 May 1961 from a heart attack at the age of fifty-three, while preparing a lecture.

Singing the world

Merleau-Ponty reminds us that speech is not a translation of our thought but the accomplishment of it. For much of my life, I thought I could speak only when I had things ready, prepared 'in my mind', and so, most of the time, I never did because they were never ready enough, or the moment had passed, or the conversation had moved on. I'm fortunate that this is one of the few real regrets in my life, that I couldn't sometimes say the simplest things to people in my life at the time. But then when you're brought up not to speak of anything that really matters, it's hardly surprising.

By the same token, language is not really a means of communication. For Merleau-Ponty, it's something far richer; it's nothing less than a way of being. In a broadcast on French national radio in 1948, he said, '[A] self only develops into a free agent by way of the instrument of language and by taking part in the life of the world' (Merleau-Ponty, 2004, p. 66). Note the radical nature of this statement. It is through speaking that we become free. Of course, it takes courage to speak. We don't know what we'll end up saying and certainly not the consequences of what we say.

Language comes not from 'I think' but from 'I am able to'. For the speaking subject, to express is to become aware of; I express not just for others but also to know for myself what I mean or want to say. For Merleau-Ponty, "[O]ur thought crawls along in language" (Merleau-Ponty, 1964a, p. 43). This is why expression can never be complete; language is always indirect or allusive, always going somewhere. This is one of the scary things about speech, whether in therapy or elsewhere. We can never know where it will take us. My own spoken words can "surprise me and 'teach me my thought'" (Merleau-Ponty, 1964a, p. 89).

We see this again and again in therapy, how often people are genuinely surprised by what they are saying. Or when we say something we may have said before, sometimes often, only to find we are saying it in a different emotional register because we are being truly heard. It is this being heard, whether in therapy or not, that can be a transformative factor. It is a minor miracle, surely, to be heard, when we feel someone has truly 'got' what we're talking about. And how devastating it can be not to be heard. Or for what we are saying to be ignored or translated by the hearer into something else altogether. This hearing ought to be at the heart of psychotherapy, but it is, precisely, what is too often missing. Many people arrive with their scripts, their prepared stories they have told themselves to make sense of their experience. But when we give them the safety and the space to let go of these, it is then they can discover, for themselves, richer ways of speaking and being, what Merleau-Ponty called, "so many ways of singing the world" (Merleau-Ponty, 2012, p. 193).

Embodiment

Merleau-Ponty reminds us that our being in the world is embodied. It is not that I have a body, but that *I am my body*. This is an inescapable fact – so obvious, perhaps, that we can lose sight of it. Without my body, I would not exist. "Existence realizes itself in the body". It is our bodies that open us out into the world and to others. "It is the lot of living bodies to close upon the world and become seeing, touching bodies" (Merleau-Ponty, 1964a, p. 16). The body establishes our first consonance with the world. Of course, we can resist this, and many do, but it can be avoided only at great personal cost. It is only through the body, a cluster of meanings, a node of expressiveness, that we can participate in the world.

So it is that we know *other* people not as spirits or minds but through their bodies, their gestures, speech, glances. Another person, Merleau-Ponty says, is "a spirit which haunts a body," and the body is "the very presence of all the possibilities contained within it when it appears before us" (Merleau-Ponty, 2004, p. 62). We see this every day in our work as psychotherapists in the different ways that individuals present themselves physically – the man who can hardly make the bell ring, the woman who holds it fractionally too long, the woman who sits as far from me as she possibly can, the people who seem compelled to have to go into the house itself to use the toilet.

For Merleau-Ponty, we are perceiving beings. It is through being embodied that we can perceive, and it is this perception that is at the heart of being human – perception understood in its fullest and richest meaning, i.e. attending to whatever is available to us through *all* our senses, not just sight and hearing, but also feeling, smelling, and tasting – and that is absolutely central to who we are. Babies can hear in the womb, and within a few moments of birth they can distinguish and respond to facial gestures. Perceiving is also always an action – it is never passive. We never cease living in the world of perception, but we go beyond it in critical thought. And, of course, we perceive through our bodies – "The perceiving mind is an incarnated mind" – we see, hear, smell, feel pain or pleasure, anxiety or boredom.

It's not that we perceive in bits and pieces and add them up, "I perceive in a total way with my whole being, a unique way of being which speaks to all my senses at once" Merleau-Ponty, 1964a, p. 50). Nor is it a deliberate act that we resolve to do, although we can, and too often do, privilege some senses over others.

Merleau-Ponty's thinking is hugely relevant to any attempt at understanding the current epidemic of eating disorders. (It says a lot that the first translation of *Phenomenology of Perception* has to explain the meaning of 'anorexia', which it does incorrectly/naively, as loss of appetite.) In its refusal of food, anorexia is a refusal of others, of the future, of life. The man who binges gives to the body what his soul lacks. But these are also ways of expressing emotions that cannot find expression otherwise; the anorexic is a parody of the self-control our culture so esteems; the binge can be an act of defiance against a very real other. Both, paradoxically, are forms of self-assertion but at the same time are directed against the body because they cannot be expressed in any other way. It is in this respect that to think of a body as something one *has*, rather than what one is, is a sort of bad faith of self-deception. It's a way of distancing and of refusing any kind of responsibility for one's actions, in the same way as 'having' some sort of 'mental illness' is a way of not having to think about the meaning of one's suffering and, in particular, that it may be a perfectly legitimate response to an untenable situation. This much, at least, we should have learned from the more thoughtful critics of psychiatry like Jules Henry, Aaron Esterson and R. D. Laing.

The enigma of sexuality

> And so we lay down arming and legging each other around as we have done since time immemorial.
>
> *(Grass, 1989, p. 4)*

Merleau-Ponty reminds us of the centrality of sexuality to who we are as human beings. If a person's sexual history provides a key to their life, it is because in it we see their manner of being towards the world, that is, towards time and other people. One's sexuality symbolizes a whole attitude towards life, whether this be one, for instance, of endless conquest or of flight and fear. For Merleau-Ponty, sex is something enigmatic. A crucial corrective, I think, to the fixed thinking of other systems of thought. Why 'enigma'? Because it *is* puzzling; it is a riddle. In therapy, this can help us to keep things open and not close them down, to put aside preconceptions and prejudices, to allow for the endless varieties and meanings of what the Scottish writer Alan Sharp termed 'many-motived ritual'.

My body can shut itself off from the world; it is also what opens me out to it and places me in a situation there. Nowhere is this more true than in the field of our sexuality. Acknowledging the limitations of philosophy in explaining the body and sexuality, Merleau-Ponty insists that the body, in its sexual being – this fulcrum and steadying factor of our life – is endlessly enigmatic. Although respectful of Freud's thinking, he is not confined by it. Sexuality is not something to be *explained* but *thought about*.

Sexual experience is something that is open, potentially at least, to everyone and always available, which opens us out to the human lot, of longing, of vulnerability. Sexuality is invariably double-edged – a source of great joy but of great misery too. As for love, one finds one's freedom not in 'a vain autonomy' but in the act of loving, in making oneself vulnerable to the desired one. Yes, Merleau-Ponty says, the experience is indeed an alienating one as it tears me away from my lone self and creates a mixture of myself and the other. Of course, this is the dilemma that many clients present: the fear of being alone, alongside the terror of being with another.

Merleau-Ponty also reminds us that the ordinary, everyday feelings of modesty, desire and love are incomprehensible if we see humans as machines governed by natural laws or even as bundles of instincts. They are relevant to man as a consciousness and as a freedom. Shame and immodesty take their place in a dialectic, a conversation of self and other, master and slave. We cannot avoid our sexuality: it's an inescapable fact of our being. For Merleau-Ponty (2012), "Sexuality cannot be transcended, and yet there is no self-enclosed sexuality. No one is fully saved, and no one is fully lost" (Merleau-Ponty, 2012, p. 174).

Destined to the world

Merleau-Ponty reminds us that we are always situated in a world in which we find ourselves and that we are always in relationship with others. There is no 'inner life' that is not a first attempt to relate to another person. "There is no inner man – man is in the world and only in the world does he know himself" (Merleau-Ponty, 2012, p. lxxiv) Consciousness is always consciousness *of something*. My consciousness is turned primarily towards the world. Above all, it's a relationship with the world. It is pointless to try to distinguish between what is natural and what is acquired, as the two are not distinct but parts of a global phenomenon.

As for introspection, what does it give me? – Merleau-Ponty asks: 'Almost nothing'. In the case of love or hate, for instance, a few pangs or heart-throbs – 'trite agitations' that do not reveal the essence of love or hate. Anger, shame, hate and love are not psychic facts hidden at the bottom of another's consciousness; they are types of behaviour or styles of conduct that are visible from the outside. "They exist on this face or those gestures, not hidden behind them" (Merleau-Ponty, 1964a, pp. 52–53). When I return to myself, Merleau-Ponty says elsewhere, from "an excursion into the realm of dogmatic common sense or of science, I do not find a source of intrinsic truth, but a subject destined to the world" (Merleau-Ponty, 2012, p. lxxiv).

A particularly important essay for therapists in this regard is 'The Child's Relations with Others' (Merleau-Ponty, 1964e), in which Merleau-Ponty sketched out a phenomenological approach to the earliest years of life. It is not that the child reflects the world of those around him or is the product of a process. Something more profound happens; the child acquires not just certain relationships but a whole way of thinking, a whole usage of language and a way of perceiving the world. This is not something that just happens to the child. The child, Merleau-Ponty says, is called upon to organize his or her experiences; the word 'organize' is crucial here for it reminds us that the development of the child is an active process. The child who knows from a very early stage indeed that she has to be 'good' will carry this way of being in the world, for better or worse, into her adult life (Merleau-Ponty, 1964e).

For Merleau-Ponty, we can never be anything other than in relation with others; our very being is intersubjective. This is why a state of mind like empathy is not a problem for him, as it has been for so many philosophers and therapists, who have looked on it as a rather suspect emotion. This is one of the times when, as someone said, Merleau-Ponty doesn't so much solve a problem but *dissolve* it. "[A] bond is tied without my needing to decide anything", he says, watching a man reach for his hat to protect against the sun that he himself feels. "I live in the facial expressions of the other as I feel him living in mine – a sign of the 'me-and-other', this is our shared humanity" (Merleau-Ponty, 1973, p. 176). The man who wrote this is a genius, the philosopher Roger Poole said in an early appreciation, not just of mind but of humanity and asks who before him would have dared write that passage and, indeed, who would dare write it now (Poole, 1974)?

Psychotherapist Natasha Synesiou, in her article, 'Boundary and Ambiguity' (Synesiou, 2014), speaks courageously and movingly of two personal experiences that bear directly on this. In a discussion of Merleau-Ponty's idea of chiasm, the idea that "every relation with being is simultaneously a taking and being taken", she recalls visiting a friend in hospital who has just undergone major surgery. Standing next to her in the recovery room, she found herself "imbibing her trauma – psychic and somatic" – she started to lose consciousness and had to leave the room before fainting. Her friend, emerging from sedation, is quite aware of what is going on. She continues:

> When my father was dying, I remember the day after his operation, walking slowly up and down the corridor with him. As I fell into step with him, holding his arm, it was as though he passed ghost-like into me. I experienced the shutting-down of his body, death's slow colonising of it, all across and in the depths of my own lived body. I knew then how it felt to be dying slowly, and I knew what I must do.
>
> *(Synesiou, 2014, p. 16)*

Like many other therapists I have had, over the years, I have experienced a number of less dramatic feeling episodes, puzzling, even disturbing, which seem to be something to do with people who've been in therapy with me at the time, a specific kind of attunement, a communication through the body. Whatever the specifics of a particular situation, they are constant reminders that communication between people is *never* solely through language.

Rediscovering the world

Merleau-Ponty reminds us of the endlessly wondrous nature of the world. He himself spoke of the 'unsurpassable richness, the miraculous multiplication of perceptible being', with its echoes of the poet Gerard Manley Hopkins' "all things counter, spare, original, strange" and the "incorrigibly plural" nature of the world. A philosopher "who made men wonder" is how one of his translators, Richard McCleary, described him (Merleau-Ponty, 1964a, p. 9). For him, phenomenology involved just "the same kind of attention and wonder, the same demand for awareness, the same will to grasp the sense of the world or of history in its nascent state" as did the great writers and artists (Merleau-Ponty, 2012, p. lxxxv). Indeed, he ended the wonderful preface to *Phenomenology of Perception*, a sort of manifesto, with the statement, "Phenomenology is as painstaking as the work of Balzac, Proust, Valery or Cezanne".

This was why he loved the painter Paul Cezanne, more than any other artist and wrote insightfully about him. In a finely nuanced discussion of his life, he said that a man's life does not explain his work but that the two are invariably connected. He puts it beautifully: "The truth is that *this work to be done called for this life*" (Merleau-Ponty, 1964a, p. 20). (I can think of so many artists – musicians, writers, painters – of whom this would be true.) And like Cezanne, he seemed to have an endless wonder at the world, at the things we so take for granted:

> The things of the world are not simply neutral objects, which stand before us for our contemplation. Each one of them symbolizes or recalls a particular way of behaving, provoking in us reactions which are either favourable or unfavourable. This is why people's tastes, character, and the attitude they adopt to the world and to particular things can be deciphered from the objects with which they choose to surround themselves, their preferences for certain colours or the places where they like to go for walks.
>
> *(Merleau-Ponty, 2004, p. 48)*

So when Cezanne paints, with "unfailing patience" an apple, "it ends up swelling and bursting from the confines of well-behaved draughtsmanship" (Merleau-Ponty, 2004, p. 39). Cezanne spoke of the 'halo' of things, which it was the task of painting to capture (Merleau-Ponty, 1964a, p. 49).

Inexplicable grace

On a number of occasions, Merleau-Ponty said that the work of phenomenology was not at all limited to philosophy but was carried out by writers and artists. "The artist", Merleau-Ponty said, "is the one who arrests the spectacle in which men take part without really seeing it and who makes it visible to the most 'human' among them" (Merleau-Ponty, 1964a, p. 18). He was writing about Cezanne, but I feel his remarks can be applied to the contemporary writer, Mavis Gallant, whom I want to look at.

Until her death in 2014, the Canadian Mavis Gallant had been writing, for more than fifty years, astonishing short stories about very ordinary people living unextraordinary lives, the sort of people we would know or certainly know of and certainly not unfamiliar to us. Her canvas is not the natural world or inanimate things, as it was much of the time for Cezanne; it was always people in relationship with one another, whether in families, couples, friends, colleagues, employers, and how they behave with one another, whether they were truthful or deceitful, kind or mean-spirited, thoughtless, hapless, manipulative and so on (Gallant, 2002, 2003).

Her eye and ear for the said and the not-said, the tiny details that make all human encounters so complex are remarkable.

Gallant herself spoke of fiction being about capturing "a climate of the mind". So there is "the faint, floating sadness" that the Paris art dealer feels when he lowers his shutters; or the meaning of the used coffee filters thrown by respectable citizens from their Paris apartments down onto cars below, "a way of saying something"; or the young woman who comes to dinner and is completely unaware of the "disaster and pain" she causes in her hosts; or a mother, whose son has gone off to enlist, wonders about other mothers and sons, "[W]hether children feel any of the pain they inflict". (After his departure, she and her sister ransack the house, "looking for clues, imaging he'd left a letter, left some love, they kept the shades drawn, as if there were another presence in the rooms, tired of daylight" (Gallant, 2003, pp. 209–210).

Although accepting and not judging of her characters' all too human failings, Gallant can also be angry. The young woman, Linnet Muir, features in a number of stories written in the 1970s and is based, I suspect, on Gallant herself. "In youth is pleasure"; she goes out to confront "the free adult world of falsehood and evasion on an equal footing; they [her late father's friends] would be forced to talk to me on an equal footing", as she goes in search of the truth of his passing. "First it was light chatter, then darker gossip, and then it went too far (*he* was ill and he couldn't hide it; *she* had a lover and didn't try", and then suddenly it became tragic, and open tragedy was disallowed.

In 'Between Zero and One', Linnet Muir has gone to work during the war in an office where she is the only women. She cannot understand why men, given so much in the way of advantages compared to women, "set such close limits for themselves and, why, when those limits had been reached seemed so taken aback" (Gallant, 2003, p. 125). There was a space of life she calls "between Zero and One" and is obsessed with working out when men reach their 'terminal point'. It's a brilliant study of male condescension, of quiet male power; the men were "rotting quietly" till pension age; no one wastes office time, but no one produces much either; the men squabble over mislaid pens, whether windows are open or shut. A girl was allowed to work there "in an ambience of doubt, apprehension, foreboding, incipient danger, and plain hostility"; she feels that "almost palpable atmosphere of sexual curiosity, sexual resentment, and sexual fear, that the presence of a woman can create, where she is not wanted." And yet, because of who she is, she is deeply happy, a period of "inexplicable grace", as if every day was "a new parcel waiting to be unwrapped" (Gallant, 2003, p. 135).

The story ends with an older woman, Mrs Ireland, who has joined the office, speaking to her and warning her against marriage. "Now you've got no one to lie to you, to belittle you, to make a fool of you, to stab you in the back". Linnet recalls: "The recollection has something to do with the blackest kind of terror, as stunning as the bolts of happiness that strike for no reason. This blackness, this darkening, was not wholly Mrs. Ireland; no I think it had to do with the men, with squares and walls and limits and numbers. How do you stand if you stand on Zero?" (Gallant, 2003, p. 147).

'Let It Pass' was a story I was tempted not to read because of its inauspicious beginning; a man, Steve, recalls getting letters from his aunt, bringing news of people he had once known but in whom he has no interest. Perhaps the kind of man one would ignore on a first acquaintance, as someone known, someone not worth paying attention to. The man, confronted by the sudden appearance of the adolescent daughter of his former wife, Lily, is forced to deal with his memories of her mother.

(The girl herself is wonderfully drawn; she thinks "adults are always where they're supposed to be" and, when she is taken to a ruined castle, complains that the Saracens, who built it, should have looked after their driveways better.)

Trying to entertain her, he finds himself not just revisiting physical places he had been to with her mother on their honeymoon but being inevitably assailed by unbearably sad memories of their short life together. He remembers the guide at one place, addressing a group but speaking "only to Lily"; he does not blame him, for he is "helplessly, caught on the rapt, sunstruck way she looked".

It's brilliantly done, the way we discover more and more with him, as he has to recall more and more. It's not just that Lily found him a disappointment but something more, almost calculated ("Lily must have seen me – my mind, my life, my future, my Europe – as a swindle") but that her whole outlook was "naturally conniving". Before they got married, he had seen her scurry out of a lover's sports shop, "a girl who could glide out of the late afternoon shadows of Peel's place, [and who] had the habits of dark doorways" (Gallant, 2003, p. 253).

But he knows, and she knows he knows, and now the telepathy that had existed between them, which once had seemed to him such a gift, becomes a nightmare. "[T]he flow of one mind into another seemed unhealthy, unwise. I prayed never to stand revealed before another human being again" (Gallant, 2003). He imagines Lily continuing to think, 'He doesn't know', as she professes her faith in the future while he whispers to himself, Let it pass. "She had more sense than any man, so she cut the sound." On the ship taking them to Europe, Lily miscarries; he knows beyond all doubt that the baby was not his;. "I was not the son of missionaries for nothing; I saw the incident as a clean sweep, the falsehood washed away, the pagan wrenched from old customs, blood sacrifice of the convert – Lily converted to me, entirely" (Gallant, 2003, p. 260). Eventually, she will leave him for a much younger man, the gardener of a neighbour, an older man who is secretly in love with the neighbour. "They had left nothing but two men who could not even comfort each other" (Gallant, 2003, p. 248).

I read not a page of this writer without encountering some insight into what it is to be a human being in a specific context or a remarkable description that truly stops me in my tracks. It is the first time I have felt the desire to read fiction with a pencil in hand to mark the passages I want to remember in the way I do when I'm reading non-fiction. I never read a story without coming away feeling somehow better, enriched. It's a bit like therapy, actually; when people are truly engaged with what they are saying and talking *to me*, as opposed to talking in my presence, the tragedies or horrors or just the all too real difficulties of ordinary life become bearable. It's the unengaged talk, the non-relating that is so much more difficult, for me at any rate.

Freedom and autonomy

Merleau-Ponty reminds us that we are born into a world that is not of our making.

> To be born is to be simultaneously born of the world and into the world. The world is already constituted, but never fully so; in the first relation we are solicited, in the second we are open to an infinity of possibilities.
> *(Merleau-Ponty, 2012, p. 480)*

Given the circumstances of its creation, written during the German occupation of his country to which he was actively opposed and published after the liberation, it's not surprising that the final chapter of *Phenomenology of Perception* is titled, 'Freedom'. For Merleau-Ponty, freedom is very much a concrete thing, rooted in our physical being in the world. We are free to act upon the world but only within pregiven limits. We are not then omnipotent, able to fashion the world as we choose; but neither are we helpless, victims of circumstances. (There is a clear echo here of Marx when he had said, almost one hundred years before in the middle of the previous century, that men make history but they do so in circumstances not of their making.) There is a realism at work that never becomes an acceptance.

More important than any statements about freedom, however, is the fact that there is a deep democratic spirit at work throughout Merleau-Ponty's thinking. There is a genuine acceptance and deep respect for what it means to be human – that, to a large extent, we are who we are and cannot be very different. "No one thinks or makes up his own mind without already being caught up in certain relationships with others", he told his listeners in his 1948 radio broadcasts (Merleau-Ponty, 2004, p. 66). The idea that no one has a privileged perspective on the world, that we all share in a continuing conversation, is profoundly democratic. Also, as Roger Poole remarked, phenomenology in Merleau-Ponty's hands, "assumes the creative presence of human freedom in perception and in thought – it is "the presence of meaning-conferring in the perceiving subject" (Poole, 1974). In other words, we are always active in the world, making choices, conferring meaning. Of course, we can always choose not to involve ourselves, but this always a choice too.

Despite the richness of his thinking, there is a genuine modesty in Merleau-Ponty's thinking that we do well to remember in our own work. When he said, in his inaugural lecture at the College de France, that philosophy limped, it was not a complaint or criticism; it was something he welcomed, it was philosophy's virtue (Merleau-Ponty, 1988, pp. 58–61). But in the end he also reminds us that moments of insight, if they are to be meaningful, have to be sustained by "a new commitment" (Merleau-Ponty, 2012, p. 482). In other words, it's not enough to understand a situation. We have a deep responsibility to change in order to meet it. This is our freedom, whether as individuals in our daily lives or as part of the world in which we find ourselves.

Acknowledgement

My love and thanks, as always, to Melissa Benn for her help in the writing of this chapter.

References

Gallant, M. (2002) *Paris Stories*. New York: New York Review Books.
Gallant, M. (2003) *Varieties of Exile*. New York: New York Review Books.
Grass, G. (1989) *The Flounder*. Boston: Mariner Books.
Merleau-Ponty, M. (1964a) 'Cezanne's doubt' in *Sense and Non-Sense*, edited by P.A. Dreyfus. Evanston, IL: Northwestern University Press.
Merleau-Ponty, M. (ed.) (1964b) 'Indirect language and the voices of silence' in *Signs*. Evanston, IL: Northwestern University Press, pp. 38–83.
Merleau-Ponty, M. (1964c) 'On the phenomenology of language' in *Signs*. Evanston, IL: Northwestern University Press, pp. 84–97.
Merleau-Ponty, M. (1964d) 'The film and the new psychology' in *Sense and Non-Sense*. Evanston, IL: Northwestern University Press.
Merleau-Ponty, M. (1964e) *The Primacy of Perception*. Evanston, IL: Northwestern University Press.
Merleau-Ponty, M. (1964f) *Signs*. Evanston, IL: Northwestern University Press.
Merleau-Ponty, M. (1973) *The Prose of the World*. Evanston, IL: Northwestern University Press.
Merleau-Ponty, M. (1988) *In Praise of Philosophy and Other Essays*. Evanston, IL: Northwestern University Press.
Merleau-Ponty, M. (2004) *The World of Perception*. Abingdon, Oxon: Routledge.
Merleau-Ponty, M. (2012) *Phenomenology of Perception*. Abingdon, Oxon: Routledge.
Poole, R. (1974) 'The bond of human embodiment', *Universities Quarterly*, (28) 4, Autumn, pp. 488–500.
Synesiou, N. (2014) 'Boundary and ambiguity: Merleau-Ponty and the space of psychotherapy', *Self and Society*, (41) 3, 13–19.

12

THIS CULTURE OF ME

On singularity, secrecy and ethics

Eugenia Lapteva

Today, if you were to enter the word 'selfie' into the hashtag bar on your Instagram account, you may or may not find yourself quite as astonished as I was to discover that there are nearly two hundred sixteen million photographs with the hashtag selfie posted on just *one* social media app. And if, spurred by this staggering truth, you then decided to type in the word 'me' instead, you might very well find yourself dumbstruck. For there are currently three hundred and twenty million, three hundred and sixty four thousand posts of different, but oddly alike, 'me's'.

From now on, it's me, me, me, my selfie and I.

Let us take a moment, for clarity's sake, to establish what the definition of this modern phenomenon is. According to the bible of information, Wikipedia, a selfie is a self-portrait photograph, typically taken with a handheld digital camera or camera phone. Selfies are often shared on social networking services such as Facebook, Instagram or Twitter. They are usually flattering and made to appear casual. Most selfies are taken with a camera held at arm's length or pointed at a mirror, rather than by using a self-timer.

Apt as this description may be, it also needs to be said that the very best way of securing a high rate of selfie likes is by tilting your chin down somewhat, pouting moderately, whilst allowing one eye to look up playfully into the camera. Not to mention the crucial post-production work – a most delicate process that involves a variety of photo filters and fine adjustments to the selfie's general fun factor and spontaneity levels.

Joking aside, the popularity of the smartphone self-portrait seems to have reached an unprecedented height across the globe. Hailed by some as a creative form of self-expression, an empowering platform for changing identities or simply a natural evolution of our need to depict ourselves pictorially, others are more critical of the trend, suggesting that it might be a sinister sign of our growing narcissism and self-obsession in a capitalist consumer society. Whichever way we choose to look at the phenomenon, the reality of it confronts us with a quandary: what does it mean to be human in an age of hyper-connectivity and electronic self-exposure?

In his remarkable book, *The Private Life: Why We Remain in the Dark*, the British psychoanalyst and literary theorist, Josh Cohen, explores some of the possible reasons as to why in contemporary culture we find ourselves in constant need of displaying our own private lives and those of others. Drawing on a number of philosophical, literary and psychoanalytic sources, Cohen refers to a particularly pertinent passage in Dostoevsky's 1864 novella *Notes from Underground*. It reads as follows:

> We find it a burden being human beings – human beings with our own real flesh and blood, we are ashamed of it, consider it a disgrace and are forever striving to become some kind of generalised human beings.
> *(Dostoevsky in Cohen, 2014, p. 198)*

In light of this statement, it seems to me that a number of very important but often neglected implications of our 'selfie-dominated' culture could be discerned. Firstly, might the surge in anonymous self-portraits be the cultural manifestation of a deeper urge to rid the self of that which resists standardization and escapes the order of visibility and, by virtue of this, of precisely what renders us human? How could this fundamental irreducibility of self be linked to our status as corporeal beings, in Dostoevsky's words, with our own real flesh and blood? In essence, what are the bonds between the burden of being human and the burden of being a singular self?

In order to try and respond to these questions, if only to inspire further thinking, I suggest that we leave the well lit reality of selfies for a moment – the familiar site of seeing where illusions of self-possession and sovereignty seemingly hold sway – and turn instead to its attending darkness and much less sharply defined space that is our psychic reality. Rather than proposing any definitive answers, I believe that psychoanalytic insights can help open our eyes to some of the subtle psychosocial mechanisms that operate within the human's different modes of relationality.

> The significance of the mother – unique, incomparable, unalterable throughout the whole of the individual's life – is rooted in these two relations [career and seductress]; she is the strongest love-object, the paradigm for all later love-relationships – for both sexes.
> *(Freud, 2006, p. 43)*

Freudian knowledge teaches us that sexuality is an integral part of human life. Challenging the ideas of his time, Sigmund Freud daringly expanded the notion of sexuality by claiming that the 'germs' of our sexual instinct are present from the very beginning of life and manifest themselves through a number of auto-erotic activities and sexual urges and impulses. He pointed out that the pleasure attached to the act of sucking at the mother's breast, for example, cannot be divorced from our primitive sexuality. Indeed, the baby's very first experiences of sensual pleasure and un-pleasure are obtained through the satisfaction, or lack thereof, of his or her vital somatic needs.

According to this psychoanalytic conception of the human being, the baby is born without a fully developed ego. From the beginning there is only id, as Freud said, and the newborn exists in a state of formlessness, a bundle of contradictory drives and instinctual energies, pressing desperately toward satisfaction at all costs. The unconscious processes in the id pay no heed whatsoever to reality; they are fearless and entirely subject to the unrelenting pleasure principle (Freud, 2006). As the American literary theorist Leo Bersani writes,

> we desire what nearly shatters us, and the shattering experience is, it would seem, *without any specific content* – which may be our only way of saying that the experience cannot be said, that it belongs to the non-linguistic biology of human life.
>
> *(Bersani, 1986, p. 39)*

Expanding on the Freudian ideas of our infantile sexuality, Bersani affirms that masochism is at once a destructive threat to life and a mode of survival that *initiates* us into the reality of social relations. Thus he advances the radical claim that human beings are in fact, ontologically, "implicated in violence almost from the beginning of life" (Bersani, 1986, p. 70). Interestingly, what we might draw from this is that human subjectivity seems to be established on the basis of an unconditional drive toward externality that on principle defies the laws of self-interest and self-preservation.

At this stage, then, before the baby has acquired the necessary cognitive capacities for reality testing and sense making, the helpless baby is at the mercy of the mother's undivided care and attention for survival. Each time satisfaction is denied, the unbearable tension caused by the excess of instinctual energy acts as a devastating break in the continuity of the baby's existence. The presence of a loving mother or caretaker is therefore imperative during this most vulnerable period in the infant's life. As the proponents of object-relations theory show, the mother enables the baby to bear these unavoidable interruptions of being (a state of 'madness' to use Winnicott's expression) and take pleasure in their momentary alleviation by acting as an auxiliary ego through which the unbound passions can be integrated and translated into more tolerable forms. Since mother and baby are not yet clearly undifferentiated in the baby's mind, the mother's unconditional gift of self as a result endows the baby with the illusion of having created his or her own psychosomatic satisfaction. The containing ego of the (m)other is consequently internalized by the baby, assimilated as part of the baby's own developing self and sense of being alive.

My point here is simply to show how in the precarious life of the infant the physical, sexual and psychic dimensions form a complex tangle of interlacing and conflicting desires that can never be fully satisfied, rendering them essentially traumatic in nature. Our primary object-relation is therefore crucial for our future existence insofar as it provides the basic ontological conditions of *being* and *giving*. These are no doubt the conditions upon which coping with the inevitable experiences of loss and lack in life, as well as creating mature and non-subsumptive relations with others, are largely (but not entirely) founded.

Returning to the passage in Dostoevsky's novella, we shall hopefully find ourselves in a better position now to appreciate why the burden of being human might be intimately linked to our being fundamentally irreducible to the general terms of understanding. Indeed, based on the proposition that our primordial masochism serves life, it would appear to be true that our entry into the world of others is conditioned upon a paradoxical modality of absolute vulnerability and ignorance of being and death: to put it in Levinasian terms, being-towards-the-other (Levinas, 1998, p. 84).

Andre Green (Green, 1996, p. 244) interestingly describes this initial ecstatic encounter with the mother in terms of an 'original madness' that will remain at the core of the subject's unconscious throughout his or her life. An original openness toward the other, which precedes self-consciousness, is thus constitutive of our subjectivity as irreducible beings and seems to lie at the very heart of what it is to be alive. As soon as we are born, we are exposed to the other person, forever binding us to what remains beyond the reach of apprehension and interrupts our ambitions of achieving complete knowledge of the self and other. The burden of being human, it would seem, marks precisely the inescapable demand upon us to *answer* to this unknowable other who gives us the gift of singularity.

Our capacities for conceptualization and phenomenalization – revealing the mysteries of the natural and social world – are indispensible to the structures of modern civilization and technological progress. Our homes, hospitals, medical treatments, various food manufacturing, welfare system and democracy are but a few examples of the astonishing advancements in the history of mankind, made possible through our cognitive capacities for abstraction. My intention here is not to make conclusive judgements about the ethics of technology as such but simply to pause for a moment and question what happens to the self, and our relations to others, if the technological demands for transparency and universality become the leading goals in society *at large*? In other words, when the right to the clandestine and singular (that which escapes the order of information and visibility) is denied ubiquitously. Is there not a risk that you, the other person in front of me, on the bus, at work, on Tinder, lying next to me in bed, turns into an objective generality towards which I lack any real sense of answerability and ethical obligation. *We are forever striving to become some kind of generalized human beings.*

Switch off and keep swiping. There are plenty more matches in the sea.

Needless to say, a carefully curated snapshot of the self can offer great satisfaction inasmuch as it grants us a comforting sense of self-certainty and control. We are the artist, critic and audience of our own being, as it were, and once we've mastered the tricks of the trade, the fleeting pleasures of instant gratification and self-affirmation are but a click, post, share, away.

Rationalization, Adorno argues, bears a striking affinity with mythology insofar as they both entail the act of subsuming particular phenomena under universal principles and concepts "in order to reduce the fearsome externality of nature to consciousness" (Cascardi, 1999, p. 30). Adorno aptly maintains that in the attempt to master our natural surroundings, the particularity of each individual object or experience becomes divorced from the realm of reason and scientific abstraction. In effect, both the realms are compromised; reason is functionalized and becomes a mere instrument of domination, and the internal complexity of the object or experience is violently reduced to a measurable element, a "clear and distinct idea" (Bowie, 2003, p. 5).

I turn on the camera on the tube – take one, two, three – close but not close enough. What do you think – hair up or down? I smudge on some more lipstick to make sure they look deep red and kissable. "You're such a babe." Thanks, but if only I felt like one. Take four, done. #selfieonthego? I upload and wait, two, three, four, five . . . six . . . approved. I feel the corner of my lip curl up. I'm OK.

"The individualism of technological civilization relies precisely on a misunderstanding of the unique self" writes Derrida (Derrida, 2008, p. 37). In *The Gift of Death* (Derrida, 2008), he gives a brilliant account of the paradox that appears to lie at the centre of our current neo-liberal individualist order. It is:

> the individualism of a masque or *persona*, a character and not of a person. [Modern individualism] concerns itself with the *role that is played* rather than with this unique person whose secret remains hidden behind the social mask.
> *(Derrida, 2008, p. 37)*

When referring to the uniqueness of a person, Derrida (2001) invokes the notion of the secret. His thoughts on the logic of secrecy paint a very different picture of the term from the one to which we are most accustomed. But I believe it can grant us a deeper understanding, albeit indirectly, of what is at stake in our relentless search for the perfect self(ie).

For Derrida, the secret of secrecy:

> does not consist in hiding *something*, in not revealing the truth, but rather in respecting the absolute singularity, the infinite separation of what binds me or exposes me to the unique, to one as to the other.
> *(Derrida, 2001, p. 123)*

In an interview published in *Points*, Derrida explains that:

> [i]t [the secret] is not a thing, some information that I am hiding or that one has to hide or dissimulate; it is rather an experience that does not make itself available to information, that resists information or knowledge.
> *(Attridge, 2010, p. 47)*

While the common belief is that in keeping a secret I am actively withholding what I already know, Derrida is clearly suggesting that secrecy is a far more complex occurrence. It involves responding to that which is kept apart and exposes me to the unique. Thus it is inextricably bound up with the experience of singularity. If we submit to this Derridean understanding of the notion of the secret, we can begin to discern how the event of secrecy relates to our essential responsibility toward one another as singular human beings. Addressing the question of responsibility in his lengthy discussion of the sacrifice of Isaac on Mount Moriah, Derrida writes the following:

> For common sense, just as for philosophical reasoning, the most widely shared presumption is that responsibility is tied to the public and to the nonsecret, to the possibility and even the necessity of accounting for one's words and actions in front of others, of justifying and owning up to them. Here on the contrary, it appears just as necessarily that the absolute responsibility of my actions, to the extent that it has to remain mine, singularly so, something no one else can perform in my place, implies instead secrecy. But what is also implied is that, by not speaking to others, I don't account for my actions, I answer for nothing, I make no response to others or before others.
> *(Derrida, 2008, p. 61)*

Herein lies the scandal and aporia of responsibility. On the one hand, responsibility insists on what is apart and kept secret (singularity and silence), and on the other hand, it impels us to speak and thus to dissolve or sacrifice our singularity in the generality of language. "Secrecy is essential to the exercise of this absolute responsibility as sacrificial responsibility" (Derrida, 2008, p. 68). Indeed, much like the primary object-relation between mother and baby, the instant of our absolute responsibility is madness. It is the essential madness, or the experience of singularity, that informs life from the very start and participates in our everyday experiences of love and responsibility *as* the secret psychic life upon which their possibility is opened up.

In conclusion, my question is: Is there an essential difference between the morality of the everyday selfie and the self-portrait as a work of art? I believe there is.

The selfie *reveals*.

Rephrasing Derrida's critique of the masked role in modern individualism, the selfie bores precisely to the extent that it claims to excite curiosity by way of showing, exposing and exhibiting the being behind its mask. Otherwise put, by unveiling everything (or attempting to do so), the selfie forecloses the singularity of the self whose essence shows itself only when it is allowed to be what it is, namely withdrawn, hidden, secret, *unknown*. In the absence of distance and invisibility, everything is calculated and the self becomes equal and indifferent. Arguably, in a world increasingly driven by technoscientific objectivity and economic profit, the culture of selfies epitomizes this suppression of irreducibility and internal complexity in favour of an identity politics ruled by the violent principles of equivalence and exchange.

I scroll down. I keep scrolling, deeper and deeper into the abyss of envy and annoyed impatience. Selfie working hard at the gym, selfie on a mountain top in South America, selfie having a FroYo, selfie going for a walk, selfie in Ibiza, selfie without makeup, selfie with makeup. I reach the bottom of the screen, pause and resume the survey one last time. However, when I put away my phone, I'm left with a strange feeling of discontent and wanting more.

The poem, writes Maurice Blanchot in *The Space of Literature*:

> . . . is the veil which makes the fire visible, which reveals it precisely by veiling and concealing it. The poem shows, then; it discloses, but by concealing, because it detains in the dark that which can only be revealed in the light of darkness.
>
> (Blanchot, 1989, p. 230)

In the space of the work of art, things are transformed into what cannot be grasped. While the utilitarian logic of our everyday communication wants primarily to rid words and images of their ambiguity, the artwork seems on the contrary to follow the curious poetic movement of secrecy that Derrida and Blanchot describe. Within the work, we often find that distance is kept and things are hidden from view. Interpretation is left open, and the person whose infinite being we can never fully know is gently disclosed precisely by *not* being entirely exposed. This movement is articulated beautifully by Blanchot:

> We feel and sometimes regret that poetry, far from reconciling the elements of language, puts infinity between them, to the point where we have to believe that the words it uses have no meaning whatsoever, and the meaning it aims for remains beyond all words. And yet everything happens as if, starting with this dismemberment, fusion became possible, the distance of this infinite distance seemed nonexistent, and from this hostility the opposition stretched out in a simultaneous overlapping.
>
> (Blanchot, 1949, p. 53)

Recall the original madness of our primary masochism and openness toward the other – the paradoxical movement of antagonistic forces upon which our capacity to give the other the gift of secrecy "without knowing, without knowledge or recognition, without thanks" (Derrida, 2008, p. 113) is based. The work of art surely also begins in this primal (con)fusion between destruction and creation.

Finally, it seems that there is a parallel between the precarious interplay of self and other in our primary experience of sexuality and the operation of the poetic work in the experience of the artist and reader. Both experiences, in virtue of their commitment to the absolutely singular other, point to a happening that explodes the limits of rational understanding and exceeds the order of binary systems. Where there is poetry, there is the enigma of singularity and thus the inescapable demand upon each individual to respond to the burden of being in a twofold way: to receive and respect the secret self.

References

Attridge, D. (2010) *Reading and Responsibility: Deconstruction's Traces*. Edinburgh: Edinburgh University Press.
Bersani, L. (1986) *The Freudian Body: Psychoanalysis and Art*. New York: Columbia University Press.
Blanchot, M. (1949) *The Work of Fire*. Stanford, CA: Stanford University Press.
Blanchot, M. (1989) *The Space of Literature*, Ann Smock (trans.). Lincoln: University of Nebraska Press.
Bowie, A. (2003) *Aesthetics and Subjectivity*. New York: Manchester University Press.
Cascardi, A. (1999) *Consequences of Enlightenment*. New York: Cambridge University Press.
Cohen, J. (2014) *The Private Life: Why We Remain in the Dark*. London: Granta.
Derrida, J. (2001) *A Taste for the Secret*. Cambridge: Polity.
Derrida, J. (2008) *The Gift of Death and Literature in Secret*, David Wills (trans.). London: University of Chicago Press.
Freud, S. (2006) 'Outline of Psychoanalysis', in Adam Phillips (Ed.), *The Penguin Freud Reader*. London: Penguin, pp. 1–63.
Green, A. (1996) *On Private Madness*. London: Karnac.
Levinas, E. (1998) *Otherwise Than Being or Beyond Essence*, Alphonso Lingis (trans.). Dordrecht: Kluwe Academic.

13
ENERGY ETHICS AND THE THOUGHT OF DIFFERENCE IN LUCE IRIGARAY

Federico Battistutta
Translated from the Italian by Manu Bazzano

The logic of the self-same

A famous sentence in Nietzsche's *Zarathustra* states: "Of all that is written, I love only what a person has written with his blood. Write with blood, and you will find that blood is spirit" (Nietzsche, 1997, p. 36).

To be thus placed, even if only to critique it, means to be willing to bleed in turn, that is, to be involved (Bataille, 1992). This position belongs naturally to the counter-tradition, given that the development of Western philosophy is rooted from its inception on a split between thought and effectuality (reality, world), between saying and doing, writing and the body, words and things. The Heidegger question, exploded towards the end of the 1980s, is its most recent and dramatic example, a source of embarrassment for the majority of contemporary philosophy and for those who had to admit, as Edmond Jabes (1991) said with his distinctive composure, how agonizing it was to have to admit that the source from which one had drunk was, deep down, polluted.

The thought of sexual difference, elaborated by philosophies within feminism nearly fifty years ago, represents a key contribution available to all – women as well as men – for the creation of an embodied philosophy.

Irigaray first studied philosophy at Louvain University in Belgium, then psychology in Paris, where she became part of the Ecole Freudienne de Paris, founded by Jacques Lacan. In 1974, she published her doctoral thesis, *Speculum, de l'autre femme*, wherein she critiques with biting irony Freud's thought as well as Lacan's on female sexuality (Irigaray, 1985). Now considered a classic of feminist literature, this book was controversial when it came out, signalling Irigaray's rupture with the Lacanian group. The *Ornicar* review, a key publication of Lacan's *logos*, will accuse her of being unethical and of lacking loyalty to a single order of discourse. In other words, Irigaray mixed psychoanalysis with other (and particularly feminist) narratives. Thinkers of the past, Irigaray writes, have produced a culture apparently valid for everyone but one that is in actual fact marked by male difference. It presents woman as the image in the mirror, as symmetrically opposite to man: woman is defined in terms of lack in relation to the fullness represented by the male. The patricide that Freud placed at the beginning of civilization was preceded for Irigaray by an even more archaic event: the murder of woman-mother, which brought about the logic of the self-same and the dominion of the one above multiplicity.

Irigaray's work is characterized by a deconstruction of metaphysics and of phallologocentric predominance that is very close to that of other authors such as Derrida, Deleuze and Guattari. Through its critique of the male-gendered subject and of the primacy of reason, it opens up the possibility of a new mode of thinking, one that is no longer logocentric.

Irigaray will grapple intensely and specifically with Nietzsche's thought, recognizing in its trajectory the most radical attempt within Western thought to break the barrier of logocentrism. Yet according to her, not even Nietzsche, prophet of the philosophy of difference, was able to smash the mirror of the self-same. Here is a significant passage of her encounter/confrontation with Zarathustra:

> Perched on any mountain peak, hermit, tightrope walker or bird, you never dwell in the great depths. And as companion you never choose a sea creature. Camel, snake, lion, eagle and doves, monkey and ass, and . . . Yes. But not to anything to moves in the water. Why this persistent wish for legs, or wings? And never gills? ". . . [I]t is always hot, dry and hard in your world. And to excel for you always requires a bridge. Are you truly afraid of falling back into man? Or into the sea?
>
> *(Irigaray, 1991, p. 131)*

Philosophy as practice

In her subsequent essays, the author will continue to delineate in greater detail the lineaments of a thought of difference and alterity. Nature, she says, is two – male and female – and we cannot leave aside the limit indicated by gender and sexual difference but act and practice the conditions that allow the cohabitation of different subjects, the most universal paradigm of which is the relation between a man and a woman.

She later became interested in Eastern thought. The West always believed itself superior to the East, considering the latter to be irremediably irrational, hence in need to be controlled. In the same way as woman represents *the other* for man, one whom man needs to enter into a relation with, so the East represents the other for the West, and only when the former is accepted and welcome can we be enlightened by it. Eastern cultures, therefore, have something to teach us; in particular, they will be helpful to us in reformulating a subjectivity that is in relation to the cosmos, overcoming the body/spirit split. Here, as it can be clearly seen, we are in the very heart of the counter-tradition. For Irigaray, we have been instructed to do whatever we like, so that the way we love is like appropriation. But having the world contained in our head, as it were, deadens life. What is captivating in experience is its irreducibility; then our response is surprise, praise, enchantment rather than repetition and appropriation.

Here philosophy becomes practice, even therapy (although the latter should not be confused with various practices of philosophical consultancy, which I see as postmodern expressions of the *business* of thought). But then already the ancient world had something to say about therapy – provided we understand the latter in a non-specialized, non-compartmentalized fashion. For instance, in his *De Vita Contemplativa*, Philo of Alexandria speaks of a Judaic religious community called Therapists (Θεραπευταί) who placed at the very heart of their way having care of the body, of one's inner world, of others and so on. "They are called therapists – Philo writes – mainly because the medicine they profess is superior to the one that is in vogue in our cities. The latter cures only the body, but the former also heals the psyche" (Leloup, 1994). He then proceeds to point to forms of suffering and to pathologies that are addressed by the members of this community, among them attachment, maladjustment, envy, melancholy and phobias.

An ethics of energy

From within this philosophy/psychotherapy discourse, I would now like to turn my attention to one of Irigaray's latest works, *A New Culture of Energy*[1] (Irigaray, 2011). In this volume too, the author, reflecting on gendered identity, highlights those elements that can better facilitate dialogue and interaction:

> To be a man or a woman means to belong to a different relational world, determined by a different rapport with the origin, with oneself, the other and the world. Such difference is a result of a different rapport with the mother, with procreation itself and with a specific body morphology;
>
> *(Irigaray, 2011, p. 112)*

Although these themes recur often in Irigaray's thinking, this time the dialogue is entirely played out on the relation between East and West on an intercultural, inter-religious terrain. She uses a slender, non-specialized language that reveals a metabolism taking place in her discourse, an energetic link between thought and action, *logos* and *physis*, speech and silence.

The entire book is imbued with an ethical tension, slight yet constant, independent of abstract imperatives derived from logomachies or strong logical deductions. What emerges instead is a kind of 'doctrine of the right way' to paraphrase Adorno's expression prefacing his *Minima Moralia* (Adorno, 1978), a sober and thoughtful *traité de savoir vivre*, or treatise on the art of living. Speaking of yoga practice, something she has done for many years, Irigaray reaffirms that the first teaching is that of refraining from harming others, "an imperative which should modestly precede the Christian injunction of loving one's neighbour as oneself" (Irigaray, 2011, p. 11). Indeed, in Patañjali's *Yoga-Sūtra* (Bryant, 2013) – a classic text and the main reference as a wider, philosophical and religious perspective on yoga beyond its uses as remedy or panacea for psychophysical balance – *ahimsa* constitutes the first basic step for the yoga disciple. This Sanskrit word, often translated as 'non-violence', is more accurately rendered as 'non-harming', an expression indicating the absence or the suppression of the desire to harm. The person who refrains from harming is literally innocent from the Latin *in-nocens*, one who does not cause harm. By not violating the dignity proper to every being, we leave the other to her or his difference, thus respecting the intrinsic order of reality and the originary aspect of all things. As Irigaray writes:

> Non-harming requires in fact taking one step ahead in our human becoming – towards a greater recognition and a greater love of the other as different from us.
>
> *(Irigaray, 2011, p. 61)*

The author turns towards a form of *ethics of energy* that centres on facilitating the production, circulation and transformation of energies. This type of ethics actively refrains from repressing these energies; it does not deprive them of that spontaneity that resides naturally in the subject, nor does it make them subservient to narratives and techniques alien to them. "The problem – Irigaray maintains – is finding a way to cultivate a natural energy which in the West is only known in the guise of instincts, drives or more or less human ... more or less reprehensible passions" (Irigaray, 2011, p. 23). Already in a previous work, comparing yoga's energetic vision (*prāna*, vital breath and principle) with Freud's hydraulic model of drives, she wrote:

> The approach of Far-Eastern traditions, especially the practice of yoga, coupled with the philosophical meditation inseparable from it, has taught me another way, a way leading not to a discharge but to an energetic recharge, to a regeneration of a culture of energy.
>
> *(Irigaray, 1996, p. 137)*

This perspective brings new and decisively important openings, when for instance, she maintains that "culture should not be any longer synonymous with submission to rules, norms or defined ideal imposed by past generations" (Irigaray, 1996, p. 24). She also writes:

> It is not about bending to existing laws, following trodden paths which are independent from us. Our very experience should instruct us and teach us to become teachers of ourselves.
>
> *(Irigaray, 1996, p. 12)*

This is effectively a path towards the subject's adulthood, towards the affirmation of the autonomy and uniqueness of each individual within the relational domain. A long way indeed from our present condition: "Our tradition has made it habitual for us to entrust our body to doctors, our soul to priests, and the spirit to professors" (Irigaray, 1996, p. 32).

Speaking, as I do here, of *energy ethics* allows us to draw together Luce Irigaray's stance to Francisco Varela *ethical know-how* (Varela, 1999). Also taking inspiration from Far Eastern sources, in particular Buddhism, Varela maintained that ethics is closer to wisdom than to reason, despite what the Western philosophical tradition has been saying since time immemorial. He made explicit the substantial difference between *know-how* and *know-what*, that is between, on the one hand, abilities and practices of immediate encounter (*savoir faire*) and, on the other, premeditated knowledge or rational judgements (*ipse dixit*). Ethics starts with the body and is not represented by abstract rules or codified procedures. Irigaray too seems to move in this direction when she speaks of non-harming, of love and compassion, seeing of the latter as a natural bridge between nature and spirit, as allowing oneself to be touched by the other's experience.

Techniques of the soul

Equally interesting is the gaze Irigaray turns to the world of yoga. Even though (or precisely because) yoga has become integral to her life, her gaze is respectful yet not devoid of critical remarks, which is not the case with so many among the newly converted. Some of her observations focus on the fact that within yoga, as with Western culture, there is no consideration in the educational process of gendered identity and the coexistence between the sexes. She denounces the generalized attitude of conceit her questions were met with. In relation to the possibilities open to a 'culture of energy', she observed:

> There is nothing to stop knowledge of energy from becoming the vehicle for a carnal and spiritual relation between man and woman, a dual and reciprocal relation, in which the genders are united as micro- and macrocosmic humanity.
>
> *(Irigaray, 1996, pp. 137–138)*

But she goes further. One of the greatest dangers a yoga practitioner can run into is, according to her, that of reducing the practice to mere technical apprenticeship of postures and various types of breathing. In this way, by subordinating one's life to a technique without fully endowing it with meaning, yoga practice is reduced to one prosthesis among others. The path thus taken will produce an ego boost, with greater interest in reaching increasingly higher levels of competitive performance.

It is timely to consider here Max Scheler's distinction between the development of 'external techniques' or 'nature techniques' characteristic of the West and the development of the 'internal techniques' or 'techniques of the soul' that are more typical of the East.

The impression one has, more than half a century after "turning East" (Cox, 1977) and having witnessed a growing interest in Eastern contemplative practices, is that this move has happened without looking closely at the problem of *téchne* as dominant characteristic of the way of being in contemporary society (and of a Western world that globalizes the entire planet) through which everything is reduced and manipulated to the level of mere instrumentality and to a product to be consumed. Did we ask ourselves whether 'techniques of nature' and 'techniques of the soul' both reveal the same objective? Or do they express something different because the latter rest on a fundamental gratuity where there is no gain or loss? By transposing instead, *sic et simpliciter*, the modalities of 'external techniques' to 'internal' ones, meditative practices become impoverished whilst remaining, at the same time ensnared within the technocratic narrative of instrumental reason, the dominant myth of the West, thus becoming unintentional missionaries of this paradigm within inner and not yet colonized regions.

Enlightenment in two

Still within the original and creative link she established with the world of yoga, Irigaray elaborates on some points that place her, compared to the majority of the relevant literature, on a decisively heretical position. Besides, a *Leitmotiv* in the book is the invitation to become ourselves bridges among different traditions. She critiques, for instance, the notion that *samādhi* (understood, at least within the yogic tradition, as the final point of the yogi's path and variously translated as union, totality, absorption, complete concentration etc.) must necessarily imply the abolition of the dualism subject/object as Patañjali and other authors maintain. She instead emphasizes how this state is reached by *maintaining* the duality, yet transforming the way we perceive it, thus achieving ecstasy in relation to the other. It is then this irreducible duality that leads me to a type of *samādhi* rooted in life itself. Here too we see emerging a keen awareness of the dual dimension, to the point where she suggests for this approach the expression *enlightenment in two*. One could perhaps describe the process Irigaray refers to in the following way. There is, first of all, a surplus of messages and perceptions one receives from the other via a radical opening, an exit from oneself, still within the subject's witnessing awareness. Secondly, starting from this widening of experience, the recognition takes place of an irreducible nucleus present in the other, which constitutes his or her most profound mystery. The latter prolongs and completes the ecstatic condition.

This brings to mind, incidentally, the work of Claudio Naranjo (1993), who proposed a meditative practice within an interpersonal context, aiming to bring together elements of Gestalt therapy and *vipassana* meditation (the latter focused on the awareness of sensorial and mental stimuli).

Beyond East and West

We also find in Irigaray a separate reflection on the link between speech and silence. To find in oneself a point of meeting of Western and Eastern cultures means, for her, giving a different meaning to both speech and silence, keeping them together rather than in opposition to each other.

The West would represent a path that recognizes the primacy of speech, while the East would be a world where greater emphasis is placed on silence. In order to be able to communicate truly and be present to my own speech, I must forever return to silence, where I find myself again by going back to the source of that which says 'I'. From that place, I also come to see that I do not know, nor will I ever be able to know everything. From there I can open myself to the truth of the other's speech. But her meditation on the rapport between speech and silence along the East/West axis is yet more nuanced. If we were to assign to the Western tradition (and primarily to Christianity) the primacy of the word, where would we then place Eastern, non-Christian authors who represent the very peak of speech and thought? Where would we place Buddha, Shankara and Nagarjuna (to name only a few within the Indian tradition alone)? And what are we to do – to quote randomly a few names from Christianity – of *hesychia* and of the Desert's Fathers, of apophaticism and the entire mystical tradition of not-knowing (from Diogenes the Areopagite onwards), of the Trappist tradition (up to Thomas Merton), or of the Quakers silent meetings?

What I am stressing here is the fact that we find problematic elements in both cultures – speech coming from silence and going back to silence – yet with different approaches and different emphases. And it is not only that. Is the objective of bridging East and West the most necessary and sufficient step, or is there more? Is it not possible today, in our globalized planet, to encounter a new and unknown scenario, a radical *novum* that no longer recognizes as satisfactory a synthesis between worlds that are already given, already known, both Eastern and Western? My answer would be yes: without polemics or particular nostalgic preference for this or that, walking on along the path of the counter-tradition, on a path that may truly go beyond East and West. Perhaps the times we live in demand it.

Note

1 The title *A New Culture of Energy*, at the time of writing, did not come out in the original French, nor has it been translated into English. All translations of passages from this book are by Manu Bazzano.

References

Adorno, T. (1978) *Minima Moralia: Reflections from a Damaged Life*. Translated by E. P. Jephcott. London: Verso. Originally published in 1951.
Bataille, G. (1992) *On Nietzsche*. Translated by B. Boone. New York: Paragon.
Bryant, E. F. (2013) *The Yoga-Sutras of Patañjali*. San Francisco: North Point Press.

Cox, H. (1977) *Turning East*. London: Simon & Schuster.
Irigaray, L. (1985) *Speculum of the Other Woman*. Translated by G. C. Gill. Ithaca, NY: Cornell University Press.
Irigaray, L. (1991) *Marine Lover of Friedrich Nietzsche*. Translated by G. C. Gill. New York: Columbia University Press.
Irigaray, L. (1996) *I Love to You: Sketches for a Felicity Within History*. Translated by A. Martin. New York & London: Routledge.
Irigaray, L. (2011) *Una Nuova Cultura dell'Energia*. Translated by Paola Carmagnani. Torino: Bollati Boringhieri.
Jabes, E. (1991) *The Book of Questions, Vol. 1*. Hanover: University Press.
Leloup, J.Y. (1994) *Avere cura dell'essere: Filone e i Terapeuti d'Alessandria*. Rome: Arkeios.
Naranjo, C. (1993) *Gestalt Therapy: The Attitude and Practice of an Atheoretical Experientialism*. Nevada City, CA: Gateways.
Nietzsche, F. (1997) *Thus Spake Zarathustra*. Ware, Herts: Wordsworth Editions.
Varela, F. J. (1999) *Ethical Know-How*. Stanford, CA: Stanford University Press.

PART IV
Therapy, language, metaphysics

Language is a given. It is the measure of us and at the same time the force we use to measure. Yet we are not slaves of language, as some would have us believe. We can create language anew, when striving to communicate something for which no words were invented yet. The images language can evoke make us feel alive or dead; we use it as both healer and weapon, while *reason* mistakes it for a tool. It is instead a form of life that acknowledges our existence in the world and simultaneously creates a quasi-existence of the world itself. The world in an important sense does not exist but for that which we can say about it, and we are saying something about it in every utterance. What we do say then, can be profound.

But what does this saying amount to? In these next pages, we will read that saying is about seeing and showing: Wittgenstein, Schopenhauer and Nietzsche – all of them visionaries of the ordinary that becomes extraordinary. These writers are spectacularly of the world encountered as they each defy linear analysis and rational twist. Instead they describe their scene, and therefore our scene, as poets and voyeurs, witnesses to sites of performance within the context of everything and yet nothing in particular: witnesses to our very existence. This stance at times refreshingly forgets psychotherapy and philosophy's compulsion to and excessive reliance on metaphysics. If at times it appears to court the latter, it does so from an *artistic* rather than *foundational* understanding: what then seems as a metaphysical stance (for example the notion of the eternal recurrence out of which Amor Fati emerges [see Chapter 17]) becomes a (momentary, necessary) act of creation rather than a longing for eternity.

14

UNDER ARREST

Wittgenstein and perspicuity

Julie Webb

Introduction

When Ludwig Wittgenstein states that "[i]t is not *how* things are in the world that is mystical, but *that* it exists" (Wittgenstein, 2001a, p. 88, §6.44), I am instantly arrested and *feel* myself to know what he means, and yet he has stated no fact in the world. He has instead described a kind of mystery that is both tangible and elusive. Amongst other things, Wittgenstein was concerned with language and description (Malcolm, 1988), not least his own claim that philosophy itself is nothing more than an activity of clarification, an activity that might lead us to perspicuous representation.

As a therapist and trainer in the humanistic tradition, I am engaged in describing and redescribing until perspicuity in any given moment is reached: that moment when we *feel* that pennies have dropped and light bulbs have been illuminated. These *feelings* of dropping into place and illumination are not only about saying but rather showing and *seeing*, a phenomenological impact of language. This chapter will consider the humanistic approach to therapy as a kind of anti-therapy, against the current tendency that sees therapy as treating the human condition as a series of problems to be solved rather than as a life to be experienced.

Wittgenstein's work has in a very important sense arrested me. I am stolen. It is a challenging task to keep up to date with current ideas and yet stay attuned to living in the truthfulness of the moment of encounter with my client, which is free from a predetermined and assumed *knowing*. I find that it is the work of Wittgenstein that yanks back the reins when I find myself falling into hubris.

Why do I express my admiration for this particular philosopher who is reputed to have been irascible, difficult and intense and who described his job of being a professor of philosophy as "absurd [and] a kind of living death" (Monk, 1990, p. 483)? Maybe sometimes I too feel that my job is absurd: I aid others in their process of redescribing their lived experience so that in some way it may be easier to bear. I often inform a new cohort of trainees that I cannot teach them anything, that any theories I offer them are merely descriptions of the work they are about to embark upon. I also inform them that nothing is hidden: we do not have to look behind a client or ourselves but rather see and trust, that everything is before us in the moment that we experience it, even the confusion, the mystery and the disturbance. I make these statements quite sincerely, and as I utter the words I experience my own feelings of inadequacy and vulnerability. I find myself smiling at the absurdity of our situation – of having to learn to be ourselves or rather to be more accurate, to surrender to the process of becoming ourselves whilst being able to hear what other persons are telling us in their moments of doubt. Perhaps I too recognize my own struggle and tendency for intense irascibility and find myself at home in the work of someone who seemed driven by the tortuous condition that is all too human: a passion to go on clarifying, a passion to reach something and all the while knowing that sometimes we cannot reach, cannot articulate, and that the mystery of the unreachable and the inarticulate are indeed clarifications in themselves.

How to live with not knowing, with not being able to reach or articulate may throw us into a kind of vertigo, unless we can create a suitable description to counter our sense of falling. I feel that it is this lack of articulation that we are primarily engaged in as therapists when we aid the client to find his own way to stabilize his fall or aid him by accompaniment during his descent or in his anxiety of ascending. Our task, as I see it, is to listen to one another and aim to do this in a spirit of openness and truthfulness. It seems reasonable to me then to assert in a Wittgensteinian sense, that *we had better be articulate*, and that does not mean to have a ready-made answer; neither does it mean being clever. For Wittgenstein, articulation is about clarity and not being clever, not least because there is nothing clever about seeing what is before our eyes – we just have to open them. This is not to suggest that any view is a complete image once and for all time and that all we have to do is locate it as though it were pre-existing somehow, but rather that we must come to recognize the view that we experience ourselves in at any given moment and further acknowledge that the view is our creation too.

One of the attractive things about his work for me is that he shows his clarification journey, or as Heaton puts it, "Wittgenstein's writing is to show his practice, not just to talk around it. In this it is like a work of art where form and content are one" (2013, p. 62). Talking therapy works like this too; as a kind of artistry, with no hiding place because our workings out and maybe wrong turns through our journey of clarification are all present in the room with us.

How do we take these wrong turns? According to Wittgenstein, "Philosophy is a battle against the bewitchment of our intelligence by means of our language" (2001b, p. 40, §109). Philosophy is the activity of speaking clearly amidst the battle of our confusion. Philosophy itself is an activity of describing that can lead to clarity and therefore may remedy our muddle. It is not a doctrine, a body of knowledge, a library of answers, a science of the mind or indeed a moral barometer.

Everything that it is not shows us what it is: a library packed full to the rafters with descriptions of what it is to be human. In the Preface to *Philosophical Investigations* (Wittgenstein, 2001b, p. ix), Wittgenstein states that he offers us "philosophical remarks . . . a number of sketches of landscapes", as descriptions of the human landscape that is always being approached afresh from different directions. 'Different directions' suggests seeing from many angles, with constant movement and refreshment, and a strong belief in the unstable, uncertain, yet creative ongoing process of becoming.

Potent description

I began my counsellor training with just this understanding in mind and had considered that counselling and psychotherapy were in fact philosophy in practice, what might be described as *description therapy* as opposed to *prescription therapy*. In his work, "Wittgenstein used alchemy of the word, for words are potential magic with a power that can transform experience" (Heaton, 2000, p. 28), and to date I have not been swayed from the notion that this is what I am engaged with in talking therapy. How often have I heard words that ignite my heart, evoke tears of sadness and raise my temper? In her powerful, immensely valuable yet often ignored work on *Fragile Process*, Margaret Warner states that "language is the expression in words of an experience that creates the image" (2008). When images are created, they can evoke and trigger all sorts of feelings within us, and those feelings can alert us to what is significant in our lives. Warner's work is pertinent because it reminds us of the power of language and how its use can be precarious, which makes it easy for us to 'annihilate' another person's experience by attempting to change it or by not paying close attention to it.

This is challenging in a profession where the dominant trend are the medical model, cognitivism, and the first tentative and as yet uncertain forays into neuroscience as a declaration of truth, fact and knowing – a profession that is fast turning to *prescriptive* technique instead of a *descriptive* methodology. That is not to say that these models have no value but rather that adhering to their explanations too tightly is at best a misunderstanding of the human condition and at worst an ethical blunder.

Wittgenstein states, "We must do away with all explanation, and description alone must take its place" (Wittgenstein, 2001b, p. 40, §109). This can be challenging because clients often arrive with a rigid, ready-made explanation of their predicament and their subsequent approach to addressing it. However, language as our "form of life" (ibid, p. 75, §241) means that, for Wittgenstein, meaning via language can only be obtained by the way it is used:

> Ask yourself: on what occasion, for what purpose, do we say this? What kind of actions accompany these words? (Think of a greeting.) In what scenes are they used: and what for?
>
> *(Wittgenstein, 2001b, p. 116, §489)*

Describing the use of language in this way alerts us to the notion that language is always 'doing' something and that words are always articulated within a context; the circumstances, predicament and situation that we find ourselves in:

> A main source of our failure to understand is that we do not command a clear view of the use of our words. Our grammar is lacking in this sort of perspicuity. A perspicuous representation produces just that understanding which consists in 'seeing connections' . . . The concept of a perspicuous representation is of fundamental significance for us. It earmarks the form of account we give, the way we look at things.
> (Wittgenstein, 2001b, p. 42, §122)

We must use ordinary language that paints a picture of the ordinary life in our view, and we must pay attention to the nuances of the arrangement of our words as we articulate them and experience them in the moment. In therapy, I must pay this type of attention to the language used by my client. If I infer meaning from *outside* my client's expression, *independently* of our encounter, not only do I miss my client, but I assume to know something of her experience that she herself does not know and that places me in the role of authority, with any possibility of ethical creation vanishing. The kind of ethics I refer to here are the ethics borne of our encounter, not as an act of equality, or acknowledgement of difference but rather a more explicit and vital act of surrender to my experience with and for the other without discounting or annihilating her experience. This subsequently becomes a delicate matter of affirmation rather than a site of justification.

Arrest and dissolve

In the therapy space, my client has arrived knowing that something is wrong; already he is on the philosophical battleground, and I join him there. It has been my experience that when particular words are used between us and we hit upon that 'perspicuous representation' that accurately describes his predicament, then just like the experience of poetry he will be stirred; he will be moved to feel something. The stirring that takes place is the truth of his experience of *seeing* that was alive in his language and can go a long way towards dissolving (not solving) his muddle and allowing space to create anew. Think of your favourite poem or lyric from a song, and notice how the words travel through your whole being, taking you on a journey of experiential delight or maybe even despair. In my experience both as a client and as a therapist, words can flow between us creating a spontaneous rhythm, and sometimes they hit the body and all at once we see something and are stirred, if not completely arrested. We have no way of knowing which words will have this impact until we stumble upon them, but when we do, we are surely stolen.

As a therapist I have no way of knowing what the client will say, what my response will be and how whatever is created will impact either one of us. For sure, as a therapist I will take my lead from the client and his language, for to begin with at least, it is *his* bewitchment that we will be battling with. This battleground is the space between what is already expressed in the client's distress and what has yet to be expressed in therapy. To understand language in the way Wittgenstein describes it, then, makes language a phenomenological process. If this were not the case, poetry, song and lyric would not be able to move us the way they do.

In the *Tractatus Logico-Philosophicus* (Wittgenstein, 2001a), Wittgenstein claims that not everything can be said: "There are indeed, things that cannot be put into words. They make themselves manifest. They are what is mystical" (p. 88, §6.522).

It is this 'mysticism' of the unsaid that Alain Badiou considers to be the transformative power of poetry, that sits at the edge of language and so does not fall prey to the "trap of theory" (Badiou, 2011, p. 176). He writes:

> A poetic composition is an assemblage that makes language say what it does not say, or that shows materially the unsaid of saying. The place of the act is thus summoned at the edges of linguistic equivocation, as the unsaid resource of the latter's powerfulness.
>
> *(Badiou, 2011, p. 177)*

This seems to point to the idea that it is the image borne from the clarification itself that finally arrests us, which is not as a result of a mathematical or logical operation, or of a scientific experiment, or of the evaluation of a therapeutic 'intervention', but rather a 'showing' of how life appears to be – the view before our eyes. The arrest that I feel being under when I am seized by the image that I experience is the 'material unsaid of saying'. When my client and I create that poetic composition, his arrest is not thinking nor saying but *seeing*, and he is *arrested* by his view.

> The antiphilosophical act consists in letting what there is show itself, insofar as "what there is" is precisely that which no true proposition can say ... this 'letting be' has the non-propositional form of pure showing, of *clarity*, and because such clarity befalls the unsayable only in the thoughtless form of an oeuvre.
>
> *(Badiou, 2011, p. 80)*

Language as an art form and a life form is a kind of 'way into' our experience – the very tool and form of life that may allow us to experience the mystery of a situation and sometimes the very awe of our existence. Badiou describes philosophy claiming propositional knowledge as a 'not':

> ... of which the fabulation about 'truth' are the clothing, the propaganda, the lies ... Philosophy is a sick and regressive non-thought, because it pretends to present the nonsense that is proper to it within a propositional and theoretical register.
>
> *(Badiou, 2011, pp. 75, 77)*

Whilst this claim may sound grand, idealistic or impossible, the words fire my passion and hit my body like a bow from Cupid because this description of philosophy is one that I also consider to describe the current state in the world of therapy. Like Badiou's description of anti-philosophy, the kind of therapy I am describing, as a chance and a dance in poetry, becomes a kind of anti-therapy, whereby the moment of clarity is shown and silently experienced outside all theoretical frameworks and bindings, and instead our conversation has articulated the view that the client sees before him, and he is all at once arrested. If one was to swap Badiou's word 'philosophy' for 'therapy', one could state that "*therapy is a not, of which the fabulation about 'truth' are the clothing, the propaganda, the lies*". Therapy is engaged with what can be described; it makes visible the human condition that is already in view. It cannot cure the human condition. I cannot be cured of my pain and suffering, my grief and longing, my desires and limitations and so forth. At best I can come to see these conditions as they can be shown to me through my activity in language and my experience of the image the words describe and clarify. Only then, as a consequence, my confusion may dissolve.

A chance and a dance

Poetry stirs me; it arrests my body. The arrest is phenomenological. The impact of poetry, then, may be likened to Wittgenstein's silent mysticism where Badiou's "authentic non-thought dwells" (Badiou, 2011, p. 79), the touching of the real. Therapy seen in this view becomes an art-like poetry where clarity is reached in thoughtless arrest, as a kind of mysterious embodiment of the description that is the image of our life. I often have this reaction when I engage with poetry. The artistry of sometimes just a few words can create such profound images of lived experience, and yet the moment I feel I have seen the riddle, touched the real, it is gone from me, and no matter how I try I cannot describe accurately what it was that I touched, but something in me will have altered. Occasionally clients come to the end of therapy and share with me that they don't really know how they have arrived at a point of clarity. They can describe specific moments that seemed to have great impact but usually end up laughing at the idea that all we did was talk! Somehow in our activity of describing, it seemed that the client touched something of the real.

This idea of authentic non-thought via the activity of pursuing perspicuous description that the client and I are involved in, has implications for the notion of empathy within the therapeutic encounter. Carl Rogers considered empathy to be one of the necessary and sufficient conditions for therapeutic personality change; he refined his ideas about empathy constantly throughout his life as he developed more and more his ideas about presence in therapy (Schmid, 2001).

In the spirit of this discussion, empathy, both valuable and powerful, becomes nothing more than my creative ability to imagine and describe, and it is upon me to widen my imaginative capacity. If I can widen my capacity and surrender to the delicate, intangible quality of empathy in order to imagine the client's world from the description she presents and allow myself to be arrested by it, then I open up the possibility to meet this person and be of assistance. Rogers states:

> When empathy is at its best, the two individuals are participating in a process which may be compared to that of a couple dancing, the client leading, the therapist following: the smooth spontaneous back-and-forth flow of energy in the interaction has its own aesthetic rhythm.
>
> (Raskin & Rogers, in Schmid, 2001, p. 157)

I often refer to therapy as a chance and a dance, both in my practice as a therapist and as a trainer. For me it is a chance and dance with words. With every word, my client describes her world, her place within it, and her place in it with others. Understanding language and empathy in this way is to understand our work as therapists as a kind of poetic ethical encounter. Ethics, as Heaton writes:

> calls for a response from the therapist using words perspicaciously, which are simple, and are ideally spoken without a touch of ill-feeling, contempt, arrogance, bias, frivolity, jargon or word intoxication. This transformational discourse does not call for theories explanations and a technical vocabulary, as it is fundamentally an ethical struggle.
>
> (Heaton, 2013, p. 31)

This ethical struggle to meet a client in truthfulness requires then a homely language and not a theoretical bias with a technical language that creates a "chatter behind their back [that becomes] the production of knowledge rather than truthfulness between two people" (Heaton, 2013, p. 27).

Language – its use, instability and slipperiness – is pertinent to the humanistic premise for the *process of becoming*. I have often engaged with my client, and we seemed to hit upon a description that illuminated something and had great power for her, only for her to arrive the following week needing to extend that description further. Empathy and ethics deem it inappropriate to fix my client to any description or momentary clarification or even fix her to a singular narrative. Instead I must come to accept that the moment has passed for both of us, and we carry on until the client can come to be able to articulate the view by herself in a way that somehow arrests her and she feels at home in it regardless of its changing face.

I have advocated surrender to becoming and invited the reader to entertain the notion of therapy as anti-therapy, as a counter to our current trend of 'quick-fix' therapy. Both of these are elucidated further by the following remark from Wittgenstein towards the end of the *Tractatus*:

> We feel that even when all possible scientific questions have been answered, the problems of life remain completely untouched. Of course there are then no questions left, and this is the answer.
>
> (Wittgenstein, 2001a, p. 88, §6.52)

Our problems seem to be created by our encounter with one another, by our phenomenological experience of being in the world, as well as by the lack of clarity that we hold about the mysteriousness of our existence. Our problems described this way suggest that they are philosophical problems and not scientific puzzles to be solved.

Of course, this idea has far-reaching consequences in counselling and psychotherapy training, an area that is fast being seized by academia and its paraphernalia of objectives, targets, *Ofsted* quality controls and grand certification leading to the status of *professional*, which seems at times to pay no heed to the philosophical discourses that underpin such a profession. To pay such heed would be to challenge the requirements of the market- and government-driven notions of well-being in order to keep a work force working, and quick-fix, six–week, problem-solving agendas. Heaton elucidates further:

> The talking 'cure' cannot be taught systematically in the way of natural sciences. It is grounded in practice rather than theory, apprenticeship rather than lectures. It must remain open to the hurly-burly of human life. Its language is incomplete and changes according to the speaker and the person addressed.
> *(Heaton, 2013, p. 62)*

Puzzles and muddles

Much is written about Wittgenstein's work, as well as the debate about which of his works are valid and claims about how much he changed his ideas from one to the other of his works. The *Tractatus Logico-Philosophicus* is the only work published in his lifetime, and, whilst Alain Badiou states that "it is certainly not unreasonable to hold that Wittgenstein has been a hero of our time" (Badiou, 2011, p. 73), he considers only the *Tractatus* legitimate as a representation of his anti-philosophy. Others consider that *Philosophical Investigations*, published posthumously, is the more important work and suggest that it puts right the mistakes in the *Tractatus*. I find elucidations in both that can show us something of the impact in the use of our language. As a practitioner in the field of talking therapy, I regard these elucidations as significant in my work.

Language as a form of life that we cannot escape is also our activity in perspicuously describing what we see before us, as we experience it – as we live it. We might call this activity 'philosophy'. Clarity may be experienced as full arrest, whereupon we come to embody the description as an artful impact of showing ourselves clearly. This showing that we experience as an *unsaid* is a phenomenological experience that may bring us relief from our muddle and create enough space for us then to make choices for our lives. This space is important because gaining clarity may not be enough, and in the end, as Taizan Maezumi states, "Of course just seeing this is not enough. You must live that life" (2001, p. 81). It seems that when we come to see, all the existential tensions of how we then go on to lead our lives anew may come flooding to the fore, even if they were implicit in our narrative all along. It seems to me that a descriptive technique supports those existential tensions and paradoxes of life such as knowing/not knowing, living/dying, certainty/uncertainty without prizing either polarity but rather acknowledging our challenge to hold these tensions and finding the courage to make new, whilst accepting as fully as is possible, that this situation we find ourselves in *is* the human condition.

Wittgenstein wrote, "[M]y talent for Philosophy consists in continuing to be puzzled when others have let the puzzlement slip away" (cited in Malcolm, 1988, p. 136). This puzzlement seems to me to be a kind of wonder that is continually making anew, and it is this attitude that keeps me engaged in my work as a therapist; an attitude, which I feel is also an acknowledgement, of the wonder that I exist at all, not as a series of problems to be solved but as flesh and blood in the process of becoming human.

References

Badiou, A. (2011) *Wittgenstein's Antiphilosophy*. Verso: London.
Heaton, J. M. (2000) *Wittgenstein and Psychoanalysis*. Icon Books: Cambridge; Totem Books: New York.
Heaton, J. M. (2013) *The Talking Cure: Wittgenstein on Language as Bewitchment & Clarity*. Palgrave Macmillan: London.
Maezumi, T. (2001) *Appreciate Your Life: The Essence of Zen Practice*. Shambhala Publications: Boston.
Malcolm, N. (1988) *Wittgenstein: Nothing Is Hidden*. Basil Blackwell: Oxford.
Monk, R. (1990) *Ludwig Wittgenstein: The Duty of Genius*. London: Jonathan Cape.
Schmid, P. (2001) 'In Comprehension: The Art of Not Knowing. Dialogical and Ethical Perspectives on Empathy as Dialogue in Personal and Person-centred Relationships'. In Haugh, S., and Merry, T. (Eds.) *Rogers' Therapeutic Conditions: Evolution, Theory and Practice, Vol. 2: Empathy*. PCCS Books: Ross-on-Wye.
Warner, M. (2008) Audio recording of a workshop on *Fragile Process* given in Milton Keynes. Online Events: West Lothian.
Wittgenstein, L. (2001a) *Tractatus Logico-Philosophicus*. Routledge: Oxon.
Wittgenstein, L. (2001b) *Philosophical Investigations*. Blackwell: Oxford.

15

A PENETRATING BEAM OF DARKNESS[1]

John Mackessy

There's a joke, from Russia I believe, about a man who always buys his shoes a half-size too small. A friend, a constant witness to his pain, asks him why he does so: "Doesn't it hurt terribly?" he asks. "Yes, *of course* it hurts," the man replies testily, "but ... when I take them off", he says, a broad smile spreading across his face, "... the relief!"

The reputation of Schopenhauer in Western philosophy is that of arch-pessimist, and the joke tallies well with his depiction of human happiness. In the world of Schopenhauer, the shoes are always half a size too tight; suffering is the core of existence and happiness but a momentary relief. There is also indication, not only from his writings but from accounts of his personal life, that he was misanthropic, misogynist and curmudgeonly. At lunch he ate alone, reserving an extra place so that no one could engage him in conversation. In a significant incident in his life, he was forced to pay ongoing compensation to a maid, who had made too much noise, for having pushed her down a flight of stairs. His best friend was his dog, Ātma, whom he would scold by calling him "Human!" when he misbehaved.

None of the central ideas in his magnum opus, *The World as Will and Representation*, completed in 1818, is glowingly optimistic. However, despite my own morbid proclivities, I cannot describe myself as a committed Schopenhauerian. To do so, one would need to attest to an 'anti-natalist' credo. Sadly, I cannot put my hand on my heart and say, as Schopenhauer does in *On the Vanity of Existence*, that it would be better never to have been born: "That human life must be some kind of mistake ..." (Schopenhauer, 2004, p. 53). His choice of the word 'mistake' is telling. It is quite different from 'accident' in that it implies volition or intention, albeit a misguided one. Willing life or *the willing of the* world is an error. This is the main thesis of his philosophy.

I welcomed the opportunity to write this chapter because in Schopenhauer I experience the clear and distinct impression of genius – a person capable of sustaining an insight tellingly different from his contemporaries' and from the world at large. In his introduction to Schopenhauer's *Essays & Aphorisms* (Schopenhauer, 2004), Hollingdale depicts this as 'obstinacy' and Schopenhauer's philosophy as an extension and justification of his pessimistic nature (Schopenhauer, 2004, pp. 22–26). I'm sure there is some truth in this, but it is an obstinacy and contrariness that, I believe, has value to anyone examining the shibboleths of culture and society, including psychotherapy.

For example, against his contemporaries and various traditions in philosophy and religion, he challenged an amorphous though palpable consensus on the positive value of life, albeit that this 'value' may be cashed out elsewhere – such as in paradise etc.

While others might be willing to paper over cracks or see a beautiful sunset at the end of the journey, Schopenhauer depicts the prevalence of suffering and brutality in existence. In considering the balance of pleasure and pain in life, he asks us to "compare the feelings of an animal engaged in eating another with those of the animal being eaten" (Schopenhauer, 2004, p. 42). This, he feels, gives us an accurate depiction of the economy of suffering/pleasure in the world. Or, more mundanely, one might reflect upon the amount of pleasure one could possibly receive though one's big toe compared to the experience of stubbing it against the end of the bed. Perhaps the *mistake* that Schopenhauer refers to is that we appear to be better 'designed' for suffering than for perfection or even for everyday happiness.

Schopenhauer is less than sanguine in asking us to think the unthinkable. He doubts not only our motives but our willingness and ability to think and have insight into ourselves. As creatures, we think when we must, as a means to an end. Behind many considerations there lies the constant question of how the world, nature and society pull the wool over our eyes or, rather, how we are complicit in deluding ourselves about life. Long in advance of Freud, he depicts us as "unknown to ourselves", as driven creatures who infrequently have insight into our own motives and then often only after the fact.

In his essay *On Ethics*, this famous misanthrope, addressing the theme of human motives and hypocrisy, writes movingly of slavery and both human and animal subjugation and exploitation (see Schopenhauer, 2004, pp. 136–139). Referring to his contemporaries, he writes that:

> *optimism*, where it is not merely the thoughtless talk of those who harbour nothing but words under their shallow foreheads, seems to me to be not merely an absurd, but also a really *wicked*, way of thinking, a bitter mockery of the unspeakable sufferings of mankind.
>
> *(Schopenhauer, 1969, p. 325)*

Schopenhauer saw optimism not only as an evasion of the truth but as a complacent and self-serving failure of compassion – a brutality towards others. Here he reminds me of William Burroughs' description of "the naked lunch", as "a frozen moment when everyone sees what is on the end of every fork" (Burroughs, 1982, p. 1).

Beyond this suspicion of our motives, Schopenhauer is, perhaps, a specialist in *disgust*, and his narrative of disgust is focused squarely on his own species. He sees humanity as different from its animal brethren in that "man is the only animal which causes pain to others with no other object than causing pain." (Schopenhauer, 2004, p. 139). Perhaps contradicting himself somewhat, he states in the same essay, "Man is at bottom a dreadful wild animal. We know this wild animal only in the tamed state called civilization and we are therefore shocked by the occasional outbreaks of its true nature" (Schopenhauer, 2004, p. 138).

Schopenhauer believes that we habitually delude ourselves, when we consider man primarily as a rational creature. Plato's Philosopher King is not extolled by Schopenhauer. So, initially I was surprised to discover that Schopenhauer's great philosophical heroes were Plato and Kant, as their philosophies are forms of 'idealism'. Oversimplifying, idealism might be associated with philosophers who try to reduce the world to ideas and to make ideas into the world. Plato and Kant would have retreated to the library at one glimpse of the salivating beast that Schopenhauer presents as man. Likewise, for them, the irrational has too much of the smell of humanity about it. It was only much later with Freud and his notion of the id that Schopenhauer's ideas regarding irrationality really began to achieve currency, if not credit.

In reading accounts of Schopenhauer's ideas, it is often easy to think one is reading Freud. For instance, when Janaway writes that:

> [m]ost importantly, the human psyche can be seen as split: comprising not only capacities for understanding and rational thought, but at a deeper level also an essentially 'blind' process of striving, which governs, but can also conflict with, the conscious portions of our nature.
>
> *(Janaway, 2002, p. 7)*

For Freud, as for Schopenhauer, this never-ending conflict, both intrapsychic and interpersonal, defines the nature of human existence.

Will

Despite acknowledging the battle of existence, Schopenhauer, like his philosophical forebears, was also in retreat from life, though not like a timid *debutante* or prissy academic but rather as a man afflicted with the pox. At the heart of Schopenhauer's philosophy is not the *logos* but the *Will*, with all its striving, iniquity and ignorance. Desire and philosophy had not really encountered one another so *physically* before Schopenhauer.

Schopenhauer sees us not primarily as free, conscious and rational agents but as beings driven by desire, particularly the desire to *be*. Yet he sees all of this in terms of *Will to Life*, often simply rendered as 'Will', which seems strange as we tend to employ 'Will' in everyday parlance in terms of individual conscious volitions and purposes. Schopenhauer, even when viewing Will at an individual level, sees it as a universal drive quite beyond us and at the heart of everything that exists.

Writing more than forty years before Darwin's *On the Origin of Species*, Schopenhauer depicts Will as a 'blind striving' to be and to become – survival and reproduction being key to this. It is interesting that, like evolution's 'blind watchmaker', Schopenhauer also sees the Will as having no end or purpose beyond this. Among his contemporaries he was thus isolated in this critique of teleological thinking. He did not believe we were progressing, just stumbling onwards with hungry bellies.

This also may help us understand Schopenhauer's economy of pleasure and pain. From a survival perspective, it may be that pain has more utility than pleasure; hence our 'design'. In this context, Schopenhauer's Will can be destructive and even 'insane' in how it pursues its 'purpose'. In order *to live*, the world consumes its own flesh and rages in murderous battle against itself. It is the egoism of Will as it becomes instantiated in the individual that sets this cannibalistic battle *en train*: Of the "inborn nature of man . . . the first and foremost quality is a colossal egoism ready and eager to overstep the bounds of justice" (Schopenhauer, 2004, p. 139). The ancient aphorism *homo homini lupus* – 'man is a wolf to man' – sums up our species for Schopenhauer.

Like Darwin and Freud, Schopenhauer views the world through the lens of a particular 'drive', with other aspects of our being 'serving' this drive. As just outlined, he sees our rationality mainly as an extension of desire, with the development of intellect being a wholly practical expression of 'the *Will to Life*'. Because of this Will, we are born into inexorable striving and a struggle for existence. Perhaps the most immediate example of this is that several times each minute we are compelled, on pain of death, to wrest something from the world – to breathe. Despite an effort to hold our breath, we are compelled to suck in that air. We consume much else and labour for our living. Even our guts and organs have *work* to do. Schopenhauer emphasized that existence demands tremendous effort just to obtain the basic necessities. There is no rest for the wicked, and we are for Schopenhauer profoundly wicked.

But how can Schopenhauer possibly justify his emphasis upon life as struggle, life as suffering – making these aspects of life ubiquitously figural in his work? He would argue, that it is not his pessimistic temperament that makes things thus but the nature and structure of *phenomenal* existence and experience itself. As soon as Will becomes divided, as happens within the phenomenal world when it is instantiated in individual persons, the individual experiences resistance – opposition from the world and from others. It experiences difference, separateness, alienation and, importantly, lack. His Majesty, the baby (to use Freud's phrase), is forced to encounter a reality not subject to his will. Or, in Schopenhauer's terminology, to be born an individual is to be born an egoist:

> [E]very individual, completely vanishing and reduced to nothing in a boundless world, nevertheless makes himself the centre of the world, and considers his own existence and well-being before everything else. In fact, from the

natural standpoint, he is ready for this to sacrifice everything else; he is ready to annihilate the world, in order to maintain his own self, that drop in the ocean, a little longer.

(Schopenhauer, 1969, p. 331)

Hence, the battle begins by the very fact of being an individual within this world, and Schopenhauer gives us a fascinating perspective on what, much later, Freud came to call 'narcissism'. He goes beyond moral judgement of 'egoism' to explain that each of us, naturally, experience ourselves as Will in its totality. He writes that "the will to live, is present whole and undivided in every single being, even the most insignificant, as completely as in all that have ever been, are or will be, taken together" (Schopenhauer, 2004, p. 142).

He believes that we experience ourselves in this way, as the "only real individual in a world" with others experienced as representations, "mere phantoms" (Schopenhauer, 1969, p. 103); yet the world refuses to comply with this sense of ourselves.

As regards the nature of the suffering entailed in this, I remember hearing the following, perhaps apocryphal, attributed to Lacan: "What does it matter how many lovers you have if none of them gives you the universe?" Desire and lack are limitless in Schopenhauer too. There is no sating the thirst of this creature that experiences itself as the whole but also as bereft, and which is 'denied' fulfilment at every turn. *This* is the 'mistake' of life under the *principium individuationis*.

This 'subject' in a world of phantoms and, with it, the questionable reality of the other bring us to a crucial difference between Schopenhauer and Nietzsche on the former's, perhaps surprising emphasis on 'compassion'. With the *principium individuationis*, the individualized Will, the stage is set for battle and for what we might now call 'narcissistic injury' and 'narcissistic rage', and, in Nietzsche, for *ressentiment* – the sly, vindictive wish for revenge of 'the weak'.

In his early life, Nietzsche idolized Schopenhauer, and, as is sometimes the case with the heroes of one's youth, he soon found him to have feet of clay. For Nietzsche, Schopenhauer became the philosopher par excellence of *ressentiment* – a man unable to affirm life, but who nurtured his grudge against the world, only to exact an "imaginary revenge" (Nietzsche, 1998, p. 22). Nietzsche felt that precisely such passive, phantastical 'revenge' lay behind another life-denying philosophy, Christianity, and its own espousal of compassion.

In the introduction to the *Genealogy of Morals*, Nietzsche explicitly frames much of this ethical thinking as a rebuttal of Schopenhauer. He writes of "the inexorable progress of the morality of compassion, which afflicted even the philosophers with its illness, as the most sinister symptom of the sinister development of our European culture". He adds that "the very *worthlessness* of compassion was formerly a point of agreement among philosophers" (Nietzsche, 1998, p. 7).

Nietzsche held that Schopenhauerian compassion is ultimately pernicious. The perceived strength of its threat occasions one of the most disparaged passages in Nietzsche's work:

> The *sickly* constitute the greatest danger to man: *not* the evil, *not* the 'predators'. Those who are from the outset victims, downtrodden, broken – they are the ones, the *weakest* are the ones who most undermine life among men, who most dangerously poison and question our trust in life, in man.
>
> *(Nietzsche, 1998, p. 101)*

Indeed what Nietzsche excoriates and rejects so forcibly in *The Genealogy* is the possibility that two qualities he associates with Schopenhauer – compassion and disgust – be conjoined. For this would lead to "'the last will of man', his will to nothingness" (Nietzsche, 1998, p. 101). So we now see where compassion, this "most sinister symptom", could lead – "Towards a new Buddhism? towards a European Buddhism? towards – nihilism . . ." (Nietzsche, 1998, p. 7).

Where Nietzsche presses forward to affirm the Will, Schopenhauer feels the endeavour to be misbegotten and egoistic, leading only to brutality and suffering. It is interesting to see how Nietzsche, a figure frequently associated with nihilism, vehemently denounces a nihilism he associates with Schopenhauer and with Buddhism.

It is true that compassion may lead one to ask, 'What of the others, those who cannot thus affirm life – the broken ones, the weak, the sickly? *What are we to do* with their "weakness" in the face of life and its iniquities?' As a therapist, I face this question every day. Engaging with these 'others' before me, with their depression and their 'weakness' has, of course, the potential to poison my 'trust in life'.

Is it perhaps more 'empowering' if I deny the base of my clients' sufferings and attribute them to 'weakness', maladaptation or cognitive distortion? Such origins may apply, but the pain and despair of humanity also say something important and valid about human experience, and it is, I believe, through compassion that we can touch this understanding. However, as regards Schopenhauer, I should say that some have indicated that, given his dark depiction of Will and thus too of human nature, it is not clear *how* the world he paints could contain altruism or how such a creature as man act from compassion. Whether this is simply a contradiction in his philosophy or indicative of a more meaningful paradox is an important question.

One of Schopenhauer's most powerful depictions of the human predicament and almost a definition of existential absurdity comes in his *Parerga and Paralipomena* (Schopenhauer, 2004):

> Our existence has no foundation on which to rest except the transient present. Thus its form is essentially unceasing motion, without any possibility of that repose which we continually strive after. It resembles the course of a man running down a mountain who would fall over if he tried to stop and can stay on his feet only by running on; or a pole balanced on the tip of the finger; or a planet which would fall into its sun if it ever ceased to plunge irresistibly forward. Thus existence is typified by unrest.
>
> *(Schopenhauer, 2004, p. 52)*

He continues that in such circumstances:

> ...no man is happy but strives his whole life long after a supposed happiness which he seldom attains, and even if he does it is only to be disappointed with it; as a rule, however, he finally enters harbour shipwrecked and dismasted.
> (Schopenhauer, 2004, p. 52)

In Schopenhauer's vision, the Will, the impetus of the runner, both originates the endeavour, the 'pursuit of happiness', and makes its fulfilment impossible. For him this *pursuit* of happiness is an absurdity – a perpetual round of Sisyphus and his boulder.

So we find in Schopenhauer the antithesis of the American Dream and consumerism's myth of ultimate satisfaction: life is *bad*, liberty *illusory*, and the pursuit of happiness is *the road to hell* . . . Remember, though, to exit through the gift shop.

Even when a happy ending is achieved, Schopenhauer would ask what happens *after* satisfaction, when the lovers walk off into the sunset or the final baddie is killed? Well, we find here the opposite pole of human experience. The runner keeps running because where need and desire end, *boredom* and *ennui* begin. For creatures like us – creatures of desire – to stop is to die, or at least to encounter *ennui*, and therein our own meaninglessness. We grow bored, we grow restless and we reach for the next thing. In a comment that could be used as a consumer warning, Schopenhauer writes:

> [T]he attained object never fulfils the promise held out by the desired object, namely the final appeasement of the excessive pressure of the will. He sees that, with fulfilment, the wish changes only its form, and now torments under another form; indeed, when at last all wishes are exhausted, the pressure of will itself remains, even without any recognized motive, and makes itself known with terrible pain as a feeling of the most frightful desolation and emptiness.
> (Schopenhauer, 1969, p. 363)

This certainly gives one pause. One of the reasons Schopenhauer appeals to me is that his work provides a corrective to some of the vacuous positivity abounding today in 'personal development', counselling and psychotherapy. Frequently, as a therapist, and certainly as a humanistic one, I hear such New Ageish nostrums as, 'You get the clients that you need'. Such an ethos of benign 'mysterious forces' is, for example, exemplified in the airport mysticism of Paulo Coelho. In his mythopoeic bestseller *The Alchemist*, Coelho has the wise Old King reassure Santiago, the seeker, that the entire cosmos is complicit in bringing his wishes to fruition (Coelho, 2005). In an alternative, Schopenhauer-inspired, anti-myth, Santiago might respond, 'Do I look like an idiot? Have you been to Palestine?'

Despite his own mystical leanings, Schopenhauer does not set up another world as a comforting alternative to the one in which you stub your toe so mercilessly without it being a 'growth experience'. The problem of suffering is not to be solved in such a specious manner.

One of the interesting things about Schopenhauer is that while he is an atheist and an ontological materialist, he is nonetheless engaged with 'salvation'. Given his awareness of the earliest translations of the *Upaniṣads* and of Buddhist texts, it is not surprising to find him drawn to the visions of liberation offered there, and let's remember that in these traditions this is liberation from the wheel of becoming, *saṃsāra* — the cycle of birth and death.

Though Schopenhauer does not affirm another world, he does find two 'worlds' within this one – those of Will and Representation, which, drawing upon Kant, can also be described as the realms of 'the *thing-in-itself*' and of 'phenomena' – the ontologically 'real' and the realm of experience. Kant holds that as all knowledge of the world is mediated by the mind and senses, there can be no direct apprehension of the real. The *thing-in-itself* exists beyond the framework of experience, including space and time. Schopenhauer, though, depicts a juncture that bridges this gap and presents itself to us both as experience and as *thing-in-itself*. This is the body.

Schopenhauer asserts that the body is Will and that through introspection we *subjectively* experience it as such. So, through direct insight into our own being, we have unmediated access to the *thing-in-itself*, which is nothing more than the *Will to Life*.

Seen from the other side, the body regarded as *object of experience* (a representation for the subject) is nothing but 'objectified will': the thing we call a hand is objectified grasping, and a mouth objectified hunger (Schopenhauer, 1969, p. 107). These depictions are telling, as Schopenhauer also holds that the desire inherent in Will is always related to *want*, a sense of insufficiency in ourselves that seeks to wrest something from the world. He writes, "All willing springs from lack, from deficiency, and thus from suffering" (Schopenhauer, 1969, p. 195).

To return to Schopenhauer's claim of an unmediated 'knowing' of this body-will, he holds that our nature and motivation as subjects, given their driven character, are revealed more clearly in our sexuality than in our thought. Desire is more transparent without the sophistry of thought, or what later in psychoanalysis came to be called 'rationalization'. He writes in 1818:

> [T]he genitals are the real *focus* of the will, and are therefore the opposite pole to the brain, the representative of knowledge, . . . the world as representation. The genitals are the life-preserving principle assuring to time endless life. In this capacity they were worshipped by the Greeks in the *phallus*, and by the Indians in the *lingam*, which are therefore the symbol of the affirmation of the will. On the other hand, knowledge affords the possibility of the suppression of willing, of salvation through freedom, of overcoming and annihilating the world.
> *(Schopenhauer, 1969, p. 329)*

In this passage, published more than eighty years before Freud's *The Interpretation of Dreams*, we find, in summary form, drive theory, the *libido*, inner conflict, repression and, interestingly, an intimation of that most controversial of Freud's ideas, a 'death drive'. Importantly, in Schopenhauer we also find a foundational story for the origins of intrapsychic conflict, our battle with ourselves.

Recently I discovered a fascinating paper by Young and Brook (n.d.), entitled *Schopenhauer and Freud*. They mention that while Freud, in a rare act of acknowledgement, cites Schopenhauer as his forerunner as regards a death drive, Schopenhauer "never postulated a positive drive to die. It was bad enough for him that death was the inevitable *result* of living; he did not think anything actually *sought* it" (Young & Brook, n.d.). Respectful of their scholarship, I would point out that even without conceptualizing such an active drive, Schopenhauer's writings *are* saturated with a longing for 'repose' and have numerous positive references to a not unwelcome end to phenomenal being. He may not posit a *drive*, but the longing in his works and his depiction of salvation might be felt to exemplify one. Freud clearly thought so.

Additionally, as others have observed, Freud's *Id* and Schopenhauer's Will bear an uncanny similarity. We should remember that ultimately Will, for Schopenhauer, is synonymous with the Kantian *thing-in-itself*, beyond space and time and all the perceptual/conceptual/logical framework of experience. This might help us to make sense of the 'primary process' of the id/unconscious. The 'primary', or primal, Will of Schopenhauer is non-temporal, unconscious, illogical, preverbal, merged/conflicted and desire-driven. No respecter of boundaries or distinctions, it wants what it wants, and it wants it now.

It may seem that all that is required beyond this to spawn psychoanalysis would be a theory of neurosis, relating the unconscious to defence mechanisms such as repression, rationalization and the like. In this regard, Christopher Janaway cites two crucial passages from the second volume of *The World as Will and Representation*:

> [T]his will . . . makes its supremacy felt in the last resort. This it does by prohibiting the intellect from having certain representations, by absolutely preventing certain trains of thought from arising, because it knows, or in other words experiences from the self-same intellect, that they would arouse in it any one of the emotions previously described. It then curbs and restrains the intellect, and forces it to turn to other things . . . We often do not know what we desire or fear. For years we can have a desire without admitting it to ourselves or even letting it come to clear consciousness, because the intellect is not to know anything about it, since the good opinion we have of ourselves would inevitably suffer thereby. But if the wish is fulfilled, we get to know from our joy, not without a feeling of shame, that this is what we desired.
> *(in Janaway, 2002, p. 59)*

And then:

> Every new adverse event must be assimilated by the intellect . . . but this operation itself is often very painful, and in most cases takes place only slowly

and with reluctance. . . . [C]ertain events or circumstances are wholly suppressed for the intellect, because the will cannot bear the sight of them; and then, if the resultant gaps are arbitrarily filled up for the sake of the necessary connection; we then have madness.

(Janaway, 2002, p. 60)

On Schopenhauer's behalf, I am reminded of George Bernard Shaw's wish to exhume Shakespeare in order to throw stones at him. In this instance, though, the posthumous assault might be better justified. But before hurling the first stone, I remind myself that Schopenhauer did not develop a psychotherapy from his ideas. Nor is it likely that he would have believed psychotherapy could effect change in the individual – for he writes that, "a man's actions are . . . not directed by his reason and its designs; so that no one becomes this or that because he wants to, though he want to ever so much, but that his conduct proceeds from his inborn and inalterable character" (Schopenhauer, 2004, pp. 144–145).

If there is room for change in Schopenhauer's philosophy, it is not change overtly striven for. For this would be simply another egoistic assertion of the Will. Rather, change comes, like the true pleasures of life, unwilled, unsought – like a gift.

There *is* a 'turning of the will' in Schopenhauer, which occurs but cannot be forced. Here Schopenhauer is very close to Buddhism and the conception of *nirvana*, the end of craving. Looking at its etymology, Damien Keown believes that a translation of *nirvana* as the *blowing out* of a flame is misleading. He feels that the gradual extinction of the flame by 'starving it of fuel' better reflects its meaning in the early Buddhist tradition (Keown, 2003, pp. 194–195). Buddhists and Buddhist scholars have long been aware of the paradox inherent in *pursuing* an end to desire, and so here we also find ourselves at a 'contradiction', one closely connected to that of 'compassion' in an essentially brutal world. The question is, 'How can creatures of Will unwill the Will?' Both Buddhism and Schopenhauer deal with this by positing a change that is not produced by the ego and that dissolves the distinction of subject and object.

Exactly how this turning, or salvation, happens without the agency of the ego is obscure in Schopenhauer, who has no Noble Eightfold Path. He is, though, clear about what precedes this change: it is knowledge, knowledge of the whole, of the *thing-in-itself*.

When you truly know what is on the end of your fork, every aspect of that animal's suffering and its kinship to you, you might lose your appetite. You understand exactly what it is that you have willed in all its reality and consequence. Schopenhauer writes that this knowledge:

> becomes the *quieter* of all and every willing. The will now turns away from life; it shudders at the pleasures in which it recognizes the affirmation of life. Man attains to the state of voluntary renunciation, resignation, true composure, and complete willlessness.
>
> *(Schopenhauer, 1969, p. 378)*

In Buddhism, too, it is seeing and knowing 'things as they are' (*yathā-bhūta*), which leads to *nirvana*. Moreover, to see things as they are is to see all phenomena as transitory and without substance – *empty*. We should note, though, that in Buddhism this emptiness is not synonymous with nihilism or meaninglessness. Schopenhauer writes:

> That we abhor nothingness so much is simply another way of saying that we will life so much and that we are nothing but this will and know nothing but it alone. But we now turn our glance from our own needy and perplexed nature . . .
>
> *(Schopenhauer, 1969, p. 410)*

Nietzsche's critique of Schopenhauer and his mode of living is telling: the man *did* resent the world. He *did* negate the value of life. His revenge *was* an imaginary one. He largely withdrew from the world to abuse it in his writings – writing, moreover, with the relative comfort of an inheritance, as a man who did not need to hold down an academic appointment and who could afford to publicly disparage the preeminent Hegel.

This picture, though, misses much. Firstly, although Schopenhauer did 'drop out' and did not have 'a job', he was no *dilettante* and not nearly as well-to-do as some have believed. He did not for much of his life live like a *bon vivant* but, instead, sought to protect a reasonable independence out of the remains of his bankrupt father's estate. Further, he knew well that his position was far better than the vast majority of humanity, and he wrote frequently of the iniquities of life for the nine-tenths of humanity not so privileged. This, in fact, was a charge of his against complacent, establishment philosophers, such as Leibnitz, who had asserted that ours is 'the best of all possible worlds', with a God-ordained minimum of suffering in it.

Finally, perhaps the value of Schopenhauer's negation is underestimated by Nietzsche. Is it a 'purely destructive' or resentful act, or is it an act of liberation? Is its aim to annihilate or, as in Buddhism, to 'go beyond', to let go of grasping at the world? Significantly, he writes that, "Behind our existence lies something else that becomes accessible to us only by our shaking off the world" (Schopenhauer, 1969, p. 404).

Conclusion

We need not share Schopenhauer's disparagement of phenomenal existence to see some value in 'shaking off' the world. As regards the work of counselling and psychotherapy, this puts me in mind of Bion's injunction to approach each session "without memory, desire or understanding" (Casement, 1990, p. 10), or we might think in terms of a phenomenological 'bracketing of the world'.

In both, there is a seemingly paradoxical attempt to 'shake off the world' in order to enter more fully into our experience of it; so, on the horns of this dilemma, we might begin to see the possibility of a 'negation' that leads not to nihilism but to engagement with experience. To extrapolate further we might even see the seeds of the concept of intentionality and hence phenomenology itself, when Schopenhauer writes, "No will: no representation, no world" (Schopenhauer, 1969, p. 410).

If, as Schopenhauer did, we look to Buddhism, there are equivalent 'negations' in various traditions. For instance, in Sōtō Zen Buddhism, *shin-jin-datsu-raku* ('body and mind fallen away') describes what may occur during *zazen* meditation. Interestingly, not cast off or shaken off but 'fallen away' or 'dropped away'.

To return to the active voice, how and how far one can 'shake off the world' and what type of 'negation' this might involve are interesting questions – especially for those of us who want to live with good appetite . . . with a side-order of Zen.

In terms of my therapeutic practice, Schopenhauer's writing has been a helpful 'corrective'. It reminds me that the realities of other people's suffering can be impossible to comprehend, particularly when I am powerless in the face of them. Aspects of my own existential predicament and the inexorable challenges of my work are difficult to engage with or even to acknowledge. It's easier to, well, do *something* else, something that feels more positive.

Just as there is a temptation towards despair, there is the temptation of a 'flight into health', towards an empty and desperate affirmation. I think we therapists frequently collude in this because we share the same desires and the same fears as our clients. So, I believe that a strain of "obligatory optimism" (Schopenhauer, 2004, p. 78) has affected therapeutic thinking and how therapy is practiced. This can involve an almost exclusive framing in terms of 'solutions' rather than staying with the felt sense of 'problems', and in this 'reframing' I feel that something is missing or has been airbrushed out. The trace of suffering is conspicuous in its absence.

Of course, in a 'consumer economy' it is hard to sell the transformation of "hysterical misery into common unhappiness" (Breuer & Freud, 2000, p. 305). A few times, I've even heard clients complain that they are not enjoying their therapy. Expectations are high, and Schopenhauer is akin to someone who spoils the party by uttering *memento mori* at precisely the right/wrong moment.

Whether Schopenhauer's brand of 'compassion' is entirely philosophically consistent with his dim view of humanity is not something I can answer. The 'tension' between these goes back to his early years and is evident even in his youthful journal: in Lyon, a teenage Schopenhauer was struck by the incongruous sight of people walking with indifference over the very place where their forebears had been slaughtered in the French Revolution (see Yalom, 2006, p. 90). Here Schopenhauer's 'dangerous' admixture of disgust and compassion is striking and, for me, forms the kernel of what he has to say about our humanity – the humanity of a species that can spawn a new culture of forgetting just a handful of years after the liberation of Stutthof, the last Nazi concentration camp. I mean no insult when I observe that Paulo Coelho was born but two years after this epoch-defining event.

I remember when I began my studies in Buddhism coming across the well-known tale of a woman whose child had died. Carrying the body, she approached Siddhārtha Gautama and asked him if he could bring back her child. He said that he would if she brought him some mustard seeds from a home in the nearby village that had never known death. At the time I saw Gautama's response as callous, whereas now I can begin to value this pointing to a shared truth about our mortality.

Strangely, though, it is not the Buddha but Schopenhauer – an obstinate, curmudgeonly and sometimes malicious man – who has consoled me by not forgetting what is on the end of every fork or what it is that we share, ineluctably, in our difficult humanity.

Note

1 The expression is from Wilfred Bion, quoted in P. Casement, *On Learning from the Patient* (London: Routledge, 1985, 223).

References

Breuer, J., & Freud, S. (2000) *Studies on Hysteria* New York: Basic Books.
Burroughs, W. (1982) *The Naked Lunch* London: John Calder.
Casement, P. (1985) *On Learning from the Patient* London: Routledge.
Casement, P. (1990) *Further Learning from the Patient* London: Routledge.
Coelho, P. (2005) *The Alchemist: A Fable About Following Your Dream* New York: HarperCollins e-books.
Janaway, C. (2002) *Schopenhauer: A Very Short Introduction* Oxford: Oxford University Press.
Keown, D. (2003) *Oxford Dictionary of Buddhism* Oxford: Oxford University Press.
Nietzsche, F. (1998) *On the Genealogy of Morals* (trans. D. Smith) Oxford: Oxford University Press.
Schopenhauer, A. (1969) *The World as Will and Representation, Vol. 1* New York: Dover Publications.
Schopenhauer, A. (2004) *Essays and Aphorisms* (trans. R. J. Hollingdale) London: Penguin.
Yalom, I. (2006) *The Schopenhauer Cure* New York: Harper Perennial.
Young, C., & Brook, A. (n.d.) *Schopenhauer and Freud* Retrieved 12 January 2015 from http://http-server.carleton.ca/~abrook/SCHOPENY.htm.

16

LIFTING THE CURSE

Wittgenstein, Buddhism and psychotherapy

Jeff Harrison

Introduction

Be warned. Wittgenstein is a cautionary thinker. 'Are you saying what you think you are? And should you be saying it?' These are the questions he asks. Given that he is mistrustful of the notion of private inner experience, these two questions and the relationship between them are not as straightforward as might first appear.

Certainly in the latter phase of his career he was not a systematic philosopher; so we should not turn him into one. It is more consistent with his approach to dialogue with him.

He asks us to look at individual problems/situations without necessarily building them up into an overarching system. That is why this chapter is presented as a series of connected thoughts and observations. The how of the saying cannot be separated from the what of the said.

He looks closely at the problematic relationship between language and reality and between so-called inner states and outer expression, including linguistic.

Whatever Wittgenstein says, we certainly *feel* as if we have a private inner life – even if that feeling and life are called into existence by relationships to others. We also have a relationship to self – even if that self is called into existence by relationships to others.

Psychotherapy offers clients a reflective space. That is, it allows or invites them to externalize material and to have it held up for reflection. We struggle to do this alone; our minds are too much like echo chambers. We can't see the wood for the trees. "I ought to be no more than a mirror, in which my reader can see his own thinking with all its deformities so that, helped in this way, he can put it right." (Wittgenstein, 1980, p. 18).

Clients come with 'issues'. It is an enduring irony that a word that means 'way out' or 'release' can also, to the client, mean something that challenges, constrains or imprisons.

In Zen Buddhism, *koans* are riddling statements that reveal the limits and distortions of a rational comprehension of world and self and challenge one to move beyond such a constrained vision. A neurosis can be viewed – and worked with – in an analogous way. The 'knotty' problems of philosophy that Wittgenstein identifies are also similar and similarly challenging, territory. All three – neurosis, *koan*, knot – reveal that the ideas we have, as well as the stories we are telling ourselves, about world and self and their interaction are unhelpful. In all three cases, increased unskilful effort in trying to solve the problem can actually exacerbate it.

Wittgenstein's own emphasis is on a move away from both the mystification and weightlessness of metaphysics and into the world of lived experience and our existential situatedness. Life is unavoidably burdensome and tensive in many ways. The call is to accept that without pulling the knots tighter.

> We have got onto slippery ice where there is no friction and so in a certain sense the conditions are ideal, but also, just because of that, we are unable to walk. We want to walk so we need friction. Back to the rough ground.
> *(Wittgenstein, 1978, PI, §107)*

The slipperiness of some of these ideas is unavoidable; the frictionlessness of their putative foundation is not.

Language can mislead us. Do we even understand the warning? Wittgenstein's 'rough ground' refers to practical groundedness, not a metaphysical substratum. In metaphysical terms – and without wishing to minimize their severity – our various forms of distress can in fact be characterized as *groundless* concerns.

What can we say, then? What *do* we actually say when we think we're saying something? Wittgenstein is a philosopher of language, communication and, almost *contra* himself, inner life.

As a client, I wish to discuss and present my 'self' – whatever its precise meaning, interactions, constitution and relationships.

We can perhaps know (be aware of) all the various meanings of the word 'self' and still not know which is being used at any given moment. Compare the subtleties of the putative relationships within the 'person-centred tribes' (Sanders, 2004). We can classify and systematize, but how do we discern what is happening in the real-life situation?

The 'family resemblances' – the common features – of any given word use may narrow the possibilities but, even then, may not make it conclusive. Conversely, in fact, 'family resemblances' can actually underline how problematic terms are.

We can say (from experience in the therapy room and from life more generally) that behaviour does *not* always match feeling. One person may report high anxiety and yet look calm; another may report moderate anxiety and look like a comic book caricature – all knocking knees and beads of sweat.

Language

Wittgenstein's emphasis is anti-scientific and anti-metaphysical. He aims for a therapeutic philosophy – one that makes sense. He is not after ultimate *or* merely empirical truths. There is modesty as well as rigour in his enterprise.

Therapy is often about moving beyond a self-concept into the fluid, organismic, non-instrumental life process. 'Worldling' replaces 'worldview' (Spinelli, 2007, p. 19). The therapist helps the client identify and challenge her static self-concept. The psychotherapeutic 'talking cure' is as much about curing certain kinds of misleading talk as about securing a cure through talking.

Wittgenstein, too, famously sought to liberate us from our bewitchment by language (Wittgenstein, 1978, I, §109).

'The lightning flashes'. Why say so? What else *can* it do? We can imagine the 'son of a barren woman' but never find one. 'Why does a giraffe have such a long neck? Because its head is so far away from its body'. We can reverse cause and effect. Quasi-mystical language can mislead (and speak truth) on many levels: "The words 'I am not' are senseless. Is this not a clear intimation that they should be true?" (Wei, 1963, p. 29).

We can applaud clear-sightedness – therapeutic or philosophical. Whether Wittgenstein risks denying us an enriching *enchantment* through language is an open question. Word-curse has its counterpart: word-blessing.

We should certainly beware of anyone who tells us what we see. But 'being enabled to see' could serve as a thumbnail sketch of what therapy entails.

The process tends to be a clearing away of undergrowth (in all senses). Any more dogmatic or constructive (rather than deconstructive) agenda may involve excessive direction on the part of the therapist.

A client may come to a therapist saying that her suffering doesn't make sense to her. We might, in turn, in a positivist vein, say to her, 'That *statement* doesn't make sense', but that wouldn't be very helpful. Especially as the sentence itself does make sense (grammatically). The better joint endeavour may in fact be to find some sense for her. In doing so, therapists, like philosophers, might home in on the meanings of the words and concepts she brings. What is her 'form of life'? Can it be changed? Can she see it differently? Can the frames of reference be altered? Can seeing afresh, seeing clearly, however painful, be a tonic truth?

A client may talk as if speaking a foreign language that she doesn't fully understand. There may be a disconnection between the words used and the emotion reported. Therapy is as much about texture (of feeling, impression, energy) as text. It is not a form of linguistic idealism. Words may be the medium of newly forged realities but not the exclusive material.

The task may be modest: to modify the picture painted on the window or to see the viability of alternatives (including erasing the painting).

A "language game" is a "form of life" (Wittgenstein, 1978, I, §23). There is no intrinsic meaning. Meaning is coloured by activity and context. In one of his most famous statements, Wittgenstein says, "If a lion could speak, we could not understand him" (Wittgenstein, 1978, II, 223). This is presumably because his impressions and concepts – his whole way of being and frame of reference – would reflect his 'form of life' and not ours. In fact, the error can be taken back a level further. The very notion of a talking lion – especially one using concepts – is implausible and anthropocentric, let alone what it might say.

So, are 'language games' and wiping the picture *from* the window compatible, or are they at odds?

Inner life

Two behaviourists have just had sex. 'That was great for you', says one. 'How was it for me?'

Wittgenstein largely refutes the notion of a private inner life. Even on those occasions where he seems more nuanced, he ascribes to it little philosophical currency. This does not make him automatically a behaviourist.

He does not deny that there is an "ineffable phenomenological quality" (Rorty, 1979, p. 103) to pain (by which he often seems to mean physical pain) but argues that there is no entirely private/secret process independent of its production and expression. "An 'inner process' stands in need of outward criteria." (Wittgenstein, 1978, I, §580)

Wittgenstein is acutely alive to how grammar can mislead us in all sorts of other ways, too: into fallacies of hypostatization (e.g. a concrete 'self'); into false or misleadingly crude dualities (e.g. subject-object); and into the inference of a non-existent *a priori* subject.

The road to hell, as we know, is paved with good intentions. Watzlawick notes that clients often get lost in a "repeated problem engendering pseudosolution[s]" (Watzlawick, 1978, p. 159). One might even say in many cases that the problem *is* how the client seeks to solve it.

We do well to recall Nietzsche's earlier warning against the 'god of grammar' (Nietzsche, 1990, 'Reason', §5). The entities that words seem to suggest, as well as the relationships between them, may have no basis in reality. But, of course, we must concede that, if our reading/speaking of the world *is* the world, they may produce that reality.

Description is valued but other, false paths can lead us to diagnosis, explanation, interpretation, and, therefore, separation, objectification, domination and imposed agendas may result.

It is bad enough that we believe in the story we tell of/as ourselves; it is worse to believe another's of us. Diagnosis is imposing a story (even the story of 'science') onto someone else.

The client's issue is a damming or diversion of life energy at the level of emotion or insight/awareness or both (perhaps it has to be both) as a response to stress/trauma (physical, psychological, existential, etc.).

Wittgenstein proposes descriptive clear-sightedness to mitigate our problems:

> And we may not advance any kind of theory. There must not be anything hypothetical in our considerations. We must do away with all *explanation*, and description alone must take its place. And this description gets its light, that is to say its purpose, from the philosophical problems. These are, of course, not empirical problems; they are solved, rather, by looking into the workings of our language, and that in such a way as to make us recognize those workings: *in spite of* an urge to misunderstand them. The problems are solved, not by reporting new experience, but by arranging what we have always known.
>
> *(Wittgenstein, 1978, I, §109)*

Many therapists have a similar approach that they may couch in the terms of phenomenological bracketing and clarification. 'What's (really) going on?' is the guiding question. 'Why?' tends to provoke more speculative storytelling, explanation and the bad spells of bewitchment. Accuracy with language/expression can literally be a part of 'coming to terms' with something.

For Wittgenstein, philosophical investigations are largely conceptual or grammatical, intending to sweep away philosophical misunderstandings (Wittgenstein, 1978, I, §90; see also Wittgenstein, 1967, §458).

Heisenberg writes: "Natural science does not simply describe and explain nature; it is part of the interplay between nature and ourselves; it describes nature as exposed to our method of questioning" (Kaplan, 2001, p. 40). If this is true of natural science, it is surely true of how we see ourselves and our world. And when we have problems in living and relating, things get more complex still. This is again why *how* we approach our problem may well be a further manifestation of it.

There is not an expectation that a client should speak as she might write, merely that the same rigour be brought to bear on not misleading ourselves (especially, as a Buddhist or Wittgenstein might add, when the very notion of a separate, inner self may be the product of such misleading).

Self, Buddhism and language

> The way to solve the problems you see in life is to live in a way that will make what is problematic disappear. The fact that life is problematic shows that the shape of your life does not fit into life's mould. So you must change the way you live and, once your life does fit into the mould, what is problematic will disappear.
>
> *(Wittgenstein, 1980, 27e)*

This might suggest philosophical maieutics.

A client comes and is confused. Her identity (the well-rehearsed life story she has told herself) is not helping her. We might ask her directly, '*Who* is confused?'

But that would probably only add to her confusion and distress. Like the Buddhist master who challenged the student to bring him the 'self' he wished to become enlightened. The student could not (and so gained insight). That story makes 'sense' if you accept that there is no 'self' to be enlightened. In therapy, we may challenge our client less directly and less extensively.

Heaton (Mace, 1999, pp. 49–64) notes that espousing the idea of no-self might engender a sense of emptiness that needs filling. There is, though, really nothing lost because there is nothing to lose; but – as we saw with our sense of an inner life – it may not *feel* like that. And feelings are not negligible – not in therapy.

"'I' is not an object; 'I' is a subject but not a part of the world. Rather it is 'a presupposition of its existence'" (Wittgenstein, 1979, p. 80). It is transcendental. A transcendental 'ground' in this sense cannot see itself.

Buddhist psychology is in many ways anti-metaphysical, but it is also 'physical' – in the experimental sense. 'Don't take my word for it', the Buddha seems to say, 'try it for yourself'.

Later, Wittgenstein saw the task of philosophy as freeing the fly from the bottle (Wittgenstein, 1978, I, §309). Those familiar with Buddhist psychology might argue that *we* are the fly in the bottle, trapped in illusory prisons, walled in by self-concepts, thought constructions (*prapanca*) and constrictions. We are still circling round the question, "What is the 'self'?" We will never answer it conclusively; we may just learn to let the question go.

Perhaps like the 'physics' of Buddhism, Heaton sees philosophical scepticism, in which tradition he places Wittgenstein, as practical and anti-dogmatic (Mace, 1999, p. 50).

Sceptikos means thoughtful or attentive. The root of 'therapy' also suggests 'attention'. Like the good therapist, the sceptic is on the *qui vive*, not bogged down in dogma.

"It is not how things are in the world that is mystical but that it exists." That is Wittgenstein (1989, 6:44) but could conceivably have been said by a Korean Zen master.

A problem for a philosopher and a problem for a client might both, in specific instances, be compared to a knot. The wise approach is not to pull at the ends but to unravel it. We need patience and attention. As in meditation, as we look with patience, we come in time to accept even our non-acceptance (Watts, 1975).

Wittgenstein, many Buddhist approaches and much therapy all seek to deconstruct error; they are about misperceptions and misrepresentations; they are bottom-up (rather than top-down) orientations. There is nothing trans-phenomenal. If we cannot begin with what is here and now, we seek to come back to it. We come to understand how we have been misled or misled ourselves – through filters, lenses, biases, cognitive distortions, introjections, thought constructs.

In Buddhism, the self is an aggregate of processes, one phenomenon amongst many. Like Wittgenstein, Buddhism seeks to uncover what is sometimes called the homunculus fallacy, the notion that we have a little man in our heads 'driving' us. He, too, of course, would need a little man driving him – and so on in an infinite regress. Philosophically, this is an error of the *mereological* kind, concerned with the interaction of parts and whole – in this case the false ascription of a whole. Sometimes we don't need something *like* we need a hole in the head; we need a hole in the head itself.

We have a *sense* of self. That is always worth repeating, and one reason for that is the weird primacy that language seems to have. Even to deny, we have first to create. 'The man who wasn't there' has to be put there in the first place before we deny his existence. This is analogous to the curse of the dyer's hand. We are haunted by any presence we refute – 'in' ourselves and 'out' there. Nevertheless, the 'projector' (self/homunculus) we imagine *in* our minds is just another image (projection) on the screen. There are thoughts but no thinker. "The idea of the ego inhabiting a body [is] to be abolished" (Wittgenstein, 1993, p. 225). If we recognized ourselves as 'emergent man', there may be less emergency *in* our lives.

The 'self' is emergent and responsive rather than eternal. It is a process of phenomenal arising. Our provisional identity is the story we tell ourselves and have told ourselves. This can be useful – as can the designation self, of course – but that does not make it ontologically real. In many ways, 'I' is a flag of convenience.

Therapy concerns itself with words *and* 'reality' (including the 'felt sense' that may or may not make itself known to others). As we figure ourselves out, we may need to reconfigure ourselves. Perhaps – and it is only perhaps – only the 'enlightened' move beyond figuration entirely. For most of us, lubricating our language and life may be sufficient. That gives us enough 'play' – the freedom to move, to become. We are dynamic verbs rather than object nouns.

A client complains of depression. 'What does depression mean to you?' we may gently ask.

There may be no private language (if language is a form of communication), but there is a private *use* of words. Most of the most important words we use (God, love, self) are indeterminate. They are deeply meaningful yet teeter at times on meaninglessness. Depression is an important word to a therapist and to the client. That is the starting point.

This may well require close attention to various conceptual markers (and oppositions) that we take for granted: inner and outer, self and other, conscious and unconscious.

The conditions that create and maintain symptoms – against which they manifest, that is – are explored, challenged and modified; and the so-called secondary gain strategies (the 'rackets') employed by the client have little or no traction in the therapy space.

In several of its early texts, Buddhism has the parable of the raft (Thera, 2006): when one has reached the farther shore, the raft one has used to get there may be discarded. Insight cannot be gained merely from ontological propositions and certainly need not linger in that form in the mind of the awakened:

> My propositions are elucidatory in this way: he who understands me finally recognizes them as senseless, when he has climbed out through them, on

them, over them. (He must so to speak throw away the ladder, after he has climbed up on it.)

He must surmount these propositions; then he sees the world rightly. Whereof one cannot speak, thereof one must be silent.

(Wittgenstein, 1989, 6.54, 7)

We may note, in the parable of the raft, that we take the raft from the near shore to the far. If one is called (and helped) by the other, however, one might imagine it better as a raft sent from the far shore.

Wittgenstein stated, "The limits of my language are the limits of my world" (Wittgenstein, 1989, §5.6). Stretching language can perhaps extend the scope of our world/experience. One is not absolved from the obligation to communicate, but one can use the consensual word 'pool' as traction for transit elsewhere.

What do we do, then, as therapists, with our models? We are human beings and, *as such*, exist in a world of models, world pictures, second-order reflection. We cannot permanently turn off that part of ourselves without diminishment or distortion. But we can see it as provisional.

Seeing beyond models and theses – seeing their provisional nature – is as desirable as training therapists without them is implausible. One abandons the raft *after* one has made full use of it. If not, therapist and client both risk drowning. We need to understand the role that the client's own 'thesis' about the world/himself has played in his engagement with 'reality' and how it has fed (into) the neurosis; so we *cannot* simply erase them all – much as we might all wish to at times.

We see again that the client's approach to a problem will, more than likely, both be determined by the problem *and* determine the problem. Similarly, what has produced the problem will be extant in our attitude to it. The therapeutic process will, on one level, facilitate the client's awareness of that and open up alternatives.

The therapist can achieve this facilitation both by raising awareness directly and by not playing along with the client's strategies of being, interaction and self-presentation.

As well as language games (concerned with context/meaning), Wittgenstein also comments on games in the more normal sense. He explains how one game can replace another, rendering the earlier one unsustainable: "But how can the new game have made the old one obsolete? – We now see something different and can no longer go on playing" (Wittgenstein, 1956, p. 100). Watzlawick (1978, pp. 124–125) sees a therapeutic application in such an observation, reading 'game' in a third way to suggest the emotional/behavioural stratagem a client may 'play' both in the therapy space and externally. It may be therapeutic in such situations for the therapist to stimulate or facilitate a different – more skillful/productive – game (without necessarily indicating to the client what she is doing).

For example, an unruly and rebellious teenager may have his behaviour reframed as existential fear of growing up and independence (and a new 'game' set in motion) by a family therapist. There is no prohibition or command, but the teenager wishes to show himself as anything but fearful and so becomes more reasonable. Further, the therapist's intervention also challenges the parents' "problem-perpetuating pseudo-solution". If they accept the therapist's explanation, they will adopt a more tolerant stance to their child (which makes that child's defiance less necessary – a virtuous circle is formed) (Watzlawick, 1978, p. 146).

Views, of course, *do* readily become static and unhelpful. Rorty, at the end of *Philosophy and the Mirror of Nature* (1979), argues that Wittgenstein does *not* take a view.

It is probably truer to say – and Rorty himself implies this – that we step in and out of views and models and theories as and when they are useful, but we ascribe to none an eternal, essential veracity. They cannot be abandoned entirely without indulging in a kind of naively romantic nostalgia for a time before language befuddled us.

Conclusion

Wittgenstein has warned us against excessive abstraction, excessive generalization, excessive extrapolation. We should heed that warning in what we seek to conclude from his writings.

Though not an out-and-out behaviourist, he nevertheless shows a suspicion of inwardness and the inexpressible. Certainly if we include body language as a language, there is a strain of linguistic idealism in his ideas. There is also, arguably, an excessive rationalism – he is rooted in conceptual meaning, apparently unconcerned with the 'meaningful'. Admittedly, the latter is an idea that positivists would dismiss as nonsense. But although a vague term, it is very *humanly* vague.

Human beings don't simply deal in *facts*. They hold values, seek meaning, are embodied, live with others, in context. The word 'fact' strains to point to something straightforward but is a highly loaded term. So, what are we to do?

Buddhist meditation offers one approach: in widening our awareness to gradually include our resistances to the unfolding of reality (as paradoxical as 'accepting resistance' may sound), we might move towards a full – and, crucially, not entirely rational/conceptual – understanding and loosening of the knot in which we are tied. When we accept what is, things tend to change.

Wittgenstein is generally subtle, but at times, too, very direct: "In the beginning was the deed" (Wittgenstein, 1993, §395). Language learning, that is the acquisition of basic language, is about natural (non-rational) reactions, associations and significations and is based on certainty (whereby the meaning of language cannot be dissociated from activity). The more sophisticated, questioning games come later – and with them the greater potential for confusion and delusion.

Clients often wish to focus on their symptoms. This is entirely understandable. Symptoms are literally 'showings' – manifestations that something is amiss. But they may be very misleading in where they seem to point. Therapists facilitate the client to look at the wider and deeper picture – such as it is for that particular client. There *is* an expansion but not to the generic – quite the opposite in fact. We learn more about how and what the client sees when her field of vision increases, and expanding that field of vision may itself be healing.

Compare, "Don't get involved in partial problems, but always take flight to where there is a free view over the whole single great problem, even if this view is still not a clear one" (Wittgenstein, 1979, entry for November 1, 1914).

An overview, a wider view, may indeed be attainable, but it is worth stressing again, in therapy we must move via the specifics of the client's life world and not force her language, frames of reference, language games or forms of life into our own (let alone any putative generality, however inclusive it appears).

This may or may not reduce tension, friction, confusion and so on. That cannot be the agenda – the client's or the therapist's. Agendas are route maps and – in good therapy – we often don't know where we are going, and we certainly cannot map out in advance how we are going to get there. All we can do – as Wittgenstein might concur – is try to avoid as many misleading signposts, false trails and dead ends as we can.

References

Kaplan, R. (2001) *Science Says* New York: Stonesong Press.
Mace, C. (Ed.) (1999) *Heart and Soul – The Therapeutic Face of Philosophy* London: Routledge.
Nietzsche, F. (1990) 'Twilight of the Idols', in *Twilight of the Idols and the Anti-Christ* London: Penguin, pp. 29–122.
Rorty, R. (1979) *Philosophy and the Mirror of Nature* Princeton, NJ: Princeton University Press.
Sanders, P. (Ed.) (2004) *The Tribes of the Person-Centred Nation* Ross-on-Wye, Herefordshire: PCCS Books.
Spinelli, E. (2007) *Practising Existential Psychotherapy: The Relational World* London: Sage.
Thera, N. (2006) *The Discourse on the Snake Simile (Alugaddupama Sutta, MN 22).* Available at www.accesstoinsight.org/lib/authors/nyanaponika/wheel048.html. Sourced on 13 December 2014.
Watts, A. (1975) *Psychotherapy East and West* New York: Vintage.
Watzlawick, P. (1978) *The Language of Change* New York/London: Norton.
Wei, W. W. (1963) *Ask the Awakened* London: Routledge.
Wittgenstein, L. (1956) *Remarks on the Foundations of Mathematics* Oxford: Blackwell.
Wittgenstein, L. (1967) *Zettel* Oakland: University of California Press.
Wittgenstein, L. (1978) *Philosophical Investigations* Oxford: Blackwell.
Wittgenstein, L. (1979) *Notebooks 1914–1918* Oxford: Blackwell.
Wittgenstein, L. (1980) *Culture and Value* Oxford: Blackwell.
Wittgenstein, L. (1989) *Tractatus Logico-Philosophicus* London: Routledge.
Wittgenstein, L. (1993) *Philosophical Occasions, 1912–51* Indianapolis, IN: Hackett.

17
AMOR FATI
Suffering to become the person one is

Devang Vaidya

Introduction

Fate is a surprisingly unexplored subject in psychotherapy. We seldom concern ourselves directly with how persons regard their life as being determined and overlook that they can have such an underlying stance, a philosophy of Fate. As therapists, we remain so focused on the particulars of our clients' difficulties that we can lose touch with their underlying stance towards their suffering. Is it dread or courage, despair or hope, apathy or concern, resistance or acceptance, resentment or love? We rarely concern ourselves with the possibility of a freedom so free that it can withstand the inevitability of the inevitable, the necessities of one's Fate. For a long period I have grappled with the idea of a third possibility that can break open this underlying dualism between freedom and necessity and between 'active' and 'passive' orientations towards life.

In today's world, surely what is required is an end to suffering. It seems disingenuous on my part to talk about loving Fate when there are billions on this earth with whom I would shudder to swap places. I admit I do not like to suffer very much. Like most of us, I have not always loved my Fate. The idea of loving my Fate unconditionally can fill me with anxiety about unimaginable what-ifs. Perhaps this is the reason for my choosing this topic. All I can hope now, with a friendly nod to Kierkegaard (1981), is that I will be anxious in the right way.

This chapter does not propose indiscriminate suffering as a moral virtue, nor does it preach love of Fate as gospel. Amor Fati is not an ideal. My reflections on Fate, and the love of one's Fate, are kept as near to person-centred therapy as possible. It should also become clear from the questions that will arise that this is still work in progress. I very much doubt that even at its conclusion – if ever there is one – I will have any definitive answers.

Nietzsche's call to love one's Fate – Amor Fati – first and foremost compels us to face our life as a paradox of necessity and freedom to bear the suffering of our

Fates. I want to bring this reflection to the practice of person-centred therapy by linking suffering with the process of 'experiencing our experience' and 'becoming congruent'. Therapeutic growth, in person-centred terms, can be regarded as an increased capacity to embody one's life experiences with self-awareness. For Carl Rogers, this can result in a client discovering that:

> he can *be* his experience with all of its variety and surface contradiction; that he can formulate himself out of his experience, instead of trying to impose a formulation of self upon his experience, denying to awareness those elements which do not fit.
>
> *(Rogers, 1961, p. 80)*

We understand this as congruence, as well as how congruence can lead to self-love, that can extend into love for others and for life itself. Rogers often observed his clients experiencing 'real affection for themselves' (Rogers, 1961, p. 73) or 'a quiet pleasure in being one's self' (Rogers, 1961, p. 87). As one of his clients put it: "I came here to solve problems, and I now find myself just experiencing myself" (Rogers, 1961, p. 80). From this we might say that successful therapy enhances the capacity to suffer one's Fate in all its complexity, as part of the process of becoming a person. Perhaps a willingness to endure suffering for becoming more congruent can be taken as an expression of Amor Fati.

From my experiences as both client and therapist, I am coming to the conclusion that incongruence remains an irreducible part of our Fate. Elsewhere I've written about incongruence as an existential condition (Vaidya, 2013), and here I'll give a brief synopsis. Firstly, incongruence is at the genesis of the self; self emerges out of a portion of the experiencing organism; therefore, whilst it overlaps with the organism to some extent, it cannot do so entirely. Secondly, due to the interconnectedness of the human organism with its surrounding environment, both congruence and incongruence are experience specific and context bound. No person can be regarded as either congruent or incongruent for all times. Thirdly, with the infinite permutations of factors that constitute our phenomenal world and with the certainty of death looming on the horizon of one's lifetime, 'vulnerability and anxiousness' are ever-present to hand. Incongruence is thus an existential given.

Congruent or incongruent, we could say that each person is Fated to suffer existentially, although the particular experiences of suffering are unique for each person. In this context, Rogers' ideas point us towards the possibility of freedom to choose the suffering that can lead us towards more congruent living. Nietzsche also advocates willingness to suffer as a freedom that must be exercised as an expression of Amor Fati.

Throughout history, this attitude of willingness to suffer for one's destined purpose has been evident in many persons whose lives continue to inspire us today. Our real test, as Vaclav Havel says (Havel, 1990a) is not how well we play the role we invented for ourselves but how well we play the role assigned to us by destiny.

Human lives are marked by a quest for discovering and fulfilling a Fated purpose, although superficially our difficulties can take the form of tensions with the boss or conflicts with a spouse. Our incongruence is indicated by anxiety about not being able to overcome the barriers to play the role that destiny assigned us.

Fate involves a movement between incongruence and congruence. This movement can be experienced as a 'dialectical dance of truth and lies' (Havel, 1991, p. ix) – and is often an intensely demanding but essentially rewarding exploration in person-centred therapy. We could go further and say that this dance is choreographed by the 'actualizing tendency', which, in the climate of Rogers' 'six conditions of therapy' takes a direction towards living more congruently. The notion of living congruently concords with Nietzsche who asked what does your conscience say? "You should become who you are"(Nietzsche, 2001, p. 152). For Rogers, this is a growth process that is "a unique and dynamic experience, different for each individual, yet exhibiting a lawfulness and order which is astonishing in its generality" (Rogers, 1961, p. 74).

'Becoming who one is', 'playing the role assigned by destiny', 'suffering one's Fate', 'becoming one's Fate' – these phrases express a fundamental commitment to living congruently within the context of the overarching existential incongruence that is a common Fate of humanity.

Emerson and Fate

One of the major influences on Friedrich Nietzsche was Ralph Waldo Emerson, the American philosopher and poet, who incidentally was also an inspiration for Carl Rogers. It is almost certain that before Nietzsche first used the term Amor Fati he had read Emerson's essay on Fate written in 1860. Here are a few excerpts:

> In our first steps to gain our wishes, we come upon immovable limitations.
> If we must accept Fate, we are not less compelled to affirm liberty.
> We are sure, that, though we know not how, necessity does comport with liberty, the individual with the world, my polarity with the spirit of the times. The riddle of an age has for each a private solution.
> The element running through entire nature, which we popularly call Fate, is known to us as limitation. Whatever limits us, we call Fate. If we are brute and barbarous, the fate takes a brute and dreadful shape. As we refine, our checks become finer.
>
> *(Emerson, 1981, pp. 346–374)*

Emerson's essay highlights the ever-present tension between free and undivided will and the ordained necessities of Fate. Nietzsche seems to have caught the spark of Emerson's enquiry. Amor Fati is its flame.

Nietzsche's first use of Amor Fati dates from 1881 (Ferrer, 2011):"Copy by R.W. Emerson. First the necessary, the needful – and this so beautifully and perfectly as you can! Love what is necessary – Amor Fati, this would be my moral" (Nietzsche, 1967, v. 2541).

For Nietzsche, loving one's Fate is necessary since Fate itself is necessary. In other words, the particular necessities of one's Fate define – set limits to – one's life and one's love. He writes: "Yes, I want to only love still what is necessary! Yes! Amor Fati is my last love!" (Nietzsche, 1967, v. 2562)

One's 'immovable limitations' act as these necessities. And it is for such necessities that one can arouse in oneself the readiness to suffer which becomes possible only when these limitations can be encountered in love. These ruminations result in the crystallization of a simple idea that what Nietzsche claims as necessary is love, and love for what is one's inevitable Fate becomes the first – perhaps the only – necessity of love.

A year later in a letter to his friend Franz Overbeck, Nietzsche sounds filled with hope and enthusiasm when he writes: "[For once I am the man of my thoughts, indeed my innermost thinking . . . I am possessed of a fatalistic 'devotion to God' – I call it Amor Fati – so that I would step into the jaws of a lion" (Nietzsche, 1882).

The German term *Gottergebenheit* that Nietzsche uses is translated here as devotion to God. It also has several other, related meanings such as submission, surrender, meekness and godliness. What this shows is that Nietzsche's commitment is not a pursuit of conquest but a determination to surrender; not demand, but prayer. This reminds us of what Han-Pile (2011) regards as the medio-passive voice and how it conveys Nietzsche's passionate move towards receptivity for an uncertain Fate that may place his very existence at risk. Medio-passivity is a linguistic stance for expressing a 'middle voice' situated between active and passive articulations. It was more common in ancient languages such as Greek and Sanskrit for conveying an attitude of 'active receptivity', or a state of willingness that lies between wilfulness and lack of will. In reflecting on Amor Fati, we find that Fate becomes a possible object of love when our stance towards it is neither wholly active – since we are not free to determine it or know it, nor is it wholly passive – since we desire to be able to choose a response.

Amor Fati holds a deeply poetic paradox as the seeming opposites of Fate and freewill. As Han-Pile (2011) explains: 'A commitment to determinism does not entail *per se* a rejection of the possibility of free will'. Conversely, she argues, it would be an error to assume that indeterminism necessarily implies freedom.

Whilst Nietzsche presents loving Fate as a real possibility, he is certainly not advocating creating suffering for one self or for others; nor is he suggesting that we merely endure our Fate passively in order to avoid suffering. He is in fact asking us to endure suffering when it is inevitable in order to sustain our passionate love of Fate.

We should note that whilst Nietzsche makes no reference to the possibility of any prior knowledge of one's Fate, he hints at the possibility of recognizing one's Fate and committing to its course. The concept of Fate does not include fore knowledge, only that it is governed by forces shaping the uncertain emergence of the world and of every individual within it. This, for me, encapsulates Rogers' person-centred notions of becoming and of the actualizing tendency. Amor Fati and suffering, together, elaborate the significance of the 'six conditions' for growing a capacity to live with increasing congruence. Nietzsche wrote:

> I want to learn more and more to see as beautiful what is necessary in things; then I shall be one of those who make things beautiful. Amor Fati: let that be my love henceforth! ... [S]ome day I wish to be only a yes-sayer.
>
> *(Nietzsche, 2001, p. 157)*

These words were written on New Year's Day, either in 1881 – or a few years before – and they sound like a resolution. Han-Pile (2011) suggests various interpretations of this and other places where Nietzsche mentions Amor Fati. One reading of the term attributes an aesthetic meaning to it. Simply put, this would mean: find beauty in your life, and begin to love it for its attractiveness. Learn to see your life as an object of your desire. Project libidinal qualities into your perceptions, and then form an amorous liaison with life. In this, however, there is an implicit assumption that the true object of love is beauty, and what is beautiful is always lovable. One should train oneself to regard that which is necessary – necessary because it is inevitable – as desirable, whereas it was initially found repellent – to see things gradually as more and more appealing, by modifying the criteria of attractiveness. One can persist with this strategy until any aversion to a situation is seen as an error and the 'object' loses its repulsive quality. If one can do this, then one has no reason to deny anything, for every occurrence can be imbued with beauty no matter how horrific; even the tragic and the traumatic can be regarded with aesthetic potential.

Whilst this sounds like a noble and a creative aspiration, it is not without some problematic implications. The attempt to convert every experience into something beautiful distorts the essence of Amor Fati. Must we beautify everything before we can love it? As person-centred therapists, do we readily adopt a similar stance to our clients and tend to construe their struggles in a 'positive' or 'virtuous' light before extending what we think is unconditional positive regard (UPR). If so, then it in fact becomes conditional upon perceiving their struggle as beautiful, as inspiring or heroic. Is such an aesthetic rendering of our clients' suffering necessary in psychotherapy practice?

We should seriously consider that genuine empathy would equally acknowledge that our clients suffer not just due to being heroic survivors or holy victims of adversity but also through their anxiety and guilt about trying to escape their Fate, sometimes even acting in 'bad faith', instead of resolutely confronting their difficulties. Can we then not offer an empathic response to their attempts at living as they do? I think we can since these distortions indicate 'incongruence'.

I doubt whether Nietzsche himself took a singular view of Amor Fati. There is another interpretation of this love of Fate. Let's consider it in the light of another quote:

> My formula for greatness in a human being is Amor Fati. That one wants nothing to be different, not forward, not backward, not in all eternity. Not merely bear what is necessary, still less conceal it ... but *love* it
>
> *(Nietzsche, 2007, p. 35)*

Whereas in the earlier version Fate is loved because it has the value of beauty, here Fate is valued because it is seen as being worthy of love (Han-Pile, 2011). The love in this case is not conditioned by its desirability for enjoyment in life. The love that is conferred here carries the meaning of *agape* – ancient Greek meaning higher love, spiritual love, whereby the beloved (person, object, situation, event) is loved for the mere fact that it exists, regardless of its usefulness or the happiness that it brings. The value of the object is assumed to be intrinsic to its existence. Its possession does not necessarily yield any material gain to its possessor.

Perhaps we can now understand how the undesired elements of one's Fate may be rendered into something akin to a catalyst for the metamorphosis of oneself – and not the modification of one's perception of the object as beautiful – that can be brought about by our physical, practical, caring love for these elements. The defining characteristic of this love, *agape*, is that it alters the former estimation of an object through a set of values of an entirely different order. The very fact that something exists is now taken as an indication of its validity even in the face of its potential undesirability. Going beyond conventional ideas of good and bad or good and evil, Nietzsche leads us to a point where we can see that any lack of goodness indicates a history of someone, something, somewhere having not been sufficiently loved. The vacant spot of a severed limb, the vacant home of a deserted lover, a friend's betrayal, a broken leg, a broken heart, an ugly scar, a brutal memory, a diseased body, a violent conflict – such a Fate that can provoke intense aversion can also perhaps become a site for love to exist.

Fate and the Fated can be regarded as the same: on one hand determined and substantial (past and present), and on the other hand, uncertain and insubstantial (future). This concurs with Nietzsche who wrote: "Treating oneself as a Fate, not wanting oneself to be otherwise – in such circumstances this is *great good self* itself" (Nietzsche, 2007, pp. 14–15).

Now one can perhaps see more clearly the resonance of this love of Fate with the concept of UPR in person-centred therapy. When Fate and the Fated are identified, loving those who are Fated becomes synonymous with loving their Fates. In a person-centred context, the self of the therapist acts as an auxiliary self of the client and exemplifies Amor Fati. There is concordance between the therapist's empathy and UPR expressed towards a client and the capacity for genuine self 'love' in a client.

Fate and freedom

The notion of Fate often has negative connotations for clients and therapists due to its meaning in common usage. It often implies a predetermined sequence of events in one's life, starting from birth and ending with death, or in some traditions, even beyond death. A fatalistic stance towards life, based on an over-deterministic view of its events, can often evoke apathy, futility or even dread.

Such a view is also inconsistent with the evolutionary view of life that is founded upon the principle of adaptation. We are shaped by a multitude of dynamically interrelated factors that influence each other's performance in the ongoing formation of life's events. For each of these factors to have been fine-tuned in advance to perform precisely in accordance with a predefined mechanism would point us towards creationism and intelligent design. For many people, the term 'Fate' remains tinged with such connotations and is therefore rejected outright. For many others, their acceptance of the notion of Fate retains a residue of such beliefs even though these beliefs may have been disavowed at the level of conscious thinking.

Equally, it can be argued, a belief in the Creator does not necessarily mean a total lack of freedom since one is also free to change one's belief or weaken one's commitment to God's will. Amor Fati therefore can be an acceptable stance to both believers and non-believers alike.

Many of our clients, who expressly favour evolution over creationism, can yet be averse to the idea of active participation in creating one's Fate. It is not uncommon to come across attitudes that are shaped implicitly by an idea of a predetermined Fate that is beyond one's capacity to influence. This is often apparent in the specific aspects of a person's life, for example, 'I am always unlucky in love', 'She was never going to be a good parent', 'Everybody knows my brother won't amount to much', 'I am a born artist', 'I can never be happy living in a small town'. Often these statements seem innocuous or merely opinionated, except that the language can reveal a tendency to take a globalized, deterministic view, as though they have access to some prescient knowledge about themselves or others.

As therapists, we tend to respond by empathizing with the emotional implications of our clients' statements. We might also attend to the finality in these statements and acknowledge it in terms of the impact on their lives. Taking the finality into account, we might say, 'You seem (to have become) helpless in your certainty of knowing that you're always unlucky (in love) and have therefore given up hope of being in a fulfilling relationship'.

We come across such a fatalistic attitude in someone who is chronically experiencing intense 'depression' or 'anxiety'. In many cases we find that such an attitude impacts every aspect of their life – rendering it either dull, unpleasant or threatening. A desirable outcome in therapy – as an aspect of congruence – is the ability to discriminate the inevitable from the changeable. The American theologian Reinhold Niebuhr (1892–1971) catches the essence of this in his popular serenity prayer:

> God, grant me the serenity to accept the things I cannot change,
>   The courage to change the things I can,
>   And wisdom to know the difference.
>
> *(Niebuhr, c. 1942)*

Amor Fati introduces the possible capacity to fiercely affirm Fate. In places, Nietzsche suggests that nothing needs ever be different before it can be loved. He even invites the same Fate to return eternally. He refers to it as a Dionysian affirmation of the world as it is (Nietzsche, 1968). Han-Pile (2011) states that here Amor

Fati receives its maximal extension: we must not only love what is necessary but love its return infinitely. We might infer Nietzsche's notion of 'eternal return' as being geared towards disturbing the inertia of unreflective human beings who seek the 'eternal' but dread the 'recurrence'.

Authenticity and finitude

In the context of therapy, freedom and necessity of Fate, as well as 'eternal return', lead to considering the meaning of living an authentic life. The notions of authenticity and temporal finitude are implicit in Nietzsche's writings. But they are of a different order and go beyond a conventional understanding of these terms. Authenticity is not a project of *uncovering* a pre-existing 'essential self' but rather of *creating* a self for meeting the demands of one's Fate. Amor Fati involves encountering the Emersonian 'immovable limitations' of our Fate in order to 'gain our wishes' rather than evading these limitations by denying our wishes.

The gist of Amor Fati for the practice of person-centred therapy is the sobering truth that both clients and therapists need the psychological capacity for facing the moral challenge to love our Fated existence. For this, overidentification with one's experiences can be hazardous. Rogers (1961, p. 80) acknowledged this by remarking on the unnecessary relating all 'sensory and visceral reactions' to one's self. This would be misunderstanding what it means to be congruent.

Self-estrangement

"The tragedy of modern man is not that he knows less and less about the meaning of his own life, but that it bothers him less and less" (Havel, 1990b).

Throughout all of Nietzsche's writings, one finds a singular concern that occupies him. This, I think, can be summed up as *man's estrangement from himself*. Self-estrangement, he seems to suggest, should cause us intense suffering, but somehow we avoid it by looking for direction and solace in external authorities and value systems. For Nietzsche, morality and transcendence can have no meaning for any who are estranged from themselves. He aims his fury at the all-pervasive corruption of moral values – evident at societal and individual levels. In *Genealogy of Morals* (Nietzsche, 1996), he points out the moral decay in morality itself and shows the consequences of this decay in terms of human beings' actions, thoughts, feelings and aspiration to power. Perhaps at its best here, Amor Fati is a clarion call for committing to the deepest values of authentic living.

Nietzsche seems to say, 'Look at your life, look what you are doing with it. Now tell me, is it any surprise that you resent your Fate? You envy your heroes, worshipping them in public but secretly hating them. Everything difficult that life gives you, rather than accepting it as inevitable, you rail against with blame – and what's more, you exploit yourself by resorting to second-hand ideals. Why? – Because you want to avoid suffering'.

Nietzsche points to a moral vacuum that many have since talked about in various disciplines. In the therapeutic journey, a person can acknowledge this moral vacuum and attempt to rebuild a new value system, personally meaningful and beyond conventional ideas of good and bad, success and failure. Psychotherapy has been termed a moral enterprise, perhaps for this reason. The person-centred approach has a set of unique and relevant formulations here.

Rogers' notion of organismic valuing process signals one path out of this self-estrangement. This is closely linked with the capacity for 'experiencing the experience', or suffering, and living with more embodiment and congruence. This can be an emotionally demanding journey. It involves acknowledging and experiencing the full force of an emotional Fate that has been disavowed, not been loved, that has been denied or distorted in mental and bodily awareness. This coming back to the organism, to one's incarnated existence, to one's Fate in the flesh, can be a pilgrimage of suffering – to become the person one is. Rogers' formulation of becoming involves both recovering the self one has become estranged from, as well as discovering the person that has yet to emerge.

In modern times, our self (self-concept) has become the ultimate article of worth for human beings, and a denial of its finitude deepens the cut of self-estrangement. Self-estrangement can conjure up illusory timelessness, where the advance of Fate can seemingly be halted or its reversal anticipated, as though we have all the time in the world. We have yet to fully digest this knowledge, embody this truth. This can be a lifetime's work. How? Through suffering. According to Nietzsche "... long, slow pain that takes its time and in which we are burned, as it were over green wood ..." (Nietzsche, 2001, p. 6). Or through becoming the experiencing organismic self, as Rogers said.

Suffering and experiencing

It has been suggested (Panaïoti, 2013) that examining Nietzsche's thoughts on suffering is the surest way to comprehend Amor Fati in all its dimensions. "One will see that the problem is that of the meaning of suffering" (Nietzsche, 1968).

Amor Fati is a challenging notion, and one of the main reasons for this is that the meaning of suffering remains elusive. Hevrøy (2011) argues that Nietzsche's philosophy of suffering can be read as a "will to freedom from resentment, that is: freedom from the sufferer's predisposition to seek revenge". He contrasts "vengefulness towards life and a Nietzschean affirmation of life" and claims that affirmation of the past and its suffering can clear the future by leaving revenge behind. The vindictive thirst erupts when one sees in suffering a sense of personal injustice that justifies resentment and vengefulness towards others even though these often serve to increase one's suffering. It is commonly acknowledged by therapists that denying all suffering can lead to more unnecessary – and avoidable – suffering that is now coupled with resentment. This can be regarded, Hevrøy suggests, as a fruitful ethical dimension of Amor Fati.

The necessity to suffer is hardly a straightforward matter of cause and effect. According to Gelvin (1991), for human beings as thinking subjects, there is invariably a question: "If this world is rational, how can we make sense of undeserved suffering? If the world is irrational, how can we justify the worth of being rational ourselves?" (p. 142).

Realizing the impossibility of answering this question can leave us bewildered by the idea of Amor Fati because nothing justifies the arbitrariness of suffering. We remain continually vulnerable to our Fates with its unknown and incalculable possibilities for suffering.

In exhorting us to love our Fate, Nietzsche does not ask us to seek out suffering. Rather, he encourages the development of sufficient capacity in us to bear the suffering that is necessary for sustaining our love of Fate. For Rogers too, "Psychotherapy ... is a process whereby man *becomes* his organism – without self-deception – without distortion ..." (Rogers, 1961, p. 103).

For Nietzsche too, the bodily life is of vital importance. Note how closely his words are in accord with Rogers when he equates the self with the body:

> Behind your thoughts and feelings, my brother, there stands a mighty commander, an unknown sage – he is called Self. He lives in your body, he is your body. There is more reason in your body than in your best wisdom. And who knows for what purpose your body requires precisely your best wisdom?
> *(Nietzsche, 1961, p. 62)*

Fate is often linked with external events. However, an organism-oriented rendering of Fate locates it in the body: not *what* happens but *where* it happens. The site of one's Fate is one's flesh. Fate is both, what happens as well as our response to what happens. In that respect, Fate has a self-generative quality. While we cannot control external events – or inner experiences – we can develop our capacity for choosing a response to them, and our response in turn also has consequences. Our entanglement with what has been Fated is not the entirety of our Fate. Between entanglement and estrangement lies the possibility of freedom that we can obtain through suffering as part of our Fate. In person-centred terms, bearing suffering is synonymous to the process of 'becoming congruent'. It is also an expression of Amor Fati.

Conclusion

The concept of Fate can be potent for eliciting from the therapeutic dialogue our clients' fundamental disposition to the facts of their existence. Person-centred therapists can meaningfully reflect on Fate with clients without committing to its superstitious or orthodox connotations.

The paradoxical nature of Fate as both freedom and necessity means that Fate is not a precoded almanac of one's future but rather an undecided, ongoing project of one's life.

Understanding Fate in this way makes it possible to conceive the possibility of affirming Nietzsche's Amor Fati as a way of committing to the essence of the person-centred approach. The task in therapy, then, is to respond to this call and to facilitate the dialogical conditions for this continuous making and remaking of our clients' Fate along with our own. UPR and empathy arise from a willingness to be with the emotional consequences of our client's Fate, intimately but without entanglement. Such an encounter can be both a vessel and an expression of love where the Fate and the Fated can be regarded as one.

Accepting the paradoxical nature of Fate also makes redundant in therapy the task of eliminating suffering. At a time when therapists have to increasingly contend with the demands of an evidence-based, procedure-driven, 'criterio-logical' practice, Amor Fati can help us to remain grounded in the necessity and sufficiency of Carl Rogers' conditions of therapy and anchor our faith in the principled non-directivity in our work. Non-directive responses of empathy and UPR convey a form of love as an "ethical compassion that involves responding to suffering in a way that people can learn and grow from suffering" (Hatab, 1995, p. 188).

The non-directive therapist neither provokes suffering nor avoids it. Rather than abjure or cure, the focus is on growing the capacity to endure suffering and foster love for one's Fate.

Amor Fati is the pinnacle of affirmation of life, not because one's life is always beautiful or pleasurable but because it is life just as it is: always and already full of being and becoming.

Acknowledgement

This chapter is a revised version of the paper given at the Person-Centred and Experiential (PCE) Psychotherapy and Counselling, Europe Symposium held at Charles University, Prague, in April 2014.

References

Emerson, R. W. (1981) 'Fate'. In *The Portable Emerson*, Bode, C., and Cowley, M. (eds.). New York: Penguin, pp. 346–374.
Ferrer, D. F. (2011) *Confrontations: Philosophical Reflections and Aphorisms*. Online. Available at www.gutenberg.us/wplbn0002821971-confrontations-philosophical-reflections-and-aphorisms-by-ferrrer-daniel-fidel.aspx?. Accessed on 14 February 2014.
Gelvin, M. (1991) *Why Me? A Philosophical Enquiry into Fate*. Dekalb: Northern Illinois Press.
Han-Pile, B. (2011) 'Nietzsche and Amor Fati'. *European Journal of Philosophy*, Vol. 19 (2), pp. 224–261.
Hatab, L. J. (1995) *A Nietzschean Defence of Democracy*. Chicago: Open Court.
Havel, V. (1990a) *Disturbing the Peace: A Conversation with Karek Hvízdala*. New York: Alfred A. Knopf.
Havel, V. (1990b) *Letters to Olga*. London: Faber & Faber.
Havel, V. (1991) *Open Letters – Selected Prose 1965–1990*. London: Faber & Faber.

Hevrøy, S. A. (2011) 'The Ethical Fruitfulness of Nietzsche's View on Suffering'. In *Making Sense of Suffering: Theory, Practice and Representation*, Hogue, B., and Sugiyama, A. (eds.). Oxford: Interdisciplinary Press. Online. Available at www.inter-disciplinary.net/wp-content/uploads/2011/04/msosufferingever11204111.pdf. Accessed on 20 March 2014.

Kierkegaard, S. (1981) *The Concept of Anxiety*. Princeton, NJ: Princeton University Press.

Niebuhr, R. (c. 1942) 'Serenity Prayer'. Online. Available at http://en.wikiquote.org/wiki/Reinhold_Niebuhr#The_Serenity_Prayer_.28c._1942.29. Accessed on 14 April 2014.

Nietzsche, F. (1882) *Nietzsche's Letters – 1882*. Online. Available at www.thenietzschechannel.com/correspondence/eng/nlett-1882.htm. Accessed on 20 February 2014.

Nietzsche, F. (1961) *Thus Spoke Zarathustra*. London: Penguin.

Nietzsche, F. (1967) *Werke. Kritische Gesamtausgabe* (Complete Critical Edition). Colli, G., and Montinari, M. (eds.). Berlin/New York: Mouton de Gruyter.

Nietzsche, F. (1968) *Will to Power*. New York: Vintage.

Nietzsche, F. (1996) *On the Genealogy of Morals*. Oxford: Oxford University Press.

Nietzsche, F. (2001) *The Gay Science*. Cambridge: Cambridge University Press.

Nietzsche, F. (2007) *Ecce Homo – How to Become What You Are*. Oxford: Oxford University Press.

Panaïoti, A. (2013) *Nietzsche and Buddhist Philosophy*. Cambridge: Cambridge University Press.

Rogers, C. R. (1961) *On Becoming a Person*. London: Constable.

Vaidya, D. (2013) 'Re-visioning Rogers' Second Condition – Anxiety as the Face of Ontological Incongruence and Basis for the Principle of Non-Directivity in PCT Therapy'. *Person-Centered & Experiential Psychotherapies*, Vol. 12 (3), pp. 209–222.

INDEX

actualizing tendency 181, 182
Adler, Alfred 21
Adorno, Theodor 5, 133, 139
The Alchemist (Coelho) 162
Alizadeh, Hossein 117
Amor Fati, in Nietzsche's work 179–89; *see also* fate
anorexia 120–1
Anti-Oedipus: Capitalism and Schizophrenia (Deleuze and Guattari) 107, 109–11, 115
anti-psychiatry 107, 109, 113
Anti-Semite and Jew (Sartre) 84, 85
anxiety, in Kierkegaard's work 24–5
a-pathy 3
Aron, Raymond 118
Artaud, Antonin 107, 110
articulation 4, 148
askesis 17
ataraxia 17
Attridge, D. 133
authenticity, fate and 186
Ayer, A.J. 'Freddie' 46

Badiou, Alain 72, 151–2, 154
Bakhtin, M. 11
Barthes, Roland 119
Bataille, Georges 5, 69
Bazzano, Manu 15, 63, 69, 96, 143
Becker, Ernest 23
becoming: in Butler's work 67–75; childhood, in Rousseau's work 96; in Deleuze's work 111; Heraclitus as philosopher/poet of 5; in Irigaray's work 140, 141, 142; nature of 68;

in Nietzsche's work 15, 180, 181, 182, 188, 189; Rogers' formulation of 180, 181, 182, 187; in Schopenhauer's work 163; in Wittgenstein's work 148, 149, 153, 155
Being and Nothingness (Sartre) 76, 77, 79, 81–2, 83, 85, 86
bellum omnium contra omnes 92
Bennet, Arnold 48
Bersani, Leo 131
'Between Zero and One' (Gallant) 125
Binswanger, Ludwig 23
Bion, Wilfred 39, 166
birds, in Kierkegaard's discourses 26–30
The Birth of Tragedy (Nietzsche) 10, 17
Blake, William 48
Blanchot, Maurice 5, 135
Bly, Robert 49
Bodies That Matter (Butler) 70
Boulton, J.T. 55
'Boundary and Ambiguity' (Synesiou) 123
Bourdieu, Pierre 119
Bowlby, John 109
bracketing 14, 166, 173
Breton, André 93
Brook, A. 164
Bryant, E.F. 140
Buber, M. 20, 109
Buddhism: compassion leading to 161; language and 170–7; nihilism and 161, 166–7; nirvana and 165–6; in Schopenhauer's work 161, 163, 165–8; Varela's ethical know-how and 141; in Wittgenstein's work 170, 173–7

Burroughs, William 157–8
Butler, Judith 5, 67–75; *Bodies That Matter* 70; desire 67–75; gender 70–2; *Gender Trouble* 70; livable life 67, 68, 70; on process/nature becoming 67, 68; recognition, desire for 67–75; *Subjects of Desire* 68–9; *Undoing Gender* 70

Camus, Albert 5, 98–104; *The Fall* 101–2; imagery 99–104; introduction 98–9; metaphor 99–102; metaphysical rebellion 98, 99; *The Myth of Sisyphus* 103–4; *The Plague* 99–100; *The Rebel* 100; *Summer in Algiers* 102–3
capitalism 48, 84, 109
Carswell, Catherine 47–8
cause and effect 13
CBT (cognitive behavioural therapy) 1–2, 3, 108
Cezanne, Paul 124
changeling 18–19
Chaplin, Charlie 118
Char, René 112
'The Child's Relations with Others' (Merleau-Ponty) 122
Christianity 2; in Camus's work 98, 100, 101; in Irigaray's work 140, 143; in Kierkegaard's work 29; in Nietzsche's work 9, 10, 12, 160
clear-sightedness, in Wittgenstein's work 171, 173
The Cloud of Unknowing (Spearing) 34, 36
Coelho, Paulo 162, 167
Cohen, Josh 130
Coltrane, John 117, 118
community 71
compassion: leading to Buddhism 161; in Nietzsche's work 12, 160–1, 189; in Schopenhauer's work 157, 160–1, 165, 167
conceptualization 132
The Confessions (Rousseau) 90
conscious: in Butler's work 68, 69; in Freud's work 109; in Rousseau's work 94–5; in Sartre's work 80, 83, 85–6; in Schopenhauer's work 158
consciousness, in Sartre's work 79–82, 83, 84, 88
contentment, in Kierkegaard's work 24, 26, 29, 31–2
continental philosophy 5
converse syndrome 55
Cooper, Robin 118
counter-cultural 18

counter-tradition 2–5, 15, 94, 114, 138–9, 143
couplework that works 50
Critique of Dialectical Reason (Sartre) 76, 77, 79, 81, 82, 83, 86

Darwin, Charles 159
Daumal, René 93
Daybreak (Nietzsche) 17
death drive 164
de Beauvoir, Simone 5, 118, 119
De Cive (Hobbes) 92
Deleuze, Gilles 5, 16, 96, 107–15; *Anti-Oedipus* 107, 109–11, 115; broken paths 107; creative delirium 115; disappointment, learning from 107–8; familialism, beyond 111; family 113–14; longing, notes on 111–13; *A Thousand Plateaus* 113; traitor's quest 108–9
delirium 109–15
Derrida, J. 68, 133–6, 138
Descartes, René 9, 48, 94
de-schooling of society, Illich's notion of 95
desire 4, 7, 65; in Bersani's work 131; in Deleuze's work 109–15; to die, in Camus's work 98; to harm, in Irigaray's work 140; in Keats's work 39, 42; in Kierkegaard's work 27; in Merleau-Ponty's work 122; in Nietzsche's work 12, 182, 183; to provoke, in Rousseau's work 96; for recognition, in Butler's work 67–75; in Schopenhauer's work 158–65; sexual, in Lawrence's work 49, 53–4, 55, 56; social, in Sartre's work 82, 88; for unity, in Camus's work 98, 103
De Vita Contemplativa (Philo of Alexandria) 139
Dharma 1, 108
dialogical 11
Dilthey, W. 16
Dionysus 7, 17, 90, 185
Discourse on Inequality (Rousseau) 90–1, 92
Discourses on the Arts and Sciences (Rousseau) 90, 91
disgust, in Schopenhauer's work 158, 161, 167
dividuum 18
doer and deed 19–20
Dostoevsky, Fyodor 130, 132
DSM-5 (APA) 98
duality 13, 42–3, 142
Dyer, Geoff 117

ego 18–19, 50, 131, 141, 165, 175
egoism 91, 159, 160
Either/Or (Kierkegaard) 25

Emerson, Ralph Waldo 181–4, 186
Emile, or On Education (Rousseau) 90, 93, 95, 96
emotive function of metaphor 101
empathy: in Lawrence's work 52, 55; in Merleau-Ponty's work 122–3; in Nietzsche's work 183, 184, 189; Rogers on 152–3; in Wittgenstein's work 153
Endless Vision (Alizadeh and Gasparyan) 117
Enlightenment 2, 91
enlightenment in two 142
Epicurus 17
epistemology 14, 46
Essays and Aphorisms (Schopenhauer) 157
eternal return, Nietzsche's notion of 186
ethical know-how 141
ethics 65; in Butler's work 67–75; of energy 139–41; language of, in philosophical practice 4; in language use 149–50, 153; in Levinas's work 118; in Nietzsche's work 16, 17, 20, 160, 187, 189; in Sartre's work 85–8; in Schopenhauer's work 157; of technology 132; Varela's ethical know-how 141
existentialism 76–7
existential psychotherapy: in Camus's work 99–101; in Kierkegaard's work 23, 24, 25; in Nietzsche's work 15–16; onto-theological approach in 108; in Sartre's work 79, 85–6
Existenzphilosophie 15–17
experiencing, fate and 187–8

Face to Face (Gordon) 118
faith: bad faith 85, 121, 183; in Camus's work 99–100; in Kierkegaard's work 25–6, 29, 31
The Fall (Camus) 101–2
false knowing 69–70
Fantasia of the Unconscious (Lawrence) 54
fate 179–89; authenticity and 186; Emerson and 181–4; experiencing and 187–8; finitude and 186; freedom and 184–6; introduction 179–81; self-estrangement and 186–7; suffering and 187–8
'Fate' (Emerson) 181
femininity 52, 71
feminism 46, 137
Fielder, Mike 117
finitude, fate and 186
force, quantum of 11–12
Foucault, Michel 17, 113, 119
Fragile Process (Warner) 149

frame of mind, philosophical 18
free association 109
freedom, fate and 184–6
Freud, Sigmund: construction of the unconscious 44; Deleuze and 107, 108; *The Interpretation of Dreams* 163–4; Irigaray on 137, 138, 140; Lawrence on 54; Merleau-Ponty and 121; Nietzsche and 21; Schopenhauer and 157, 158, 159, 160, 163–4; *Schopenhauer and Freud* 164; on sexuality 130–1, 137; "Where it is, I shall be" 109; work and love 48

Gallant, Mavis 124–6
Garrison, Jimmy 117
Gasparyan, Jivan 117
The Gay Science (Nietzsche) 13, 17
Gelvin, M. 188
gender: in Butler's work 70–2; in Irigaray's work 138; in Lawrence's work 53–4, 55; in Sartre's work 79
Gender Trouble (Butler) 70
Genealogy of Morals (Nietzsche) 13–14, 18–19, 160, 161, 186
Gestalt therapy 142
The Gift of Death (Derrida) 133
God 2; in Keats's work 34; in Kierkegaard's work 24, 28, 29–30; in Lawrence's work 45–6; in Nietzsche's work 13, 18, 182, 185; in Pascal's work 62
Goldstein, Kurt 12
Gottergebenheit 182
Grass, G. 121
gratitude, in Kierkegaard's work 30–2
Green, Andre 132
groundedness 170
group, notion of 71
Guattari, Felix 96, 107, 109–11, 113, 115, 138
Gurwitch, Aaron 118

Hadot, P. 17
Han-Pile, B. 182, 183, 185–6
happiness, Schopenhauer's pursuit of 162
Hardy, Thomas 48, 50, 54
Havel, Vaclav 180
Heaton, J.M. 148, 153, 154, 174
Hegel, G.W.F. 68–9, 72, 81, 90, 91, 113, 166; *Phenomenology of Spirit* 5, 19, 20, 67, 68
Heidegger, M. 14, 15–16, 19, 24, 109, 137
Heisenberg, Werner 173
Heraclitus 2, 4, 5, 15
Hevrøy, S.A. 187
Hinduism 46

Hippocrene 39
Hobbes, T. 92, 93
Hölderlin, F. 90
holistic perspective 94
homo homini lupus 159
homosexuality 70, 72
homunculus fallacy 174
Hopkins, Gerard Manley 123
hubris 18, 147
Human, All Too Human (Nietzsche) 17, 18
human being: in Bersani's work 131; in Camus's work 102; in Dostoevsky's work 130; fate and 183, 186, 187, 188; in Freud's work 131; in Gelvin's work 188; in Hobbes's work 92; in Kierkegaard's work 26–30; Maslow on nature of 95–6; in Merleau-Ponty's work 121, 126; in Nietzsche's work 20, 183, 186, 187; psychoanalytic conception of 131; in Rousseau's work 92–6; in Sartre's work 85–6; in selfie-dominated culture 130, 131, 132; van Deurzen's elements in 24; view of 3; in Wittgenstein's work 176, 177
Husserl, Edmund 14, 15, 16, 20, 118
Husserl, Malvine 118
hyper-rational 10, 48
hyper-rationalism 48, 52, 53

Ibn al-'Arabi 112
id 109, 131, 158, 164
the Ideal 10, 48
identity: in Butler's work 67, 69–73; ethics and 4; fluency 34–5; in Irigaray's work 105, 139, 141; in Keats's work 34, 35, 42–3; in Nietzsche's work 16; politics 16, 135; in Sartre's work 78–81; in Wittgenstein's work 173, 175
Illich, Ivan 95
imagery, in Camus's work 99–104
immanent 7
immovable limitations 181–2, 186
in absentia 5
individualism: in Derrida's work 133–4; in Nietzsche's work 10
individuum 18
infant sexuality 54
inner life: in Nietzsche's work 10–11; in Wittgenstein's work 172–3
'In Praise of Philosophy' (Merleau-Ponty) 119
internalization of man 10
intersubjectivity 20, 68, 105, 114
'Intimates' (Lawrence) 49–50
Introduction to Kierkegaard (Pattison) 25

Irigaray, Luce 5, 65, 105, 137–43; enlightenment in two 142; ethics of energy 139–41; *A New Culture of Energy* 139; philosophy as practice 138–9; self-same, logic of 137–8; soul, techniques of 141–2; *Speculum, de l'autre femme* 137; Western and Eastern cultures, beyond 143

Jabes, Edmond 137
Janaway, Christopher 158, 164–5
Jensen, H.M. 29, 32
Jones, Elvin 117
Jung, Carl 21, 35

Kant, Immanuel 13, 158, 163, 164
Keats, John 5, 7, 34–44; *see also* negative capability; 'Ode to a Nightingale' 34, 36–42; uncertainty and 34–6, 41–4; X-factor 43
Keown, Damien 165
Kierkegaard, Søren 5, 23–32; anxiety and 24–5; contentment and 24, 26, 29, 31–2; *Either/Or* 25; gratitude and patience 30–2; introduction 23–4; lilies and birds, discourses on 26–30; love and 24–7, 31; outline 24; *The Sickness unto Death* 25, 30; *Upbuilding Discourses in Various Spirits* 24, 25–6; *Works of Love* 23, 31
Klein, Melanie 109
knowing; *see also* not knowing: in Buddhism 166; in Butler's work 67–70; in Keats's work 39; in Schopenhauer's work 163; in Wittgenstein's work 147–9, 155
Kristeva, Julia 5, 73

Lacan, Jacques 19, 68, 137, 160
Lady Chatterley's Lover (Lawrence) 50–4
Laing, R.D. 107
language 2–3, 4, 145; in Blanchot's work 135; Buddhism and 170–7; in Derrida's work 134; of ethics 4; games 172, 176, 178; gender norms and 70; in Irigaray's work 139; in Keats's work 42; in Merleau-Ponty's work 119, 122, 123; self and 170–7; in Wittgenstein's work 147–55, 169, 170–8
Lapassade, Georges 95
Larkin, P. 51
Law of Excluded Middles 46
Lawrence, D.H. 5, 7, 45–56; British public's inability to accept 50; capitalism, socialism and 48–9; *Fantasia of the Unconscious* 54;

'Intimates' 49–50; introduction 45; *Lady Chatterley's Lover* 50–4; legacy of 46–9; love relations and 49–50; procreative sexuality and raising children 54–6; *The Rainbow* 48, 52–3, 56; relationships of 47–8; sex, desire and 49–54; 'The Snake' 48; 'Song of a Man Who Has Come Through' 55; *Sons and Lovers* 55; tenderness and 50–2; *Women in Love* 48, 52–3
Lawrence, Frieda 47–8
Lebensphilosophie 15–17
Lessing, Doris 51
Les Temps Modernes 84, 118
'Let It Pass' (Gallant) 126
Leviathan (Hobbes) 92
Levinas, Emmanuel 109, 118, 132
Lévi-Strauss, C. 95, 118
liberation psychologist *see* Sartre, Jean-Paul
liberation psychology 88
lightning 11
lilies and birds, in Kierkegaard's discourses 26–30
limitations 181–2, 186
logos 2, 7, 137, 139, 158
longing, in Deleuze's work 111–13
love: in Badiou's work 72; in Deleuze's work 112, 114; in Derrida's work 134; in Freud's work 130; in Gallant's work 125, 126; importance of 105; in Irigaray's work 139, 140, 141; in Keats's work 36, 41; in Kierkegaard's work 24–7, 31; in Lawrence's work 45–56; in Merleau-Ponty's work 121–2; in Nietzsche's work 179–89; parental 78, 88

Madison, G.B. 2
Maezumi, Taizan 154
many-motived ritual 121
Marino, Gordon 23
Marx, Karl 5, 81, 82, 91, 93, 127
Marxism, Sartre's 76–7, 79, 81, 82–3, 86
Marxism and Subjectivity (Sartre) 83
masculinity 71
Maslow, A.H. 95–6
May, Rollo 3, 21, 23, 25
McCleary, Richard 123
McDaid, Carol 117
McLuckie, John 31, 32
meditation 1; in Camus's work 100; in Irigaray's work 140, 142, 143; in Nietzsche's work 14; in Rousseau's work 93, 95; in Schopenhauer's work 167; in Wittgenstein's work 174, 177

Merleau-Ponty, Maurice 5, 16–17, 105, 117–27; 'The Child's Relations with Others' 122; destined to the world 122–3; embodiment 120–1; freedom and autonomy 127; inexplicable grace 124–7; introduction 117–18; life and context 118–19; *Phenomenology of Perception* 118, 120–1, 124, 127; rediscovering the world 123–4; sexuality, enigma of 121–2; singing the world 119–20; *The Structure of Behaviour* 118
metaphor: in Camus's work 99–102; emotive function of 101
metaphysical rebellion 98, 99; *see also* Camus, Albert
metaphysics 145; in Irigaray's work 138; in Nietzsche's work 14, 15, 17, 19; Plato's 17; in Wittgenstein's work 170; Zen and 108
Methuen 53
mindfulness 1–2, 12, 30, 108
Mindfulness-Based Stress Reduction 2
Minima Moralia (Adorno) 139
Modern Times 118
mutual recognition 68–9, 74
mysticism: airport, Coelho's 162; Heideggerian 16; silent, Wittgenstein's 152; of the unsaid, Badiou's 151
The Myth of Sisyphus (Camus) 103–4

the naked lunch 157
Naranjo, Claudio 142
narcissism 10, 129, 160
narcissistic injury 160
narcissistic rage 160
naturalistic 4, 11, 16
natura naturans 111
nature 2; of becoming 68; of fate 181, 188, 189; Heisenberg on 173; of human existence, defined 158; in Irigaray's work 138, 141–2; in Merleau-Ponty's work 123–4; in Rousseau's work 90, 91–2, 93, 94, 95–6; in Sartre's work 88; in Schopenhauer's work 157, 158, 159, 160, 161, 163, 166; of the self 18, 34; in selfie-dominated culture 132, 133; state of nature and nature of the state 92
need, in Sartre's work 82–3
negative capability 7, 34–44; conclusion 43; description of process 36–42; duality and identity 42–3; introduction 34–5; uncertainty, modes of inhabiting 35–6; X-factor 43
negative psychology 10, 20
Neill, Alexander 95

A New Culture of Energy (Irigaray) 139
Niebuhr, Reinhold 185
Nietzsche, Friedrich 4; *see also* fate; *The Birth of Tragedy* 10, 17; cause and effect 13; *Daybreak* 17; doer and deed 19–20; existential/phenomenological psychotherapy 13–15; *Existenzphilosophie* 15–17; *The Gay Science* 13, 17; *Genealogy of Morals* 13–14, 18–19, 160, 161, 186; *Human, All Too Human* 17, 18; individuum and dividuum 18; inner life 10–11; *Lebensphilosophie* 15–17; middle works 15–18; philosophical frame of mind 18; quantum of force 11–12; reading well, reading slowly 10; on Schopenhauer 160–1, 166; self and 9–21; *Thus Spoke Zarathustra* 19, 137; truth 15; *Twilight of the Idols* 13; weakness 12–13; will to power 12, 111
'Night of Fire,' Pascal's 58–63
non-harming 105, 140, 141
Notebooks for an Ethics (Sartre) 85
Notes from Underground (Dostoevsky) 130, 132
Not I but the Wind (F. Lawrence) 47
not knowing; *see also* knowing: in Butler's work 69–70, 74; in Irigaray's work 143; in Keats's work 35; in Wittgenstein's work 148, 155

Obscene Publications Act 53
Observer 117
obstruction, in Rousseau's work 93
Oedipus 45, 55–6, 109, 110, 111
On Ethics (Schopenhauer) 157
On Learning from the Patient (Casement) 168
On the Origin of Species (Darwin) 159
On the Vanity of Existence (Schopenhauer) 156
onto-theological 4, 16, 108
optimism, in Schopenhauer's work 157, 167
organismic valuing process 71, 187
Ornicar review 137
the Other 67, 69–70, 72–4
otherness 16, 41, 69, 72, 80, 108, 112
Overbeck, Franz 182

Parerga and Paralipomena (Schopenhauer) 161–2
Pascal, Blaise 5, 7, 58–63
passivity: in Keats's work 34, 42; in Lawrence's work 55; relational 55; in Sartre's work 86, 182
pathos 3
patience, in Kierkegaard's work 30–2

Pattison, George 25–6, 29, 32
performativity 70
personal development 72, 162
person-centred therapy 95, 107–8, 179–89; Amor Fati for practice of, in Nietzsche's work 179–89; organismic valuing process 71; Rogers and 95, 107–8, 179–89; therapeutic growth in terms of 180
perverted 96
phenomenalization 132
phenomenologists 13–15
phenomenology: in Hegel's work 5, 19–20, 68; in Merleau-Ponty's work 118, 120–1, 124, 127; in Nietzsche's work 14, 16; in Schopenhauer's work 167
Phenomenology of Perception (Merleau-Ponty) 118, 120–1, 124, 127
Phenomenology of Spirit (Hegel) 5, 19, 20, 67, 68
Philo of Alexandria 139
philosophical anthropology 16
Philosophical Investigations (Wittgenstein) 149, 154
philosophy; *see also individual philosophers*: of being/becoming 15; counter-tradition and 2–5, 15, 94, 114, 138–9, 143; horror of becoming machine-like 48–9; introduction 1–2; life or death 45–6; traditional 2–3, 100; as a way of life 3–5
Philosophy and the Mirror of Nature (Rorty) 177
physical theatre 107
Pippin, R.B. 19, 20
The Plague (Camus) 99–100
Plato 2, 14, 17, 158
Plessner, H. 16
Points 133
politics 65; in Deleuze's work 115; in Lawrence's work 45, 46, 51; of liberation, in Sartre's work 83–8; Marxist 82; in Nietzsche's work 16, 17; psychotherapy as political act 87; in Rousseau's work 92–4; selfies and 134–5
Poole, Roger 123, 127
Poppeliers, Willem 55–6
Porter, Steve 32
Port-Royal des Champs 58, 62
practico-inert 82, 83
praxis 83
pre-reflective awareness 80, 82
pre-reflective consciousness 79–82, 83, 84, 88
pre-reflective understanding 79–80
principium individuationis 160

The Private Life: Why We Remain in the Dark (Cohen) 130
process of becoming 67, 148, 149, 153, 155, 180
psychoanalysis: in Deleuze's work 108–11, 113–14; Freud's, Nietzsche's ideas in 21; introduction 2–3; in Irigaray's work 137–8; in Lawrence's work 54; May's existential, Nietzsche's ideas in 21; in Schopenhauer's work 163–4
psychology: Adler's individual 21; Buddhist 174; Gestalt 118; humanistic 86, 95; Irigaray's study of 137; Jung's analytical 21; liberation 88; Merleau-Ponty's interest and 118–19; negative 10, 20; Nietzsche's 9–21; Roger's non-directive 95; Sartre's existential 76–88
psychotherapy 65, 145; *see also* existential psychotherapy; in Camus's work 98–104; counter-tradition and 2–3; fate in, in Nietzsche's work 179, 183, 187, 188; intersubjectivity and 20, 68, 105, 114; introduction 1–5; in Merleau-Ponty's work 117–28; in Nietzsche's work 15–17, 20; note on 86–7; as political act 87; psychotechnics and 1–2, 3, 109; rooted in the body, in Lawrence's work 54–6; in Sartre's work 76–88; in Schopenhauer's work 157, 162, 165, 166; self-awareness and 96; training 72, 154; uncertainty and, in Keats's work 34–44; in Wittgenstein's work 169; Zen and 108

quantum of force 11–12

The Rainbow (Lawrence) 48, 52–3, 56
Rank, Otto 21
Raskin, Nathaniel J. 153
rationalization 133, 163, 164
The Rebel (Camus) 100
recognition: in Butler's work 67–75; desire for 67–75; double helix of 65; in Hegel's work 20; in Irigaray's work 140, 142; in Lawrence's work 48; mutual 68–9, 74
reflective consciousness 79–82, 86
Reich, Wilhelm 55, 95
ressentiment 160
'The Rhine' (Hölderlin) 90
Ricoeur, P. 101
Rilke, Rainer Maria 46
Rimbaud, A. 93, 114–15
Rogers, Carl 23, 44; client-centred therapy 95; Emerson and 181; on empathy 152–3; formulation of becoming 180, 181, 182, 187; organismic valuing process 71, 187; overidentification with one's experiences 186; person-centred therapy 95, 107–8, 179–89; on psychotherapy 188; Rousseau and 95; six conditions of therapy 181, 189
Rorty, R. 5, 177
rough ground 170
Rousseau, Jean Jacques 5, 90–6; *The Confessions* 90; debt and acknowledgement to 94–6; *Discourse on Inequality* 90–1, 92; *Discourses on the Arts and Sciences* 90, 91; *Emile, or On Education* 90, 93, 95, 96; overview of 90; pathologies of civilization 90–1; pedagogy of liberation 93–4; *The Social Contract* 92–3; state of nature and nature of the state 92; working on oneself 92–3

Sagar, K. 50
Sartre, Jean-Paul 5, 76–88; *Anti-Semite and Jew* 84, 85; *Being and Nothingness (B&N)* 76, 77, 79, 81–2, 83, 85, 86; consciousness, dialectic of 79–82, 83, 84, 88; *Critique of Dialectical Reason* 76, 77, 79, 81, 82, 83, 86; existentialism 76–7; *The Family Idiot* 76; fundamental project, notion of 77, 80–1, 83, 84, 86, 87; introduction 76; later works of 81–2, 88; Marxism 76–7, 79, 81, 82–3, 86; *Marxism and Subjectivity* 83; need 82–3; *Notebooks for an Ethics* 85; politics of 83–8; Sartrean Dialectic 81; scarcity 82–3; *Search for a Method* 77, 82
Sartrean Dialectic 81
scarcity, in Sartre's work 82–3
Schacht, Richard 16
Scheler, Max 16, 141–2
Schérer, René 96
Schmid, P. 153
Schopenhauer, A. 5, 17, 108, 145, 156–68; *Essays and Aphorisms* 157; *On Ethics* 157; Freud and 157, 158, 159, 160, 163–4; Nietzsche's critique of 160–1, 166; *Parerga and Paralipomena* 161–2; reputation of 156; *On the Vanity of Existence* 156; will 158–66; *The World as Will and Representation* 156, 164
Schopenhauer and Freud (Young and Brook) 164
Search for a Method (Sartre) 77, 82
'Searching for Couplework That Works' (Duffell) 50
secondary gain strategies 175
self 105; in Buddhism 174–5; in Butler's work 70; as a changeling 18–19; in

Deleuze's work 110–11; in Dostoevsky's work 130; in Irigaray's work 137–8; language and 170–7; in Nietzsche's work 9–21, 180, 184, 187, 188; in Rogers' formulation of becoming 187; in selfie-dominated culture 129–36; sense of 34, 35, 42, 73, 80–4, 87, 88, 132, 175; in Wittgenstein's work 173–7
self-awareness 18, 67, 96, 180
self-consciousness: in Butler's work 68; ethical, in Hegel's work 20; in Green's work 132
self-estrangement, fate and 186–7
selfie-dominated culture 129–36
self-same, logic of 137–8, 164
sense of self 34, 35, 42, 73, 80–4, 87, 88, 132, 175
'Serenity Prayer' (Niebuhr) 185
Sexual Grounding Therapy, Poppeliers' 55–6
sexuality: in Butler's work 70, 72; Freud on 130–1, 137; infant 54; Lacan on 137; in Larkin's work 51; in Lawrence's work 51–5; in Merleau-Ponty's work 121–2; in Rousseau's work 96; in Sartre's work 79; in Schopenhauer's work 163; in selfie-dominated culture 135
Shaw, George Bernard 165
The Sickness unto Death (Kierkegaard) 25, 30
silence: in Derrida's work 134; in Irigaray's work 139, 143; in Kierkegaard's work 26, 29–30, 31–2; in Rousseau's work 93
'The Snake' (Lawrence) 48
The Social Contract (Rousseau) 92–3
socialism 45, 46, 48
Socrates 17
sole self 41
Solitaries 58, 62
'Song of a Man Who Has Come Through' (Lawrence) 55
Sons and Lovers (Lawrence) 55
The Space of Literature (Blanchot) 135
Speculum, de l'autre femme (Irigaray) 137
speech: in Irigaray's work 139, 143; in Merleau-Ponty's work 119, 120
Spinoza, Baruch 5, 111
Stoics 17
The Structure of Behaviour (Merleau-Ponty) 118
Subjects of Desire (Butler) 68–9
suffering, fate and 187–8
Suicidal Behaviour Disorder 98
Summerhill 95
Summer in Algiers (Camus) 102–3
sympathetic centres 53
Synesiou, Natasha 123

Taalmod 32
talking cure 171
Taylor, C. 19
tears of joy, in Pascal's 'Night of Fire' 58–63
technology 132–3
tenderness, in Lawrence's work 50–2
teriaca 59
therapeia 41
therapeutic growth 180
Therapists (Θεραπευταί) 139
therapy 2, 4, 105; *see also* psychotherapy; client-centred 95; in Deleuze's work 107–15; description therapy as opposed to prescription therapy 149–50; Gestalt 142; humanistic approach to, in Wittgenstein's work 147–55; in Kierkegaard's work 23–32; language in, in Wittgenstein's work 171–6; in Merleau-Ponty's work 107–15; modes of inhabiting uncertainty, in Keats's work 34–44; obligatory optimism and, in Schopenhauer's work 167; person-centred 95, 107–8, 179–89; Poppeliers' Sexual Grounding Therapy 55–6; for recognition, in Butler's work 67–75; school of, in Nietzsche's work 14
thing-in-itself, Kantian 13, 163, 164, 165
A Thousand Plateaus (Deleuze and Guattari) 113
threshold experience 7
Thus Spoke Zarathustra (Nietzsche) 19, 137
Titanism 18
Todd, Oliver 100
Tractatus Logico-Philosophicus (Wittgenstein) 151, 153, 154
traditional philosophy 2–3
transcendent 7
transcendental 7, 174
transparency, in Rousseau's work 93
truth, in Nietzsche's work 15
turning East 142
Twilight of the Idols (Nietzsche) 13
Tyner, McCoy 117

uncertainty: in Keats's work 34–6, 41–4; in Sartre's work 84; in Wittgenstein's work 155
unconditional positive regard (UPR) 183, 184, 189
unconscious: in Deleuze's work 109, 110, 111, 114, 115; in Freud's work 44, 131,

164; in Lawrence's work 45, 46, 54; in Schopenhauer's work 164
Undoing Gender (Butler) 70
unsaid 4, 151, 154
Upaniṣads 163
Upbuilding Discourses in Various Spirits (Kierkegaard) 24, 25–6

Van Breda, Herman 118
van Deurzen, Emmy 24
Varela, Francisco 141
vipassana meditation 142
volitional centres 53

Wagner, Richard 17
Warner, Margaret 149
Watzlawick, P. 172, 176
weakness, in Nietzsche's work 12–13
Weil, Simone 118
"Where it is, I shall be" (Freud) 109
will: to power, in Nietzsche's work 12, 111; in Schopenhauer's work 158–66
Will to Life, in Schopenhauer's work 158–9, 163

Wittgenstein, Ludwig 147–55, 169–78; arrest and dissolve 150–2; articulation 4, 148; Buddhism and 170, 173–7; chance and a dance 152–4; description therapy as opposed to prescription therapy 149–50; inner life 172–3; language 171–2, 173–7; perspicuity and 147–55; *Philosophical Investigations* 149, 154; puzzles and muddles 154–5; *Tractatus Logico-Philosophicus* 151, 153, 154
Women in Love (Lawrence) 48, 52–3
Wood, James 100
work of art 16, 134, 135, 148
Works of Love (Kierkegaard) 23, 31
The World as Will and Representation (Schopenhauer) 156, 164

X-factor 43

Yalom, Irvin 31
The Yoga-Sutras of Patañjali (Bryant) 140
Young, C. 164

Zen 107–8, 167, 170, 174